The Ideal Student

The Ideal Student

Deconstructing Expectations in Higher Education

Billy Wong and Y.L. Tiffany Chiu

Open University Press

Open University Press
McGraw Hill
8th Floor, 338 Euston Road
London
England
NW1 3BH

email: enquiries@openup.co.uk
world wide web: www.openup.co.uk

First edition published 2021

A catalogue record of this book is available from the British Library

ISBN-13: 9780335249251
ISBN-10: 0335249256
eISBN: 9780335249268

Library of Congress Cataloging-in-Publication Data
CIP data applied for

Typeset by Transforma Pvt. Ltd., Chennai, India

Praise page

This clearly written and engaging book will be of interest to HE practitioners, students and researchers who want to support more inclusive learning environments. Drawing on their own innovative empirical research, Wong and Chiu tease apart differing perceptions of the 'ideal' university student, exploring useful and informative variations, meanings and implications for practice.

Professor Louise Archer, Karl Mannheim Professor of
Sociology of Education, UCL Institute of Education, UK.

Wong and Chiu's recommended and timely account provides us with opportunities to both reflect upon and deconstruct what we believe The Ideal Student to be. Applicable at undergraduate and postgraduate levels, the importance of this research resides in its implications for practice in higher education.

Dr. Richard Race, School of Education, University of Roehampton, UK.

This is a timely and important book which conceptualises the ideal student in higher education. The book also offers a multi-stakeholder perspective on the ideal student based on the extensive empirical research. The concept of the ideal student advances our understanding of why some students excel in their university study while some do not. It has practical implications for improving retention and student success in higher education.

Dr Feng Su, Head of Education Studies, Liverpool Hope University, UK

This is a rigorously informed and illuminating reconsideration of the notion of the Ideal Type of student in higher education. This mixed methods study successfully explores the concept of the ideal student from the perspectives of students and university staff. It makes an important contribution to the debates around higher education expectations of students and demonstrates as a diverse group, students bring different experiences and aims to the university. Whilst the construction of 'the ideal type' has fixed and limited expectations of students to the detriment of their educational opportunities, this book identifies opportunities for staff and students to engage in a reconstruction of what it means to be a higher education student and thereby address inequalities in the teaching and learning experiences of students. A very readable and thought-provoking book.

Professor Gill Crozier DPhil, FRSA, University of Roehampton, UK

This is a detailed exploration of the implicit assumptions made by higher education staff and students that underpin their views of what makes an 'ideal' student. Drawing on a two-year mixed methods study, it makes many interesting points about the perspectives of both groups, and how they inform various social processes within contemporary higher education.

Professor Rachel Brooks, Department of Sociology, University of Surrey, UK

The book by Wong and Chiu invites reflection and discussion about what staff and students in higher education expect and anticipate of each other. Based on solid empirical work, combining qualitative and quantitative data, the book offers an insight into the perception of whom and what the ideal student is. The results deserve to be studied and discussed in their own right, but the book also calls for further research and discussion about similarities and differences, nuances and changes and about what is expressed and what runs under the surface and behind our backs. The book is a valuable contribution to the conversation about higher education, what it is and could be, including about diversity and inclusion.

Professor Lars Ulriksen, Department of Science Education, University of Copenhagen, Denmark

Contents

Figures and tables

Acknowledgements

The seeds of this book were planted in 2014 when Billy completed a professional development programme linked to the accreditation of Fellowship of the Higher Education Academy (FHEA) in the UK. The idea of the ideal student started as a simple summer project, with the aim to improve our teaching practices and understandings of students. Our interest in student experiences grew and we began doing small-scale qualitative studies in each of the following three summers as we explored the academic success of 'non-traditional' students. These data encouraged us to revive our interest in the concept of the ideal student. We received funding from the British Academy/Leverhulme Small Research Grant (SG 170137, 2017–2019) to develop our thoughts, which has led to this book. We are grateful to the funders and grant reviewers for their confidence and support, especially Gill Crozier who wrote the reference.

There are many people we would like to thank. We want to acknowledge the support of our research assistants, Myrto Nikolopoulou and Meggie Copsey-Blake, for their help with data collection and the literature review, especially on graduate attributes. We would also like to thank our student researchers Dana Chow, Maja Wojtynska, Nadia Gjerdingen and Shiyao Ke. Our project benefited from Imperial's StudentShapers programme, which supports partnership in learning, teaching and research between staff and students.

Our special thanks go to Jen DeWitt, who was our consultant and adviser for the quantitative part of the project. Without her help, we would have struggled with the survey analysis. We want to thank colleagues who supported our survey data collection, especially as gatekeepers to their students. We are especially appreciative of the support and enthusiasm of Freddie Page, Hilary Harris, Julia Choate, Magda Charalambous and Steve Connolly, who were brave enough to try out the ideal student survey as a tool for student induction.

We want to thank the support of our colleagues at the Institute of Education (University of Reading) and the Centre for Higher Education Research and Scholarship (Imperial College London). We are grateful to our friends and colleagues who offered their valuable time and expertise to provide constructive feedback on different chapters and sections of this book, especially during the coronavirus pandemic. Our sincere appreciation goes to Alan Floyd, Camille Kandiko Howson, Carol Fuller, Eliel Cohen, Emily Dawson, Kate Hoskins, Jen DeWitt, Jo Horsburgh, Lars Ulriksen, Martyn Kingsbury, Olympia Palikara, Órla Murray, Pengchong (Anthony) Zhang, Peter Kemp, Rachel Brooks, Susana Castro-Kemp and Suzanne Graham. Whilst the revision process has also brought out our mutual friend, *Imposter Syndrome*, we have learnt to be more comfortable in sharing our ideas and thoughts, even if it is, and probably always will be, a work in progress. We convinced ourselves that the ideal student project has the potential to make a difference now, so why wait?

We would like to acknowledge that the book includes elements from our previously published work in open-access articles, namely *AERA Open* (Sage), *British Journal of Sociology of Education, Educational Review, Journal of Further and Higher Education* and *Studies in Higher Education* (all Taylor & Francis). These articles are included in the reference list. Our thanks also go to Laura Pacey and Clara Heathcock at the Open University Press for their encouragement and prompt replies to our questions and queries. We thank Yu-Ting Wong, who helped us with the layout of the supplementary tables in Appendix 3. A line of code reduced hours of manual copy-and-paste into a few minutes of formatting.

The book would not be possible without the participation and support of students and staff. We thank them for their valuable input. Writing this book has been challenging, but all in all, we found it enjoyable and thought-provoking. We hope this book will offer interesting and inspiring insights for our readers.

Billy Wong and Y.L. Tiffany Chiu

1 Introduction

You may be intrigued, curious or even sceptical when you read the title of this book, *The Ideal Student*. It would be easy to conclude here and say that there is no such thing because what it means to be an ideal student can vary from person to person. Yet, the complexities of the concept of the ideal student are exciting to explore and we invite you to hear us out. This book discusses what it means to be an ideal student in contemporary higher education. We look at it from different perspectives, starting with the basic definitions before we move on to the conceptual, empirical and practical implications. Essentially, we argue that the concept of the ideal student offers a transparent and timely space for us to reflect, explore, discuss and appreciate the different views and expectations of university students. We want to understand the shared but often implicit assumptions and desirable expectations that students and staff have about the roles and responsibilities of university students. When expectations of students are unclear or assumed, some will struggle or even be disadvantaged, which has implications for student welfare and social justice. The ideal student concept therefore challenges key stakeholders such as students, staff and university leaders to really think about what they expect and desire of university students, beyond the minimum requirements (e.g. for retention, progression or completion of their degrees).

We want to know, how is the ideal student imagined and envisioned? To what extent are characteristics of the ideal student realistic and achievable? Are certain students more or less likely to aspire to, identify or even embody characteristics that are considered to be desirable? Are there any features of the ideal student that are widely shared and recognised? What about differences in opinions and values, especially between staff and students? More broadly, how do people from different social backgrounds and positions construct their ideal student? As these questions suggest, there can be multiple formations of the ideal student and the purpose of this book is to deconstruct and analyse how university staff and students, from different disciplines and universities, construct and negotiate their own ideal students.

Defining ideal

The word *ideal* is often used to describe our dreams and aspirations, such as the ideal house, the ideal car, the ideal holiday or even the ideal job. Most of us will have at least some ideas about these scenarios. The word ideal can also be applied to social roles and positions, for example the ideal citizen, the ideal partner, the ideal boyfriend/husband, the ideal girlfriend/wife, the ideal employer/employee or worker, the ideal teacher and, of course, the ideal student. In everyday practice, the term ideal candidate is often used in job advertisements to outline the requirements and expectations of the successful applicant, even though the selection process may include considerations of implicit or hidden factors that reflects internal priorities (Chiu 2019). We could extend the use of ideal for institutions and establishments, such as the ideal school, the ideal hospital or even the ideal society, which would invite deeper philosophical debates. For example, we could go all the way back to ancient Greek philosopher Plato and the *theory of Forms* or *Ideas*, which highlights the importance of imagination between abstract and concrete realities (MacIntosh 2012). We know this is an oversimplistic interpretation of Plato's work and even if we just focus on individual roles such as that of a student, the concept of ideal is sufficiently complicated. Our aim in this book is to explore and discuss the concept of the ideal student in higher education. We want to know what is desirable and ideal in a university student, according to staff and students themselves.

Dictionary definitions of the word *ideal* typically include the word *perfect* in parts of its clarifications (e.g. 'a standard of perfection', Merriam-Webster.com), while the broader interpretations of ideal would mean 'a standard or principle to be aimed at' (Lexico.com), even though it is likely to exist 'only in the imagination' (Dictionary.com). In other words, ideal can be interpreted as an imaginary vision or target that is largely shaped by prior experiences, knowledge, views or ideas. It is important to state that our conceptualisation of the ideal student does not mean perfection or the best, as the rest of this book will argue (especially Chapter 3). There are, of course, other words and terminologies that appear similar to the ideal student, such as the model student, the brilliant student, the outstanding student, the excellent student, the high-achieving student, the successful student (e.g. Nyström et al. 2019; O'Shea and Delahunty 2018; Picton et al. 2018; Wong 2015) and, as suggested already, the perfect or best student. The differences between a good and an ideal student are discussed in Chapter 8.

We acknowledge that these words and their dictionary definitions can sometimes overlap and even be considered as synonymous with each other, but each descriptor, arguably, has a slightly different meaning and implication, especially when applied in specific contexts. There are important nuances but the keyword *ideal* truly captures the essence of our research and starting points, which, for us, were also inspired by Max Weber's (1949) theory of *ideal types* (see Chapter 2). Essentially, we want to highlight what is expected of students in higher education. These expectations constitute an ideal because it represents our aspirations or targets, even if in practice these ideals may be difficult to realise. While we view ideals as mainly conceptual and as existing to provide us with conjectural reference points, there are also practical implications (see Chapter 9). We are aware that the notion of ideal is riddled with presumptions and ambiguities, and these concerns, as well as potentials, are discussed conceptually and empirically throughout the book.

Before that, it is important for us to situate the context of the ideal student concept in the field of higher education.

The context of higher education

Over the last few decades, an increase in graduates has become a priority for many governments and their educational policies around the world in response to the 'knowledge economy' (Marginson 2011, 2016). Globally, the graduate population is on the rise, driven by the promise that a degree will enable better employment opportunities and economic prosperities (Brown et al. 2011; De Vries 2014; OECD 2017). In 2017, over half of all adults aged 25–34 in the UK, Canada, Japan and Korea were degree-educated, with the US, Australia, Norway, Switzerland and Sweden expected to surpass the halfway mark imminently (OECD 2018). The growth in higher education has generally been positive, especially when we consider how exclusive universities were in the not too distant past. The university student population is now more diverse than it has ever been, especially in the UK (the context of this book), and hopefully this trend continues into the next decade (AdvanceHE 2019). There are, of course, still many issues and problems from access to participation to outcome, and there are fantastic and critical works which have explored these issues in-depth (e.g. Burke 2012). Our purpose here is not to delve deeply into these debates, because that merits a separate book, but to provide sufficient context so that we can explain the purpose of, and inspirations for, our research.

There are two premises to our research. First, we recognise that there are now more people going into higher education from a wider range of backgrounds. Sometimes referred as *non-traditional* students, we have seen an increase in students who are the first in their family to attend university, as well as students who are traditionally underrepresented in higher education, such as those from low-income households, minority ethnic/racial backgrounds, over the age of 21 and with a declared disability. Second, key stakeholders such as university staff, students and higher education institutions most definitely have expectations of university students, be it stated or unstated. These expectations and ideas can have real consequences for students when there are mismatches of values and practices, especially if the expectations held of students are not clearly or explicitly communicated.

Understanding and managing expectations

With the ever-changing demands and expectations of university staff and students around the world, we believe the concept of the ideal student has the potential to challenge existing and unspoken assumptions of students that can have unintended and negative consequences for social equity, particularly in countries that operate with a higher education market (e.g. Australia, England, New Zealand and the US, where universities compete for student as consumers who pay tuition fees). The ideal student concept is about managing expectations between different stakeholders, especially staff and students (Wong and Chiu 2019a). Universities are more focused than ever before on the student experience, especially the services and support available to current and pro-spective students (BIS 2016). This trend has urged universities to review their learning and teaching strategies, thinking beyond the transmission of knowl-edge to consider pedagogical transformation that creates a more supportive and interactive environment for students (Burke et al. 2017; Evans et al. 2015; Wong and Chiu 2019b). Given this context, the ideal student concept provides a more explicit and transparent recognition of the different expectations held of higher education students from different stakeholders. This understanding is important for the growing diversity of students, especially for those from non-traditional as well as international backgrounds. We aim to minimise the possible disadvantages due to differences in what is now expected of university students.

With a heterogenous university student population, there are also more inequalities of experience. A plethora of research has investigated the strug-gles and challenges of non-traditional students in higher education, such as the student experience before, during and after their degrees. These studies, along-side many others, discussed student attainment, aspirations and university readiness, as well as broader identity concerns of university belongingness, including inequalities of gender, social class and ethnicity (e.g. Cotton et al. 2016; Kuh et al. 2006; Richardson 2008; Thomas 2011). Many studies have also explored university students' transition, retention and adaptability, where dif-ferences or clashes in cultures, values, identities and practices between higher education institutions and non-traditional university students have been high-lighted (e.g. Bathmaker et al. 2013; Bowles and Brindle 2017; Holmegaard et al. 2017; Hughes and Smail 2015; Laing et al. 2005; Leathwood and Read 2009; Lowe and Cook 2003; Marshall et al. 2016; Meehan and Howells 2018; Reay et al. 2010; Schömer and González-Monteagudo 2013; Turner and Tobbell 2018; Willcoxson et al. 2011; Wong 2018; Wong and Chiu 2019c). These studies have illustrated the barriers and struggles of non-traditional students in higher educa-tion, which are also linked to growing concerns around student wellbeing and mental health, especially around stress, anxiety and self-harm, driven by the various challenges of university study (Baik et al. 2019; Brown 2016), including feelings of uncertainties about the higher education experience and process. Many of these issues are also applicable to international students, some of whom navigate language challenges, if different to the host country, as well as broader cultural differences and practices (McDonald 2014; Murray 2016).

In short, we know that hidden and implicit expectations of students have long disadvantaged those who have struggled to understand or *play* the higher education game. These students are typically from non-traditional backgrounds but can also include international students. The UK government, for instance, wants to welcome 600,000 international students by the year 2030, up from 460,000 in 2018 (ukcisa.org.uk). Whilst widening and improving access into uni-versity is important, we need to ensure that all students are provided with an equal chance for success through the removal of structural barriers, including implicit assumptions. As each student who enters higher education is likely to have their own thoughts and imaginations of what university is about, the ideal student concept offers a more specific and explicit understanding of what is expected of university students (see also Balloo et al. 2017; Hassel and Ridout 2018; Money et al. 2017). For university staff and students, a greater awareness and transparency of what constitutes the ideal undergraduate provides an opportunity to reflect and articulate the relationship between thoughts and practices. This is essential for inclusivity, as what one does might not always align with what one thinks and values, thereby conveying unintended or mixed messages.

The ideal university student

The concept of the ideal student is a distinctive and unique contribution to higher education research. Whilst the scope of our project is on the ideal undergraduate, the ideal student concept can also be applied and adapted for students in postgraduate study, which would merit additional research.

Research on the ideal student is scarce, often dated and disparate. In the 1950s, Becker (1952) wrote about the ideal pupil and reported that schoolteachers tend to value middle-class children and their values. In the 1960s, Brown (1960) and Torrance (1965) explored the personality traits of the ideal student and concluded that academic competence and aptitude were the fundamental basis of an ideal student in higher education. Literature from educational psychology, which is overwhelmingly quantitative, has also focused on individual factors as key predictors for academic success, including self-belief, motivation, preparation, learning styles, personality traits and the practice of self-regulated learning (Burger and Naude 2019; Komarraju et al. 2011; Lee and Lee 2012; Richardson et al. 2012; York et al. 2015). However, academic success – especially attainment – is not necessarily an attribute of the ideal student in higher education (Wong and Chiu 2020). More recent studies related to the ideal student were mostly conducted in schools (Bradbury 2013, 2019; Harkness et al. 2007; Maslovaty et al. 2008), including a focus on the ideal teacher (Arnon and Reichel 2007; Robson 2018). In general, these studies reported the ideal pupil to be attentive, disciplined, obedient, respectful, responsible and punctual.

The beginning of university often coincides with the start of students' adulthood and the age of independence (typically 18, but can be up to 21), which can be an exciting but also terrifying period of transition, particularly for those who live away from home for the first time. Some will thrive and settle in seamlessly, but many others will need to learn and adapt as they navigate and negotiate their newfound roles and responsibilities as a university student. For instance, university teaching typically places more onus on the individual to prepare or read before/beyond a lesson. There is often a leap from their school learning which is typically more confined and structured. Entering university could also challenge students' self-identity. The highest achievers in one school may suddenly find it difficult to maintain such status in a competitive university as other students were also the highest achievers in their respective schools.

What we know is that the limited research related to the ideal university student has reported academic skills, abilities and attainment to be highly desirable in students by lecturers in Sweden, which included staff from biomedicine, chemistry, engineering and physiotherapy (Thunborg et al. 2012). In Denmark, tutors have envisioned the ideal physics undergraduates to be interested, committed, modest and clever (Ulriksen 2009). In our earlier research, we found social science lecturers in England to construct their ideal students as prepared, engaged, committed, critical, reflective and progressing, whilst highlighting the insignificance of student attainment (Wong and Chiu 2020). From these literatures, we can say that although the ideal university student may vary by discipline, institution or even country, these expectations and ideals, at the very least, offer current and future students an indication of the attributes that are valued in their respective contexts. The intention of this book is to deconstruct the ideal student in higher education, with the focus on the UK context.

Why is this research important?

As the global higher education sector continues to place greater emphasis on student rights and demands (Brown and Carasso 2013), it is crucial that expectations of students are clearly communicated between educators and learners so that potential mismatches of expectations can be appropriately addressed. The concept of the ideal student can reduce uncertainty and anxiety that some students may have about what lecturers and the university expect from them, beyond the minimum expectations or even the 'average' or 'typical' student. By uncovering some of these ideal characteristics, students and staff would be better informed and will have the opportunity to discuss, negotiate and reflect on their similarities and differences about ideal expectations of students at university. As such, the concept has the potential to enhance the quality of learning and teaching as it encourages us to appreciate the different visions of what it means to be a university student.

We believe in the need for greater openness around what is ideally expected of students at university, and critically reflect on these shared desirable student characteristics and whether it privileges certain social groups over others. A stronger and perhaps even shared understanding of what is expected of ideal students could also alleviate the mismatches of values and expectations and potentially strengthen the staff–student relationship – a key influence in students' academic progress and outcome (Rockoff 2004). The aim of this research is not just to highlight mismatches between the views of staff and students, but to also invite students and staff into the same conversation to discuss what is or should be desirable and expected of undergraduate students. There is scope for students to be more active learning agents as their voices and viewpoints could be better recognised, valued and even rewarded (Burke et al. 2016). We also want to promote a mindset that recognises and appreciates the holistic aims of higher education, such as the importance of transferable and higher-order skills development, rather than, say, an exclusive focus on academic outcome/ attainment in formal assessment.

This book will be particularly useful and relevant for university staff and practitioners across all disciplines, particularly those with responsibilities in teaching and supporting learning, curriculum design and pedagogical development. As staff and students are both active agents in shaping their respective roles and responsibilities, our discussions of the ideal student will encourage readers to reflect and relate the findings to their own experiences, especially the different ways in which conversations about the ideal student correspond to their contexts. In the final chapter of this book (Chapter 9), we offer practical ideas and activities that can be adopted by staff in their own practices to support student transition and progression, as well as to better manage student expectations of higher education through greater transparency and mutual understanding.

The concept of the ideal student offers a fresh and exciting approach to comprehend desirable expectations of university students. An appreciation of our respective ideals is important because universities around the world continue to change and adapt to government policies and ideologies. Our aim is to interrogate how the notion of the ideal student is understood, interpreted and recognised, as well as challenged and negotiated by university staff and students. In doing so, expectations of students will be more transparent and better managed, which is important for openness and equality. Implicit rules and practices can breed inequalities, especially by social class, where more/less privileged students operate with different resources and dispositions to navigate their higher education journeys (see Chapter 2). We believe that our conceptualisation of the ideal student has the potential to disrupt some of these structural barriers, starting with the emphasis and reflection that unspoken rules or hidden expectations of students are made more explicit and transparent. Until we have an honest and open conversation about our respective ideal university students, the impact of well-intended initiatives to support university students may not be maximised.

The research study

This book draws on a two-year mixed-methods study funded by the British Academy and Leverhulme Trust, with the aim to map out the different characteristics of the ideal student in UK higher education. Further details of the research methodology can be found in Appendix 1. In short, the data included 33 hour-long focus groups with 132 university staff and students, as well as a questionnaire completed by 1,043 participants. Whilst the data were collected in the UK, especially in England for the focus groups, it is hoped that the issues we cover are relevant and applicable to universities worldwide, and particularly pertinent in higher education contexts that are driven by a market mechanism.

For the focus groups, participants were asked to discuss their respective views and interpretations of the concept of ideal *per se*, including the potential problems and possibilities as we refine our collective understanding of the ideal student and the characteristics that are considered desirable for students in higher education. Participants came from five universities across three English regions, including both pre-92 and post-92 institutions, from the broad disciplines of the applied sciences, arts & humanities, natural sciences and social sciences. Pre-92 universities are typically considered to be more research-oriented, especially *Russell Group* universities. Post-92 universities are mostly former polytechnics, with a history of being more teaching-oriented. Data were thematically analysed with support from the software *NVivo 12*.

Our ideal university student survey was developed empirically from focus group data alongside existing literature and related questionnaire items. Of the 1,043 participants, we had 700+ students and 300+ staff from 20+ pre- and post-92 UK universities across the four abovementioned broad disciplines. The survey included 50 items on various ideal student characteristics. Respondents were asked to rate the items on a 5-point Likert scale: 'not important (1)', 'slightly important (2)', 'moderately important (3)', 'important (4)' and 'very important (5)', in relation to their own views of the ideal university student. All questions were optional, and participants' demographic data were collected to enable interactional and regression analyses. Using the software *SPSS 25*, exploratory factor analysis was carried out with statistically significant 'factors' to be discussed as key dimensions of the ideal student in higher education (and more importantly, how these items, or 'factors', differ between different participants and their demographic backgrounds).

Essentially, we wanted to know what university staff and students had to say about the concept of ideal, as well as their own constructions of the ideal higher education student, and how these may differ due to their respective roles and subject disciplines.

Outline of chapters

This book is organised into nine chapters, each designed with a clear focus and logic that takes the reader through a journey to appreciate and understand the aims and purposes of this research and its implications.

This chapter has introduced the ideal student project and its rationales, alongside an overview of the higher education landscape. The importance of our focus on the concept of the ideal student was discussed. In Chapter 2, we review a range of empirical and theoretical literature to support the development of the concept of the ideal student. In Chapter 3, we highlight the concerns as well as potentials of the concept of the ideal student, drawing on our empirical data. Chapters 2 and 3 therefore provide the conceptual foundations for our thinking on the ideal student, using existing studies and ideas to formulate and review our understanding, followed by qualitative data to elaborate how the notion of the ideal student *per se* is understood and conceived by university staff and students.

Chapter 4 moves on to the attributes of the ideal student, with a descriptive mapping of the various ideal student characteristics that were articulated by our participants. In other words, Chapter 4 presents and describes the items used in our ideal university student survey, which lays the foundation for Chapters 5, 6 and 7, where we discuss the ideal student characteristics as expressed by different types of respondents, drawing on both quantitative and qualitative data.

Chapter 5 focuses on the similarities and differences between staff and student views of the ideal student characteristics. Chapter 6 considers how the ideal student is constructed differently according to university type (i.e. *pre-92* and *post-92*) and discipline (e.g. *STEM* and *SHAPE* subjects). Chapter 7 explores the social identities and inequalities associated with the characteristics and conceptualisations of the ideal university student, such as variations by gender, social class, ethnicity and age.

In Chapter 8, we focus on the views and identities of students, especially their personal identifications with the ideal student. Here, we discuss the question, *is the ideal student me?* and explore the factors that appear to influence how students associate with the ideal student identity. In particular, we make comparisons with the identity of the *good student* as we further develop and consolidate our understandings.

In Chapter 9 we focus on the implications of our study for practice, with suggestions and examples of the application of the ideal university student survey to support student transition and progression. Here, we bring together the key messages from earlier chapters as we set out our aspirations and next steps for higher education research and practice.

There are also three appendices. Appendix 1 provides full details of the research methodology, Appendix 2 presents the final list of items in the ideal university student survey, while Appendix 3 includes a number of supplementary tables from the survey analysis.

Summary

Chapter 1 introduced the concept of the ideal student in higher education, which aims to promote a more transparent conversation about what expectations are held of university students. We argued that the concept of the ideal student offers a fresh and useful way to explore and reflect on contemporary higher education teaching and learning practices, with potential implications for social justice and inclusion. The ideal student should be thought of not only as a conceptual tool but also a practical construct that encourages critical self-reflection, explicitness and transparency about our ideal expectations of university students.

2 Understanding the concept of ideal

With the background of the research already explained, the purpose of Chapter 2 is to offer a deeper insight into the educational literatures that will help us understand the concept of *ideal*, especially in the context of university students. To do so, we will explore the relevant theories and discuss how these ideas are potentially useful in our conceptualisation of the ideal student.

As mentioned in Chapter 1, our theoretical inspiration came from Max Weber's theory of *ideal types*, which ultimately informed our use of the word *ideal* when thinking about desirable expectations of students. Yet, we also recognise and acknowledge that it is important for us to situate our thinking within other existing concepts and literatures. We want to further explore and discuss these related ideas as it will undoubtedly help us to better contextualise and consolidate our thinking and understanding of the ideal student. More specifically, in addition to *ideal types*, this chapter will also review concepts and literature on *imagined and social identity*; *possible selves*; *being a university student* and *graduate attributes*. The latter, we believe, may also be interpreted as the *ideal graduate*. We appreciate there could always be additional ideas or research that are relevant to exploring the concept of ideal, but it would be unrealistic for us (or anyone) to include all possible literature that may be related.[1] The ideas we discuss below will help us to establish a strong foundation on which to think about and theorise the concept of the ideal student. In the next chapter, we also consult the views of our participants as we work towards a working definition that reflects our approach to defining the concept of the ideal student.

---

1 As we stretched our thinking and review of relevant work, an argument can be made for a number of studies to be included in our discussion. However, to enable a more focused discussion of the key ideas that ultimately shaped our thinking, the following writers and ideas were not included, even though their research could arguably be contextualised in our current project, and certainly worthy to explore in the future. These include Margaret Archer's (1995) realist social theory, Tony Becher and Paul Trowler's (2001) academic tribes and territories, Basil Bernstein's (2000) pedagogic device, Dorothy Holland and colleagues' (1998) theory of identity-in-practice, Ernesto Laclau and Chantal Mouffe's (2014) hegemony and socialist strategy, Bruno Latour's (2013) modes of existence, Karl Maton's (2000) legitimate code theory, Wally Morrow's (2009) epistemological access, and Brian Street's (1994) autonomous and ideological model of literacy.

Ideal types

According to Weber, the purpose of *ideal types* is to provide:

> comparison with empirical reality in order to establish its divergences or similarities, to describe them with the *most unambiguously intelligible concepts*, and to understand and explain them causally. (1949: 43)

In other words, Weber considered ideal types to be an abstract concept that allows us to think about society and social phenomena. He conceived ideal types as the mental constructs that we develop to make sense of, and comparisons with, reality. For Weber, ideal types are crucial to the functioning and stability of societies because individual members of society can associate their own views and experiences with these ideals, as a point of reference, to further construct, develop and negotiate their social understanding and interactions. For example, ideal types can help us to appreciate and comprehend the roles of schools and teachers, which are constructed and developed over time through lived experiences and reflections, as well as through different ideas, expectations and anticipations about their roles and responsibilities. Weber (1978: 21) believed that anyone can construct ideal types as long as they can act 'in a rational way'; 'has complete information'; 'is totally aware of what he/she is doing' and 'does not make any mistakes'. These criteria, of course, are unrealistic in reality but serve as an important reminder that ideal types are essentially figments of our imaginations, with the purpose to be critically compared with reality (and adjusted as appropriate) so that ideal types are not out-of-touch with what happens in everyday life interactions and experiences (Swedberg 2018).

Ideal types can therefore support the functioning of societal normality by being part of the socialisation process that provides us with the dispositions to interpret, react and respond to the complexities of everyday life occurrences (Stemplowska 2008). For instance, knowledge of the ideal body temperature, amount of sleep, weight or blood pressure allows us to compare with an agreed, accepted, dominant or popular standard. These ideals provide a transparent benchmark, which can still be challenged and revised if necessary. Such ideals are also achievable, even if only temporary. Although the ideal state or range in these examples are in quantifiable metrics, the construction of ideals can also be qualitative, with richer descriptions but also broader interpretations and therefore even disagreements. Yet, all ideals serve the same function, which is to make transparent and explicit the expectations or visions. More specifically, Weber (1978) mentioned that ideal types can be useful in at least three ways – for *terminological* purposes, for *classificatory* purposes and for *heuristic* purposes. According to Swedberg (2018: 189–190), 'clarity is always important, and classifications are useful, but the heart of a good sociological analysis consists of coming up with new ideas in analysing social reality, verified by the facts'. We concur with this view as we attempt to create a working definition of the concept of the ideal student in higher education, supported by quantitative and qualitative evidence (see Gerhardt 1994).

Like beauty, ideals can be in the eye of the beholder, especially at the individual level. However, our collective ideals, or ideal types, are shared at the societal level and likely to be part of dominant discourses (Burr 2015). Although by no means unanimous, these discourses, including ideals, would constitute the prevailing views and expectations. Whilst we recognise that ideals can have unintended and negative consequences, such as stereotypes, we believe that by unpacking our own ideals of the university student will encourage a more transparent conversation about the student practices that are rewarded or punished in higher education.

We stress that the ideal student is not meant to be a direct reflection of specific individuals with particular attributes. Rather, following Weber's (1949, 1978) theory of ideal types, the ideal student constitutes a collective recognition of the range of features that we find desirable across a spectrum of students. Interestingly, some scholars have focused on the notion of *non-ideal* and argued that 'the best way of realising the ideal is through the recognition of the importance of theorising the non-ideal' (Mills 2005: 166). In other words, we could also identify what is *not* desirable as a way to support formulation of our visions and ideals. For our study, this could also mean an understanding of the characteristics that we do *not* expect in an ideal university student. Similarly, this means we could also consider the *least/minimum* as well as the *most/maximum* that are expected of students. By exploring what the ideal student is *not*, we could be building a better understanding of what the ideal student *is*, although we ought to be mindful of the context. Moving beyond our main inspiration, the rest of the chapter will now consider other key ideas and literature that we feel are relevant to the concept of the ideal student.

Imagined and social identity

The first related and complementary ideas we explore are the notions of *imagined identity* and *social identity*, which we think can potentially enrich our thinking and understanding of the concept of the ideal student. We will also make brief references to more established and popular concepts, namely *imagined community*, *imagined geographies* and *social imaginaries*, to provide possible links and contextualisation. The common keyword here is *imagined*, which is defined as 'to form or have a mental picture or idea of something' (see dictionary.cambridge.org). This definition certainly seems to be in sync with Weber's ideal types.

We initially took note of the concept of *imagined identity* in a paper by De Ruyter and Conroy (2002), who wrote about the importance of ideals in the formation of identity. To put it simply, an imagined identity refers to the visions of what, where and perhaps who we wish to be in the future. The key argument here is that ideals are significant and integral to identity development, even if they are imagined. If an identity is *unimaginable* or deemed impossible or unthinkable, then the probability of the individual even contemplating the development and embodiment of such identity would be very low. An imagined identity is therefore also about what is considered feasible, possible and therefore imaginable. The ability to envision our futures is thus important in the formation and development of our aspirations and sense of selves, which we explore later under the concept of *possible selves*.

We argue that the notion of imagined identity can also be situated within the plethora of research on social identities. To keep it brief, prominent writers have argued that our identity is a social construction and development that is always *in process* (Hall 1990), it is performative (Butler 1990), it is relational (Lawler 2014) and it is intersectional (Collins and Bilge 2016; Crenshaw 1991). Social identity is generally regarded as fluid and entangled within complex relations of power. Our identity can therefore be thought of as a continuous project of social constructions, constituting an ongoing process of negotiation within multifaceted structural and agentic relationships. According to Wenger (1998), identity is a negotiated experience through the lived experiences and practices of our environments (i.e. community of practice). Whilst the people around us can contribute towards a collective sense of identity, say, within an academic community, the practices of individuals are also moulded by departmental and institutional forces and values, through gradual socialisation and normalisation (Fitzmaurice 2013; Kreber 2010). In other words, the identities and roles of students and staff are influenced by the (real or imagined) communities of practice in which they are engaged, which can be specific to a discipline or university. On a personal level, Gee (2000) and many others have argued that our identity essentially boils down to the certain kind of person that one wants to be and be recognised as. As such, while our imagined identity may shed light on what we strive to achieve, typically for ourselves, we must appreciate that these imaginations, if they are to be realistic or intelligible, will also be influenced by expectations of others, especially since social identities are only sustainable through recognition by self and by others.

We want to briefly mention the popular term *role model*, which is defined as 'a person looked to by others as an example to be imitated' (see Lexico.com). A role model is an identity that is widely celebrated and regarded as a template for others to learn or reproduce (Collins 1996; Merton 1968). In everyday life, people may self-identify or be identified by others as a role model, such as in a classroom, a workplace or by community members (see also Teigen et al. 2000). On some levels, role model operates in a similar way as the concept of the ideal student, but the former is typically named and embodied by particular individuals whilst the latter is more abstract, with traits and characteristics that in reality may not exist or only be found across a spectrum of students. The concept of the ideal student unveils our ideals, including our visions and imaginations.

Beyond the focus on the individual, the concept of imagination has of course been written extensively alongside the word community, most notably in Benedict Anderson's seminal book, *Imagined Communities*, first published in 1983. The research is focused on nations and nationalism, especially the idea that whilst individuals never realistically know all community members, individually 'in the minds of each lives the image of their communion' (Anderson 1983: 49). In other words, individuals imagine themselves to be a part of a national community that shares a history, language and perhaps even particular ideas and beliefs. These imaginations can provide people with a sense of belonging through constructions of mental images of what 'people like us' are supposedly like. Similarly, Edward Said (1978) talked about *imagined geographies*, especially around Western imaginations and (mis)conceptions of Eastern cultures, which were often perceived and constructed as inferior. More recently, philosopher Charles Taylor (2004) wrote *Modern Social Imaginaries*, building on the work of Anderson (1983). Taylor is interested in how people imagine their common and collective social life in the context of multiple modernities in Western societies. We acknowledge that our coverage of these concepts is limited but our interest here is more on the concept of imagined identity and how these plausible visions are relevant in our conceptualisations and constructions of the ideal student.

In short, the notions of imagined community, imagined geographies and social imaginaries are mostly concerned with the abstract, national and societal levels of imaginations. In the context of our research, we can perhaps interpret these perspectives of imaginations to be how students might envision their university communities, including their imaginations of fellow university students and what it means to be a university student (at their own institutions as well as more generally across the higher education sector). Nonetheless, the concept of imagined identity seems most consistent with the notion of ideal types and the overall focus of our research.

Possible selves

The notion of *possible selves* is widely accredited to a 1986 paper by Hazel Markus and Paula Nurius, who developed the concept to provide a conceptual link between cognition and motivation. The paper is built on the vast literature base in psychology, especially around self-concept and self-efficacy. Similar to imagined identity, Markus and Nurius argued that our possible selves constitute the ideas of what we expect to become, what we wish to become and what we are afraid of becoming. It is, in their words, 'how individuals think about their potential and about their future. Possible selves are the *ideal selves* that we would very much like to become' (Markus and Nurius 1986: 954). This elaboration, as far as we understood it, mirrors the concept of imagined identity and is consistent with Weber's theory of ideal types.

Whilst Weber (1949) stated ideal types are important for social functioning, Markus and Nurius (1986: 954) argued that a key purpose of possible selves is to 'mediate personal functioning'. Thus, the emphasis here is more on the individual and their range of selves, or identities, that are conceived as possible and probable. As with theories on social identity, Markus and Nurius also envisioned possible selves as being shaped, influenced and even limited by an individual's past experiences and personal encounters. Constructions of our possible futures are therefore not boundless because our scope of possible selves is inevitably reflective of our rather particular 'sociocultural and historical context ... [and] immediate social experiences' (1986: 954). As such, possible selves can simply be the expected views of ourselves for the future, including what we hope to become as well as what we fear of becoming. The theory of possible selves is popular in the US, especially in social psychology and research into student goals and aspirations (e.g. Oyserman et al. 2004; Pizzolato 2007; Rossiter 2009).

In the UK, Stevenson and Clegg (2011) applied the lens of possible selves to explore how undergraduates imagined their future selves and employment pathways and reported that some students struggled to construct their possible futures due to the dire state of their current challenges or constraints. As a notion for understanding motivation and self-concept, Erikson (2007) suggested that our approach to possible selves should place greater emphasis on personal agency and experience in the formation of future selves and move away from imaginations that are too abstract or superficial. Thus, possible selves should precisely be selves that are possible and realistic, rather than just wishful or even delusional thinking. In their introduction to the edited volume *Possible Selves and Higher Education*, Henderson, Stevenson and Bathmaker (2019) explore the applicability of possible selves in higher education, with theoretical and empirical insights that incorporate sociological thinking and an explicit recognition of the role of social inequalities such as gender, social class and 'race'/ethnicity. A number of researchers contributed to that collection and one of the central messages is an appreciation that possible selves and futures are imagined within structural barriers and exclusionary practices. In other words, students cannot just imagine their future selves in any way that are desired because their imaginations are also shaped and limited by their past and present social positions and dispositions, demographic backgrounds and sociocultural contexts (see also Harrison 2018).

Being a university student

Students from non-traditional or underrepresented backgrounds often encounter social inequalities and barriers, which can shape their identities and experiences of university as a place not for 'people like me' (see Chapter 1). Becoming a university student is an identity that is increasingly fluid and fragile, especially with the higher education market and the shifting roles and responsibilities of institutions, staff and students (Brown and Carasso 2013). In this section, we provide a brief overview of the inequalities as experienced by university students, especially those from non-traditional backgrounds. Our focus is then on literatures we identified that are particularly relevant to our research on the ideal university student, namely the book by Ronald Barnett (2007) on being a university student in an age of uncertainty, Lars Ulriksen's (2009) concept of the *implied student*, and Rachel Brooks' *EuroStudents* (2016–2021) project on the construction of university students in Europe.

Higher education, and education more generally, is often celebrated as the engine of social mobility (especially by the government). A degree certificate can be an entry ticket for 'graduate-level' jobs, which is counted as a marker of 'success' in university league tables and metrics (e.g. Graduate outcomes by

HESA). However, educational opportunities and outcomes are not equal. Sociologists have long argued that the production and reproduction of social inequalities are particularly prominent through the education system, which effectively functions to benefit those from more privileged backgrounds (Bourdieu and Passeron 1990). As social beings, we develop and mature under specific environments and conditions, which facilitate and shape our comprehensions of, and approaches to, the world.

As such, the experiences and benefits of education are not the same for every student because of their unequal starting points, with differences in prior knowledge, dispositions and resources (Bourdieu 1977, 1986). The socially privileged are better prepared and equipped than the socially and economically deprived. Higher education is no different, with hidden rules, assumptions and expectations that appear to favour those from more privileged backgrounds (Elliot et al. 2020; Portelli 1993). Bathmaker et al. (2013) explored the university experiences of working-class and middle-class undergraduates and highlighted the advantage of the latter group in terms of access to valued capital, such as securing internships and participation in extracurricular activities, as well as their dispositions to play the higher education game or understand the implicit or hidden rules (which can result in rewards or punishments).

The university experiences of non-traditional students can be highly complex, and the struggles of *fitting in* have been a useful notion of enquiry in UK, US, Canadian and Australian higher education research (e.g. Collier and Morgan 2008; Groves and O'Shea 2019; Leese 2010; Lehmann 2007; Meuleman et al. 2015). In short, students from working-class/first-generation at university, minority ethnic, disabled and/or mature backgrounds are more likely to feel alienated at universities (especially in 'elite' universities) and less likely to access or possess academic resources, knowledge and dispositions (e.g. Dong and Lucas 2016; O'Shea 2015; Reay et al. 2010; Shiner and Noden 2015; Walkerdine 2011). These studies, and many others, have explored issues related to student transition, progression and attrition, as well as their economic, social and cultural challenges due to unfamiliarity with higher education (e.g. Crozier et al. 2008; Fuller 2014; Leathwood 2006; Leathwood and O'Connell 2003; Munro 2011; O'Shea 2014; Thunborg and Bron 2019; Tinto 1993; Ulriksen et al. 2017).

Here, implicit and occluded expectations of students can disadvantage those who struggle to understand but also powerless to play (and win) the higher education game, which is especially pertinent for students from underrepresented backgrounds (Jones 2018). For a more equitable outcome and experience, there is an urgent need to disrupt the system and empower students to recognise and renegotiate the rules of higher education, especially those that are implicit or even hidden, which links back to the foundations of the ideal student concept – to promote mutual understandings and explicit expectations.

We believe the concept of the ideal student can provide students, especially those less familiar with higher education discourses, a better and clearer understanding of what is valued and expected at university. The concept of the ideal student has the potential to bridge differences, manage expectations and therefore reduce the uncertainty that some students may have about what lecturers and the university expect from them, as such unfamiliarity can contribute or exacerbate existing social inequality. We also recognise there is a potential dilemma between understanding the tacit and explicit norms and expectations, and the dangers around the reproduction of power and dominant discourses if students, especially those from non-traditional backgrounds, are encouraged to learn and adjust their values and practices to be in sync with what the establishment (i.e. university) expects of students. Our overall view, however, is the belief that transparency should take precedence, which can then offer potential scopes for change and renegotiation on what is currently valued and expected of students. Below, we include a short review of selected literatures which are particularly relevant and complementary to our understanding of what it means to be a university student.

A will to learn

In the book, *A Will to Learn*, Ronald Barnett (2007) invites us to think about what it means to be a university student through what he calls an *ontological turn*. Barnett offers a deep philosophical discussion on the notion of being and becoming a student as he concludes that 'in a genuine higher education, the student not merely undergoes a developmental process, but undergoes a continuing process of becoming ... marked by the student's becoming authentic and coming into herself' (2007: 62). Indeed, Barnett cautioned that students' *will to learn* and *will to offer* are rarely questioned in the literature as it is often assumed by their enrolment and presence at university. As such, his arguments are centred on the concept of *will*, notably the willingness to learn and to be a student, for understanding student progression.

Whilst the will to learn can be gained or lost, Barnett argued that an authentic student in higher education ought to take responsibility for their own learning, which includes the *qualities* of being diligent, respectful, resilient, self-disciplined, open and persistent. He also suggested that 'a will to learn; a will to engage; a preparedness to listen; a preparedness to explore; a willingness to hold oneself open to experiences; a determination to keep going forward' (Barnett 2007: 102) are *dispositions* that university students ought to develop, alongside self-belief. Furthermore, these dispositions and qualities should be assessed differently, even if tacitly. For example, dispositions may be assessed 'simply through students' willingness to submit themselves for assessment', whilst qualities may be assessed 'through the marking schemes for different assignments' (Barnett 2007: 110). Barnett does acknowledge, however, that the assessment of these dispositions and qualities might be counterproductive as students might just morph into these 'desired dispositions and qualities, rather than come into them through an authentic engagement with their educational experiences' (Barnett 2007: 110). We revisit this dilemma in Chapter 3 using our empirical data.

The implied student

From Denmark, Lars Ulriksen (2009) introduced the concept of the *implied student* to appreciate the relational and contextual expectations of students, including structural constraints and sub-disciplinary preferences. Ulriksen argued that the curriculum and culture of the discipline and institution offer students 'a set of frames for what is possible if the practice should still be considered as a legitimate and comprehensible way of engaging with the study' (Ulriksen 2009: 522). In other words, a student's course of action and approaches to his or her learning are more or less conditioned and regulated in light of certain perceived situated expectations and assumptions, be they implicit or explicit, and hence generate *implied* action. Thus, the implied student would reflect the dominant discourses and expectations. However, Ulriksen also suggested that as students themselves are the ones who take part in and interact with their studies (in his term, 'a structure of action'), there would be more than one way of doing the study in that some might not conform to the structure of the academic and disciplinary curriculum and context.

More importantly, implied does not necessarily mean desirable, although implied does entail some mutual recognition, even if implicit. For instance, the implied role of a lecturer is often beyond teaching, as it also includes a range of administrative duties and other responsibilities that are reasonably expected of that role. In a recent strike action by academic staff in the UK, the phrase 'implied terms' was used by human resources to highlight the unwritten and unspoken duties of lecturers that are apparently 'deemed to be too obvious to be written down' (BBC 2019). Ulriksen's work has also been applied in the context of doctoral students (Lindvig 2018) and museum visitors (Nicolaisen and Achiam 2019), where societal and institutional norms would generate specific expectations and assumptions of these respective roles.

The concept of the implied student therefore highlights the implicit rules and expectations of students, especially the unstated but assumed knowledge or experience of the role which offers an analytical framework to investigate what teachers, programmes and institutions assume about their students. As such, while the concept of the implied student emphasises structures and conditions, it also seems to entail an aspiration that strives for greater explicitness. Building on this, our conceptualisation of the ideal student intends to bring this transparency to the fore, while at the same time foreground the desirable expectations of university students to provide a space for university staff and students to discuss and negotiate what is desirable, possible and realistic.

Eurostudents

Funded by the European Research Council, the *Eurostudents* project (2016–2021) is led by Rachel Brooks, with the aim to explore how university students are conceptualised across six European countries (Denmark, England, Ireland, Germany, Poland and Spain), including the explicit and implicit assumptions that are commonly made about higher education students. This five-year study aims to explore similarities and differences across nations, as well as how university students are constructed by policymakers (see Brooks 2019a, 2020), policies, the media, universities and students themselves. As such, this work is very relevant to our own research. For instance, Brooks (2019c) explored the construction of university students within national policy documents across European countries and found considerable differences in the positioning of students as 'objects of criticisms'. Here, some countries construct university students in more positive terms, whilst others are more critical about student quality, numbers and their progress (see Brooks 2018a, 2018b). Brooks also discussed the concept of investment, especially between students as individual investors or as a societal investment, which contributes to debates about the purpose of higher education. In short, there are national differences in what it means to be a university student in dominant policy discourses and her research challenges the view that there is homogenisation across European higher education (despite, for example, the celebrations of the *Bologna Process*, which involved a number of European countries).

More importantly, Brooks (2019b) argued that the idea of Europe constitutes an important *spatial imaginary* for Europe's universities (see also Watkins 2015), where socially held stories about particular places and spaces are collectively produced, shared and reproduced (see also Anderson's *imagined communities* earlier). These *spatial imaginaries* can shape the ways policymakers and policies construct higher education students, especially as European citizens, because Europe, as Brooks (2019b) argues, continues to constitute an *idealised space* for many nations within Europe. A key takeaway message for us here is the power of imaginations and ideals, which aligns with our focus on the concept of the ideal student. In their forthcoming edited collection, Brooks and O'Shea (2021) will also explore a range of dominant constructions of higher education students from around the world, for instance as consumers, future workers and learners. As what it means to be a university student continues to change and be influenced by national and international policies or ideologies (see also Schömer and González-Monteagudo 2013; Ulriksen et al. 2017), it is ever more important now to be transparent about our expectations and ideals of higher education students.

Ideal graduate and graduate attributes

A related concept to the ideal student is the *ideal graduate*, which focuses on the desirable features of graduates, especially from the employers' perspective (Ingram and Allen 2019). Arguably, the ideal graduate can also be thought of as a proxy for another prominent concept, *graduate attributes*, which are often publicly advertised and branded as the range of skills and qualities that students are expected to develop from the holistic education offered by that university. In this section we provide a review of the notion of graduate attributes as we appreciate the role of institutions in the construction of their desirable and ideal graduates.

In countries such as Australia, New Zealand and the UK, the higher education market has prompted universities to justify their value and worth, which has encouraged the development of graduate attributes. Our conceptualisation of the ideal student constitutes the desirable expectations of university students, which, we argue, are not all that different to graduate attributes and the ideal graduate (Mireles-Rios and Garcia 2019).

Graduate attributes can be defined as 'the qualities, skills and understandings a university community agrees its students would desirably develop during their time at the institution' (Bowden et al. 2000: 3), which are inextricably linked to employability (Spronken-Smith et al. 2013). Whilst other terms, such as graduate outcomes, graduate skills, graduate profiles, graduate qualities and graduate capabilities are also used in the literature, these are more or less synonymous with graduate attributes, especially in Australasian literature where most existing research is published (Barrie et al. 2009). In the UK, most universities have adopted a version of graduate attributes to promote the expected characteristics that their own graduates should embody upon graduation (Normand and Anderson 2017; Wong et al. forthcoming). Yet, little is known about the extent to which these graduate attributes, which are essentially institutional expectations of their ideal graduates, are shared by staff and students across disciplines and universities. We believe this is where our concept of the ideal student has the potential to inform future developments of graduate attributes (see Chapter 9).

In alignment with the ideal student concept, graduate attributes are meant to indicate to prospective and current students the range of qualities and skills that they should develop by graduation (Barrie 2012). Whilst these graduate-level skills are marketed as desired by graduate employers (Green et al. 2009), the graduate attributes promoted by the universities themselves often vary due to the competitiveness of the higher education sector and the importance for universities to be different or distinctive so as to attract students (Normand and Anderson 2017). Thus, there are numerous graduate attributes, although many are often variants of similar qualities, such as communication skills, critical awareness and cultural competence.

Graduate attributes are designed to be relevant and applicable for all graduates, but Jones (2009a, 2009b) found discipline-specific interpretations and meanings for the same attribute (e.g. critical thinking), which is not always the same. As such, there remain different opinions, or even disagreements, about the constituents of graduate attributes. According to Barrie et al. (2009), there are eight interacting stages for implementing graduate attributes: conceptions; stakeholders; implementation; curriculum; assessment; quality assurance; staff development; and student centred. We argue that the last two elements, focusing on staff and students, should be considered first and foremost in conceptualising expectations of students, be it upon graduation, as graduate attributes or during university, as ideal students at university. As key educators and learners, their views and expectations of university students would offer us a bottom-up approach to interpret what it means to be a university student. In Chapters 5 and 6, we will discuss how the ideal student is constructed differently according to students and staff, as well as by university types and broad disciplines. Although graduate attributes are marketed as the *outcome* of university learning, we believe the *processes* of learning are also important to appreciate how desirable student qualities might be developed and consolidated over the course of the degree journey.

For early career researchers in academia, the Careers Research and Advisory Centre (CRAC) has also published a Researcher Development Framework (Vitae 2011), which describes the knowledge, behaviour and attributes of successful researchers through four domains and 12 qualities. Perhaps we can interpret this as a possible template for the *ideal researcher*.

Summary

We appreciate that the concept of ideal is peppered with assumptions and uncertainties, but our starting point is that desirable expectations of university students do exist for key stakeholders such as staff, students and institutions, even if subtle, tacit or even subconscious. Sometimes, these ideals are explicitly communicated, such as graduate attributes, but more often than not they are implicit and implied, especially from the views of staff and students.

In this chapter, we explored a range of theories to strengthen our understanding of the concept of the ideal student, with a particular focus on the notions of ideal types, imagined and social identity, possible selves, being a university student (including the will to learn, the implied student and policy constructions of higher education students) and, finally, graduate attributes. These ideas help us to appreciate that, ultimately, the ideal student is simply what we desire and expect of university students and can be seen as a kind of imagined and social identity that is considered possible and therefore imaginable. The construction of the ideal student entails an ongoing process of negotiation within its situated contexts.

3   Conceptual concerns and opportunities

Whilst the previous chapter discussed the theories that underpin our conceptualisation of the idea of the ideal student, we recognise that in practice and everyday life, the term ideal student can trigger a range of assumptions. Indeed, few of our participants admitted holding a degree of scepticism and uncertainty about the meanings or implications of the concept itself when first invited to take part in the research. From their participation, we witnessed rich and reflective discussions on the challenges but also opportunities afforded by the concept of the ideal student.

Chapter 3 therefore explores how the *concept* of the ideal student is understood, interpreted and recognised by university staff and students. We present the voices of staff and students in our focus groups, who extensively discussed their thoughts and understandings about the concept *per se*. Here, we begin by sharing their concerns and reservations, which include the issues of definition, metric and achievability, before we discuss the potentials and possibilities of the concept that are also recognised by staff and students. This chapter draws on empirical evidence to further develop our understandings and we conclude with a holistic discussion and a working definition of the concept of the ideal student. With the foundations in place, we then explore the range of ideal student characteristics in Chapter 4.

For transparency, the content of this chapter is primarily based on an open access article we published in the journal, *Studies in Higher Education* (Wong and Chiu 2019a).

The challenges

The concept of ideal is not straightforward, even if we ignore the added layers of complexity when discussed in a theoretical, philosophical or epistemological context. Different disciplines may have their own take on this, so the debate could be endless. What we are interested here are the views of university staff and students, especially when asked to discuss and articulate their thoughts about the *concept* of the ideal student in our focus groups (FGs).

Subjective meanings

Some participants, as anticipated, initially linked the word ideal to perfection because most dictionaries tend to treat these words as synonyms (see also

Chapter 1). Others raised concerns about our respective interpretations of what is considered ideal, because what it means to be an ideal student can vary, especially between staff and students, who are likely to hold different priorities and preferences (see also O'Shea and Delahunty 2018). For example, Eric (FG11, Staff) commented that 'each one of us has our own thoughts, views and defining features of what we would like to see a student be and become', whilst Elise (FG4, Student) questioned 'ideal for who? ideal for you? or ideal for the uni?'. As there could be multiple interpretations and constructions of ideals, our participants are concerned that 'there's not a singular understanding' (Roger, FG9, Staff) of the ideal student because 'it could mean so many different things to different people' (Simon, FG17, Staff) and 'everyone has different opinions' (Elon, FG23, Student). The challenge of subjective interpretation is recognised, as well as the potential power play with regards to whose ideals are recognised or celebrated and whose ideals are suppressed or ignored. We touch on this again in Chapter 7 when we explore the social identities of the ideal student.

When participants were asked to describe the characteristics of their own ideal student, a few struggled to consolidate their thoughts because, as one member of staff admitted, 'when I thought about the best students I've ever worked with, they wouldn't conform to a single ideal. They have different strengths and they come in different combinations' (Anto, FG16, Staff). In other words, there is a range of characteristics associated with the ideal student and these characteristics seem to be spread across different individuals, which aligns with Weber's (1949) theory of ideal types (see Chapter 2). Here, we also note the synonymous use of the term 'best student' alongside the concept of ideal, which highlights the unconscious but ingrained associations of these similar words. Unlike the ideal student, however, the accolade of the best student is typically accredited to an individual, as the 'number one' student within a domain, such as a sport, subject or even school.

Markers of the ideal student

On the prospect of becoming an ideal student, some of our participants believed that most university students, in one way or another, 'have the qualities of potentially being ideal but just not all' (Reham, FG13, Student). As Dennis (FG3, Student) elaborated, 'some people will hit more criteria, some will hit less'. For instance, 'I might have four out of these six characteristics. Therefore, I'm not the ideal student' (Holly, FG1, Student). Here, recognition as an ideal student, by self or by others, seems to follow a list, where the status of being ideal is only possible when all criteria are met. Yet, these views also imply that it is possible or even common for students to embody some of these ideal characteristics, even if not the full range, whatever these may be.

Relatedly, there are also concerns around the metrics of the ideal student. Staff in two focus groups deliberated at length about the challenges of 'assessing' the ideal student from a more objective standpoint. Unlike coursework assignments and outcomes, which can be quantified through explicit learning outcomes, marking criteria and grades, some staff suggested that 'choosing the metrics will be difficult' (Francis, FG17, Staff) for the ideal student because 'those things aren't measurable [and] aren't assessed' (Will, FG19, Staff). Drawing on their own preferences in students, Kathy (FG17, Staff) queried 'how do we judge curiosity?', for example, whilst another asked, besides a reference letter, 'how do you quantify to an employer … that the student has a good attitude?' (Jofra, FG19, Staff). Essentially, questions are raised here about the objectivity of recognising (or assessing) different ideal student characteristics, although we remain to be convinced that an objective paradigm is required or appropriate.

Some participants rightly feared that a list of ideal student characteristics could create a *hierarchy*, as some attributes will inevitably be valued more than others. The concern here is that the identification of ideal student characteristics might limit 'opportunities for expression' as aspirational students could, in order to become ideal, all end up 'in the same way … [with] no variations' (Zheng, FG13, Student). While our respondents acknowledge that the availability of a list 'would be great … for some people because they need that clarity', a list 'could be limiting' for others (Ella, FG7, Student). In other words, by specifying *what is* considered to be ideal, we are simultaneously inferring *what is not* ideal. This process of inclusion and exclusion has power implications around dominant and marginal discourses, with an underlying concern about the extent to which ideal student characteristics might privilege or disadvantage particular groups. Yet, we believe that an occluded and unspecified range of desirable attributes is even more problematic as these actively contribute to inequalities in student experiences and outcomes due to their unfamiliarity with higher education (Crozier et al. 2008; Johnston 2010; see Chapter 1).

Achievability

Another conceptual challenge raised by participants is the *achievability* of the ideal student identity, with suggestions that 'to have an ideal student, you'd need an ideal lecturer … an ideal institution, an ideal society and none of those things coexist' (David, FG10, Staff). While David admitted that 'we can maybe imagine what an ideal student might look like', his sentence concluded with 'but it doesn't exist'. Interestingly, David later asserted that 'we have to be *real* with them [students] about our expectations', which implies that the ideal student can be unrealistic and, ironically, not ideal *per se*. This apparent contradiction is also illustrated in a student discussion (FG2, Student):

Rachel: It's not reality to be that ideal. I think it would be really difficult to have all of these aspects at once.
Sally: It's not very ideal.
Dennis: Yeah. It's not. It's not ideal because … everybody's different so you can't expect everybody to be this one category of student.

The tension here, dubbed when the ideal is *not* ideal, is interlinked with perceptions of reality and the plausibility of students to embody the ideal student identity or all ideal student characteristics. Concerns that being an ideal student is beyond the reach for most if not all students bring to question whether the ideal student is really a reflection of our own ideals and desires. We revisit this apparent conundrum later in the chapter. If the ideal student – as interpreted by some participants – is not considered as ideal, is it possible to reimagine a more realistic ideal student? Or perhaps the ideal student, as one member of staff commented, is precisely 'not the typical student, but beyond typical, the sort of student that you would like to have' (Maria, FG18, Staff).

So far, we have highlighted the challenges perceived by students and staff about the concept of the ideal student, from definition to interpretation to identification. As the focus groups progressed, there were growing appreciations that the concept of ideal has the potential to champion explicit expectations of university students. As one student later commented, 'even if [the ideal student] is not feasible, we do have these ideas' (Cindy, FG13, Student), as there is recognition that these presumptions can shape their actions and practices. Similarly, one member of staff acknowledged that they 'definitely tap into ideas about what student is better or worse, or preferable ... because I do have views' (Oliver, FG10, Staff). We consider these preferences and views as components of their own ideal student, which we explore below.

The potentials

Staff and students, when probed, all offered their views and expectations of university students. These expectations, we argue, constitute their constructions of the ideal student because these features are desirable, valued and ideal. As individuals may desire different traits in university students, the aim would be to collate a range of perspectives to highlight the collective views. As one participant remarked on our research, 'I think it's a really interesting study. It's a challenge because I think you're working with an abstract there on what ideal means, but you may be able to unpack the components of what this troubled word means' (Eric, FG11, Staff). Having discussed some of the challenges above, we now focus on the potentials of the concept, drawing again on our participants' conceptualisations of the ideal student, some of which respond to the challenges as we aim to further develop the concept.

Clarifying the meaning of ideal

The definitional link between *ideal* and *perfect* was disputed by some participants in other focus group discussions. One member of staff argued that 'I wouldn't be thinking of a perfect student even when you ask the question ideal ... [because] in some ways, we're looking for the *idealised* student ... the ones that we would like to teach' (Eva, FG18, Staff). Here, the ideal student is also understood to reflect ideals, desires and preferences, which can include imperfections or rooms for improvement, whilst the term perfect seems to entail flawlessness.

As Ayra (FG8, Staff) explained, 'we can think of ideal student in a different way, which is that ideal student is the one who we see as progressing … and not already perfect'. Considering this, we argue that the disassociation of ideal student from being perfect is important, as the latter interpretation can be a popular but rigid and misinformed perception about the concept of ideal.

Some participants considered the ideal student to exist only as characteristics, rather than as a specific person. As one member of staff clarified, 'actually what you're looking at is the attributes around the ideal student' (Will, FG19, Staff); to paraphrase, the ideal attributes desirable of university students. One student suggested that there should be 'basic … [and] common characteristics' expected of the ideal student, such as 'attending lectures, writing down notes, being independent, being inquisitive [and] asking questions' (Suvi, FG13, Student). While these different characteristics are explored in Chapter 4, the concept of the ideal student aims to offer students and staff an open thinking space to populate attributes that are considered to be ideal, by themselves as well as by others. For some, there are certain baseline expectations and ideals of university students that should transpire across levels of study, disciplines and even institutions or countries, such as attendance.

Others, however, argued that features of the ideal student are not universal but change according to context. According to Xin (FG13, Student), 'what is ideal shifts according to who we're being taught, you're like morphing into different images of an ideal student'. Another student agreed that while 'there are things that they [staff] want us to be at the end of the day', the ideal student can 'vary from where you are or the institution you are in' (Muna, FG5, Student). Here, students acknowledge and appreciate that ideals can be relational, suggesting that being an ideal student may be more likely in some settings than others. It is important, therefore, that conceptualisations and constructions of the ideal student consider and reflect on any contextual priorities, such as disciplinary or institutional specific values (see Chapter 6). As one member of staff reflected on how their views had evolved during the focus group:

> I was coming prepared to give you a lovely little speech how there is no such thing as an ideal student. Right now, it hit me that I've worked for quite a few years in different universities and I remember one thing – the one thing I miss actually [is] that no one ever dared to come to class unprepared … You could not imagine any students in [pre-92/elite] institutions setting foot in class without having done at least two-thirds of what they were supposed to do. (Angel, FG9, Staff)

The comment above highlights two points. First, initial concerns or rejections of the concept of ideal student can be mitigated through deeper discussions and self-reflections. Second, expectations of students can vary by university (e.g. pre-/post-92 institutions, see also Chapter 6), who tend to attract different student profiles. We acknowledge that there may be contextual expectations of students specific to individual universities or even disciplines, but we also have voices, which suggest that there are foundational student characteristics that are *universally desirable* in higher education (see Chapter 5).

Existing but hidden applications of ideal

Interestingly, our students also said that the term ideal student is rarely used by their tutors, even when expectations of students are communicated, which are instead often written in module/programme handbooks. As one group discussed (FG12, Students):

Diana: There's a booklet that says everything you have to do; you have to be present a certain percentage of the time, you have to achieve certain grades otherwise you don't pass, you have to attend this and this and meet this.

Stefan: But the tutors or the university … haven't labelled that as the ideal student …

Diana: No, they didn't, it would be like the minimum you have to do to be here.

Here, expectations of students are set out as the minimum requirement, which might be useful for monitoring purposes. By comparison, the ideal student goes beyond the minimum as it sets out the desirable features of students, although ideal does not necessarily mean the best or the highest (grade). Here, we wonder to what extent staff expectations that are beyond the minimum are made explicit in module/programme handbooks.

Our participants also discussed the importance of explicitness and the dangers of presumptions, which, as existing literature can attest, can result in or further reinforce social inequalities. As Oliver (FG10, Staff) recognised, 'I think students do increasingly need more explicit guidelines … we shouldn't assume that they know' about the demands of university, whilst another believed that the concept of the ideal student 'can be quite helpful because it can set a series of yardsticks to measure against' (David, FG10, Staff). As such, the concept of ideal can offer students an opportunity to situate, reflect or compare themselves with the features that are considered to be desirable in a university student. Similarly, Francis (FG17, Staff) said that 'students here want to understand exactly what you want from them. They get really frustrated and anxious if they feel like they don't know exactly what to do … so give them a list'.

As can be seen, the concept of ideal student can offer a clearer and more concrete attempt to spell out expectations of students, at the desirable rather than the minimum level. An unpacking of these ideal expectations of students can also provide students with a *viable template* to develop as higher education students. These views were also expressed by students, who associated the ideal student with a prototype that sets out the desirable features of students:

Lecturers could say at the start of the year, this is what the ideal student did last year, and this is what we expect of you. So, if you want to try and push yourself and be that ideal student then … students can do what the criteria say if they want. (Dennis, FG3, Student)

Here, our students appreciate the availability of guidelines for those who wish to be an ideal student. Whether or not a student could or should aspire or develop to be an ideal student merits a deeper discussion, the premise is that expectations of ideal students should be transparent, explicit and, most importantly, realistic. In sum, it is clear that desirable expectations of students exist, on the part of both staff and students, which we conceptualise as the ideal student.

Is there a conceptual conundrum?

So far, we have argued that the concept of the ideal student provides a platform for expectations of students to be shared, discussed and negotiated. We established that being ideal is not the same as being perfect, in the sense of flawlessness, as being an ideal student can also mean future improvement or progress (Wong and Chiu 2020). For students, this concept offers an indication of the type of student characteristics that are valued by tutors and an opportunity to self-develop, negotiate and embody these attributes, if realistic and desirable. For staff, the ideal student promotes self-reflection of the student features that are most appreciated, recognised or even rewarded. Staff can also ensure that their expectations of students are realistic and mutually understood, with a better awareness of areas where students might need further support.

The ideal student aims to promote transparency and explicitness about the desirable characteristics in a student, so that students, especially those from non-traditional backgrounds, are not disadvantaged due to their unfamiliarity and inability to 'play the higher education game' (Bathmaker et al. 2013). It is important to emphasise that the ideal student is meant to represent our ideals, and not the irony where the ideal student is instead considered *not* to be ideal because it is unrealistic or impossible. We reiterate that our conceptualisation is ultimately underpinned by Weber's (1949) theory of *ideal types*, a mental construct that reflects the breadth of desirable features, which can vary by context. Ideal types, and indeed the ideal student, would constitute the collectively agreed range of ideal attributes of a range of students, rather than an individual (see Chapter 2).

We acknowledge that the concept of the ideal student is still a work in progress. There are legitimate concerns that need to be addressed and discussed, including the conundrum of whether an explicit approach towards understanding the ideal student characteristics could result in a *list of ideals* that can potentially confine alternative (and *unlisted*) expressions of student practices and identities. The process of specifying and identifying what characteristics are considered as ideal is intertwined within complex power relations, especially between staff and students but also wider social inequalities such as gender, class and 'race'/ethnicity. For example, the voices of staff are fundamental in the construction of ideal student characteristics, although it is equally important for students to be engaged in this process, given the rise in student–staff partnerships in higher education (Healey et al. 2014). Ultimately, we want to provide students with the opportunity to consider and make their own meanings out of the range of desirable characteristics of an ideal student, which is central to inclusive and diverse learning practices. More broadly, implicit rules and practices can breed inequalities, especially by social class. Transparency plays a key role to reduce inequalities caused by assumptions, as well as to manage and negotiate differences, if any, in expectations between staff and students, especially those from non-traditional as well as international backgrounds.

While staff and students might have varied views about the ideal characteristics of university students, our analysis did not find any notable differences between their respective views of the concept of the ideal student *per se*. We must also remain vigilant and aware as to whether our ideal student characteristics might advantage or disadvantage particular social groups, and what countermeasures could be in place to support students to develop the desirable characteristics that are valued and rewarded. For instance, these might include supplementary skills workshops or a holistic approach that embeds the development of ideal student characteristics as part of students' university education. Despite the concerns of an explicit approach, we believe the damage of an implicit approach is worse, as unspoken assumptions and expectations of students offer limited guidance to develop as university students, especially for those who are less familiar with the learning and practices in higher education.

The ideal student may consist of a range of attributes, but these are not absolute and are intended to reflect the situated ideals and desires of students in specific contexts and circumstances. As mentioned already, the ideal student should reflect the realistic ideals of stakeholders, such as staff and students, rather than an imagination that is far-fetched and improbable. In other words, the ideal student characteristics should be desirable but also realistic, even though no individual is expected to embody the full spectrum of ideal attributes. We do not envision the ideal student to be a means to an end, or to have a status of being accomplished or achieved, but rather as a continuous process of reflecting, being and becoming, in relation to the ideal features of university students. Identifications with the range of ideal student characteristics are likely to be ongoing, partial and rarely, if ever, static or complete. And even if complete, this association is temporary and always 'in process'.

The concept of the ideal student also champions a shift in paradigm from minimal requirements (e.g. attendance and attainment for progression) to desirable outcomes. The concept aims to promote an indicative but not prescriptive range of ideal student characteristics that enables a more transparent staff–student relationship that we believe can contribute to a fairer and more equitable higher education. The rules of higher education are explicit and implicit. The former often reflect official guidelines and procedures, especially the minimum expectations; the latter are malleable, ambiguous and even assumed, including our desirable and ideal features of university students that we emphatically argue do exist.

We want to encourage key stakeholders, especially staff and students, to thoroughly reflect and explicitly note down the practices and values that are desirable for university students. Universities and staff could then play a proactive and collaborative role to support students to develop the range of identified student characteristics that are considered as important within their respective contexts (see Chapters 5 and 6). For students, especially those from non-traditional backgrounds, university constitutes a new and even foreign environment, which is often very different from their prior experiences of education in schools (Johnston 2010). The ideal student can highlight the differences as well as the gaps in expectations of students between schools and universities, contributing to student transition into higher education, both in practice and research (see Chapter 9).

Our working definition thus far is underpinned by the keywords of desirability, imperfection and realism. As such, we argue that the ideal student constitutes *the desirable but realistic expectations of students in higher education; ideal is not about perfection, or being the highest or the best.* In the following chapters, we explore how this concept operates at the individual and collective level, especially between staff and students (see Chapter 5), and across disciplines and institutions (see Chapter 6). With a greater understanding of the ideal student, differences in expectations of students can be appropriately addressed, but until an honest conversation takes place about our respective ideal students, we are wary of the missed opportunities to maximise the impact of the support that universities already provide to students.

As subsequent chapters will attest, discussions of the concept of the ideal student have not only provoked curiosity and cynicism, but also offered insights into its potential value for practice.

Summary

Chapter 3 used qualitative data to explore the views of university staff and students on their understandings and concerns about the concept of the ideal student *per se*. We discussed the key challenges and potentials of the concept. In essence:

- There are concerns about the subjectivity, markers and achievability of the ideal student.
- However, the potentials and possibilities afforded by the concept are also appreciated and acknowledged, where the availability of *viable templates* can reduce uncertainties on what it means to be a university student.
- A working definition of the ideal student is provided, which is captured by the keywords of desirability, imperfection and realism.

 **4**

The eight dimensions of the ideal student

In this chapter, we want to map out the different characteristics of the ideal student, a difficult task given that we all have our own views. Some of these may be similar but there are bound to be different priorities and emphasis between individuals. We do not expect a single or unanimous vision about the ideal student, especially the characteristics considered to be ideal and desirable of university students. The chapter aims to provide a descriptive overview of the characteristics that informed the ideal student survey, which consists of 50 items. Further details are provided in Appendix 1, especially on how the survey was developed, distributed and analysed.

In short, our analysis of the survey revealed eight factors, or dimensions, of the ideal university student. These are provisionally labelled as: *Diligence & Engagement, Organisation & Discipline, Reflection & Innovation, Positive & Confident outlook, Supportive of Others, Academic skills, Employability skills* and *Intelligence & Strategic approach*. These are listed by order of their relative importance according to the survey outcomes, which are discussed in Chapters 5, 6 and 7.

In this chapter, we describe the constituents of these eight dimensions, with a focus on the meanings and definitions of the 50 student characteristics, or items, that we developed. We discuss how each survey item was formed, which drew primarily on our focus group data as well as existing literature, as we provide insights into the fluidity of the descriptors that are used to articulate different thoughts and ideas about the ideal student. Below, we describe the survey items, which have been grouped under one of the eight dimensions. We include their item numbers as originally assigned in the survey for ease of reference (see Appendix 2). Whilst we have kept it concise, this is inevitably a long chapter because we included the empirical data that supported the emergence of the survey items. The 50 items we used in the ideal student survey should not be seen as a complete or exhaustive list but rather as a range of plausible characteristics to consider in our constructions of the ideal student. There may be characteristics that you feel are important but are not featured, and if that is the case, we are pleased that you are thinking more deeply about this. We revisit the implications of our project in Chapter 9, with practical suggestions on how to use the survey items for teaching and learning.

Diligence & Engagement

This first dimension consists of nine items that broadly captures students' learning attitude and work ethic, such as enthusiasm, dedication and effort. Below, we expand on each item and present the data which informed their development and inclusion in the ideal student survey.

Enthusiastic, passionate, engaged and/or motivated in learning (item 1)

The first item in the ideal student survey is perhaps the most compacted, with four adjectives collated into one descriptor. We recognise and appreciate that each adjective could potentially be an item on its own, but our analysis of the words and descriptions that students and staff used to explain their meanings prompted us to group these as one item, as these terms are often used interchangeably and discussed together in their constructions of the ideal student. Statistically, the keywords in item 1 were mentioned at least 104 times in our focus group activity, where participants brainstormed their 'top five' most important features in an ideal student. As such, item 1 was by far the most popular item as it constituted over 10% of all the characteristics (n = 795) that we gathered about the ideal student from the focus groups.

In the context of higher education, our staff and students seem to have interpreted enthusiasm, passion, engagement and motivation in learning as synonymous or interrelated practices. The use of one adjective is often supplemented by another, even in the same sentence, when asked to elaborate on the characteristics that are important in an ideal student. For example:

Holly: So, having that *enthusiasm*, that sort of comes in with being interactive and being *engaged* rather than just sitting there thinking I'm bored, why am I here?

Finlay: I think *motivated* is more about what Holly's saying, like you have that *enthusiasm* and then you stick with that *enthusiasm*. (FG1, Students)

> I put *passionate* because I think if you're more *passionate* about this course, stuff comes more naturally ... and you're more *engaged*. (Ben, FG7, Student)
>
> Ideally, you'd have a student that is very *engaged* and *passionate* about the discipline. (Sian, FG19, Staff)
>
> For my second [on the list] I put *motivated* and *passionate*, which is hard to define that I think there has to be some kind of driving force behind you just wanting to do the degree. (Shirley, FG20, Student)

Item 1 is therefore the most popular expectation of students in an ideal world and our decision to group these four adjectives into one item reflects the inter-changeable ways in which students and staff have described their ideal students. We acknowledge that for concepts such as 'engagement' and 'motivation', there can be a deeper level of theoretical and analytical interrogation (Kahu 2013; Kusurkar et al. 2011; Trowler 2010). For the purpose of our study and the everyday applications and understandings of these descriptors, we feel item 1 sufficiently captures the broad acknowledgement of the importance of enthusiasm, passion, engagement and motivation for university learning.

Dedicated, focused and/or determined in learning (item 2)

Item 2 refers to dedication and determination, which include being focused in and committed to academic learning. As above, we present the meanings and interpretations of these keywords from our participants:

> *Dedication* [is] like making sure you're on time to lectures, doing reading, doing your work promptly on time, meeting deadlines, having the discussions in class. Just making sure you're *focused* in your learning. (Dennis, FG3, Student)

> I put *determined* ... if you're *determined*, it'll push you doing the others. You need that force to learn. So, at the end, you just gotta be *determined*. (Irene, FG7, Student)

> My second ranking is *determined*. So, a student who knows why they are taking a module and course and has the ability and *dedication* to achieve for their own gain. (Eric, FG11, Staff)

We appreciate that item 2 is closely related to item 1 but felt that there is enough of a difference to merit a separate description. Several participants such as Holly (FG1, Student) recognise that '*dedication* ... sort of ties in with enthusiasm', although Jane (FG12, Student) felt that '*dedication* is one step further than motivation, it's just that little bit more action'. In other words, being dedicated, focused and determined seems to be a more specific description of how students could approach learning, which is also related to adjectives such as resilience and tenacity (see Brewer et al. 2019; Holdsworth et al. 2018), even though these exact words were rarely used by students and staff to describe their ideal student.

Disciplined, diligent and/or respectful in learning (item 3)

According to the *Oxford Dictionary* (2010, see Lexico.com), being disciplined is defined as 'showing a controlled form of behaviour or way of working', being diligent is understood as 'having or showing care and conscientiousness in one's work or duties', and being respectful means 'feeling or showing deference and respect'. These three words constitute item 3, which aims to describe a particular aspect of student behaviour and practice, namely being disciplined, diligent or respectful in learning.

Our participants agreed that the ideal student should have respect for others, such as teachers, fellow students and the learning environments. Sienna (FG1, Student) explains that poor punctuality and attendance are not only disruptive for learning but also '*disrespectful* to the lecturer and all the work that they've put in'. In everyday communication, Stefan (FG12, Student) feels that it is imperative for students 'just to *respect* people's social positions and views in life, not that you agree, you just show *respect* for them'. Relatedly, the ideal student should also be *disciplined*, which is interpreted as actually 'doing what they say they'll do ... [such as] say I will do two hours of revision and they actually do the two hours of revision and do it with a purpose' (Ella, FG7, Student). The word *disciplined* can also be applied in the context of time management, which is a separate student characteristic (item 18). The term *diligent* can be associated with work ethic (see also item 7), although it has been used in the context of students' conscientious practice, such as 'showing up to class ... [and] take good notes' (Jay, FG28, Student) as well as the mental preparation that students undertake for difficult or laborious assignments.

Overall, we feel the meanings of being disciplined, diligent and respectful in learning form a coherent cluster of interrelated ideas that support our mapping of ideal student characteristics.

Responsible and/or professional in learning (item 4)

Being responsible and professional is the crux of item 4, which refers to the ways in which students are sensible, accountable, serious and mature in their approach to learning. In other words, the ideal student is expected 'to assume *responsibility* for their own learning' (Eric, FG11, Staff). For Tyson, this means:

> I don't want them knocking at my door every two minutes, but I want them to take *responsibility* for doing some of their own learning and interpretation, coming to me with interesting questions rather than just ructions. (Tyson, FG18, Staff)

In other words, being responsible is about students taking ownership of their role as active learners, and not as passive recipients of knowledge (Nelson 2018). The second keyword, being professional, has been described alongside how students should conduct themselves at university as if it were the workplace:

> The ideal student is like the training to become the ideal worker, in a sense. It's about being *professional*. If you cannot make it [to a class], email your lecturer to let them know why you're absent ... justify yourself as if it was your workplace. (Grace, FG5, Student)

Here, the ideal student would be professional in the sense that they would take responsibility and ownership for their own actions, which is arguably also an indication of maturity. In an earlier study (Wong and Chiu 2020) we reported that social science lecturers value maturity in an ideal student, by which we do not mean age, but students who 'want to be there for a reason' (Daisy, FG7, Student).

Good attitude, willingness and/or behaviour in learning (item 5)

Item 5 is made up of the keywords that can potentially be all-encompassing, especially with the word attitude, which could arguably cover most items in the whole survey. As such, we also included the keywords of willingness and behaviour in this item to provide a better steer towards our intention to explore the importance of students' approach, mentality and mindset in learning. In general, our participants agreed that a good attitude is more about effort than outcome, with the focus on the ways in which students conduct themselves in their learning. For example:

> If I had to pinpoint anything that I needed from a student, it would be that they have a *willingness* to be a student. (Flora, FG14, Staff)

> There's going to be some parts of the course which you're just not as drawn to as others, but I can still have the right *attitude* about it ... I can still sit there, make notes, pay attention, and participate, and so that's why I put that as number one. (Sienna, FG1, Student)

> I put behaviour, just because your *behaviour* heavily impacts everyone else. I feel like if you have disruptive *behaviour*, even if you're a really nice person, you can't be the ideal student because you disrupt everyone else. Chatting amongst yourself while the lectures happening is distracting for everyone. (Lorna, FG1, Student)

We were informed by a range of data in the construction of item 5 but to keep it concise, we only include a few excerpts above to highlight how staff and students considered the importance of attitude, behaviour and willingness in learning.

Good preparation and/or readiness in learning (item 6)

For some people, the ideal student should be prepared and ready to learn. Arguably, being prepared also reflects one's attitude to learning, which is the keyword in item 5. However, this statement is more specific. For staff, the ideal student is someone 'who takes their education seriously' (Angel, FG9, Staff) and therefore comes '*prepared* for the classes in advance, such as reading around the topic to be discussed' (Roger, FG9, Staff). As Tricia explains, 'I expect the students to do the pre-reading before lecture and to come to class *ready* to engage, *ready* to contribute' (Tricia, FG11, Staff).

Similarly, our students believed that the ideal student 'should come *prepared* to the lecture ... know what the topic is and *ready* to learn' (Gola, FG25, Student). In a separate exchange (FG2, Students), one student shared her commitment to learning through good preparation and readiness:

Sally: Real talk. I got to get outta my house early. I wake up at six in the morning. Get *ready* to leave my house by seven fifty-five. Get here around, yeah ... I'm here like twenty minutes before the actual lesson, all *prepared.*

Rachel: See, that's the ideal student.

Hard-working and/or studious in learning (item 7)

Perceptions of the ideal student as a hard-working or studious person is not difficult to envisage. The importance of study and work ethic was often inferred by staff and students in our focus groups. There seems to be a general acceptance that at university, 'if you don't *work hard*, you're not gonna get anything out of it' (Ella, FG7, Student). As such, a hard-working or studious student would 'always try to stay on top of lectures and on top of tutorials' (Tej, FG26, Student). For instance:

> The ideal student is someone who, you know, shows up to lectures, goes home and studies, and has their head down *working hard* all the time. (Kobe, FG21, Student)

The keyword studious has also been used to highlight the importance of hard working, as well as being focused and scholarly. Item 7 is closely related to items 9 and 10, as discussed below.

Do more than required and/or go the extra mile in learning (item 9)

Perhaps a level up, the characteristic of doing more than required or going the extra mile focuses on the extent to which students are willing or prepared to do additional or extra work in their approach to learning. In our earlier study we found that going the extra mile seems to be an attractive trait in lecturers' construction of the ideal student (Wong and Chiu 2020). Data from our focus groups with staff and students also support this:

> I think an ideal student would be someone who takes on *extra* things, so like does extra performances, does *extra* work ... or rehearsals and stuff like that. (Jane, FG12, Student)

> Students who are passionate about their subject ... would go the *extra mile* to learn more about it, to gain knowledge about it ... the ideal student has put extra effort in. (Kyle, FG26, Student)

> I have met students who I would say are ideal or close to ideal. They have that motivation and they're very, very interested in learning. They will go beyond. If you say, 'Read this paper' and they'll go *beyond*, and they will pick up other papers that they're interested in, because they've got that intrinsic motivation to go ahead and to do that. (Callum, FG15, Staff)

As illuminated above, the ideal student would be someone who goes above and beyond what is typically expected or asked of them, which may be driven by their passion about or attitude towards learning (see also items 1 and 4).

Always trying their best in learning (item 10)

In a similar vein as the preceding two items (items 7 and 9), the last statement under the first dimension (*Diligence & Engagement*) is interested in the efforts and mentality of the ideal student, which is symbolised by the motto of always trying their best. According to Wong (2016), the discourse of 'trying my best' focuses on the process of learning and participation, rather than the outcome, such as the grades awarded. Good attainment is desirable but not necessarily expected. Education itself is highly valued. Thus, the keyword for students who try their best in learning would be effort, which is likely to be a reflection of their learning attitudes (see item 5). Here, we included some data to enrich our understandings of what is meant by trying their best in learning:

> You are not motivated all the time, sometimes you have to learn things you don't like. Still, you do the *effort to actually learn* and be conscious of the opportunities, you have to be able to learn all those things for [yourself], is important in an ideal student. (Mia, FG4, Student)

> The ideal student is someone who always attends their lectures, does *the best to their ability*, completes the work, keeps up with deadlines. (Ben, FG7. Student)

> As long as the person is giving, putting in *their best effort* in whatever it is. That's the ideal student. Even if it's not achieving the best grades, as long as you *do your best*, and you *try your hardest*. That's what I think is the ideal student. (Irene, FG7, Student)

Organisation & Discipline

The second dimension of the ideal student is *Organisation & Discipline*, which includes five survey items that can be summarised as being efficient, punctual and rule-following. Unlike the first dimension, where the items are mostly sequential (by how the survey was originally written), the number gap between each item is a lot more sporadic (i.e. item 11, then item 18, before items 41, 42 and 46). As before, further details of each item are provided below.

Good attendance and/or punctuality (item 11)

Item 11 is a relatively straightforward statement and refers to the regularity of students to attend and participate in their scheduled learning without much lateness or absences. In other words, the ideal student should turn up to their classes, on time. In the focus groups, the use of the phrases good attendance or good punctuality are often discussed alongside keywords which appeared in other items, such as respectful (item 3), professional (item 4) and attitude (item 5), under the dimension *Diligence & Engagement*. Such interrelatedness reminds us that the individual survey items and their keywords can sometimes overlap when describing the ideal student, although we believe item 11 presents a clear statement on timekeeping and being present. As far as Daniel (FG3, Student) is concerned, it is important for the ideal student to be good with their *'atten-dance* and being *prompt with attendance*, not walking in ten minutes late to lectures'.

Good organisational or time management skills (item 18)

This statement is about the ability of the student to be efficient and effective with their time and preparations for learning. The ideal student should be good with their organisation and management of time, which can range from every-day life situations such as getting ready for class to the longer-term planning of learning and assessments and how to balance between different priorities. As Sally (FG2, Student) explains:

> It's a pretty similar. So, you have *time management*. So, it's *organisation*. You have to *organise* with everything. You have to know when your deadlines are, what work you have to do, what readings you have to do.

Beyond the university, Natasha (FG6, Student) said time management is also about managing a balance between study and family commitments:

> I'll drop my kids before coming here … I used to work Monday to Saturday, but I have to take off those days, just to *organise* yourself … it all comes to *organisation*.

Finally, there is also recognition and a conscious effort by some staff to develop and promote students' organisational skills:

> We certainly need to support students with *organisation*. I try to be really supportive about that. I often say that half of doing a degree is *organisation*. I try and be supportive about all the different challenges they got on tugs their time for work and family. (Rebecca, FG8, Staff)

Seek support when needed (item 41)

According to some participants, the ideal student should be able to seek support, or ask for help, if and when that is needed. Our previous research on the experi-ences of non-traditional university students identified one of the key barriers to their academic success was a reluctance to seek support from staff, due to fears but also self-pride (Wong and Chiu 2019c). In the focus group discussions, both staff and students made comments on the importance of the ideal student to recognise and accept that asking for help is a common or even expected part of the student experience. An example is shown below (FG6, Students):

Elaine: You are in the class and you don't really know what is going on, you will *need the guidance* to that. You can *ask your tutor or you speak with your colleagues*. Take some guidance from them ... You know, some people will think they know it so I don't want to *ask* so that people don't laugh at me. No. An ideal student, you can never know it all.

Anna: You can't feel ashamed about it.

Henry: You are here to learn.

Similarly, staff also value and appreciate students who are able to come forward and ask for support:

> If they notice that something is going wrong, they should *seek help* early ... Some students they would just never come forward, and I can't stand it. I find that very difficult to see. I would say my ideal student, hopefully ... will *search for some advice* or *seek help* ... when they need it. (Teresa, FG15, Staff)

On-time submission of assignments (item 42)

It might be a surprise for some that the expectation of students to complete and submit their assignments on time was mentioned as a characteristic of an ideal student. Here, students and staff spoke of the importance to meet deadlines, which is most likely an extension of the keywords of organisation and time management (item 18). For example, Sally (FG2, Student) said that 'an ideal student should always be able to submit before the due date'.

In fact, the act of on-time submission of assignments is also very relevant to – and perhaps an example of an outcome of – a number of keywords that are core to other survey items, such as being focused (item 2) and responsible (item 4), with a good attitude (item 5) and preparation (item 6) in learning. In other words, item 42 here could somewhat be seen as an 'objective marker' of the ideal student, where students who are able to submit their assignments on time are also more likely to be organised, responsible, prepared and so on. Of course, there are legitimate and acceptable circumstances where students may need extensions, but in general, it is probably fair to say that meeting deadlines is an ideal expectation of students at university.

Follow university or teaching instructions, rules or procedures (item 46)

The final item under the dimension *Organisation & Discipline* refers to the importance of students to observe rules and regulations. We are interested in the extent to which the ideal student should follow university procedures or tutor instructions, akin to the phrase 'do as one is told' or a 'code of conduct' (Dennis, FG3, Student). For example, these could be the rules of study etiquette, such as the respectful use of study space or the fulfilment of a homework as set out by the tutor. It is interesting to note that the data which contributed to this item did not only stem from discussions of what is most important, but also what is least important, in an ideal student, at least in the context of their own degrees. The excerpt below illustrates how rule-following may also vary by discipline (see Chapter 6):

> I don't know, like, science, math, engineers, the expectation is *just following the rules*, follow the formula and just follow the route that you're supposed to go. But for us [in the social sciences] it's a very critical thinking, out of the box. (Xin, FG13, Student)

Reflection & Innovation

The third dimension, *Reflection & Innovation*, considers the ability of students to be thoughtful about the choices and decisions they make, as well as their initiative to be proactive or creative about their ideas and thinking. We appreciate that being reflective *per se* does not necessarily mean being innovative, or vice versa, and so it is important to remind ourselves that all dimensions are provisional and grouped together statistically with the purpose to provide us with meaningful and manageable interpretations. This dimension has eight items, each of which is discussed below.

Curious, inquisitive and/or open-minded about learning (item 8)

The vision of an ideal student as someone who is curious, inquisitive or open-minded about learning is consistent with the boarder philosophy of education as a journey of personal and knowledge development. Learners ought to be receptive to and intrigued by learning. In educational psychology, these keywords may be associated with self-determination theory (Ryan and Deci 2000), especially the notion of intrinsic motivation, where students want to learn because the learning experience itself is rewarding or satisfying. Below is a longer quote which captures the importance of being open-minded about learning, as well as being reflective, which we discuss later in item 31:

> My expectations really ... is that they're *open-minded*, that they're *open* to new ideas. And they're willing to embrace new ... or willing to contemplate new ideas. Things that they haven't experienced before. And not just dismiss it out of hand but to think, okay let's see. For everything that they do, there is something that they can learn. If it goes well, that's brilliant. If it doesn't go well, it's still brilliant. Because they can still work out why it may not have gone well and what they could have achieved differently, or how it could have been conducted in a different way. (Andrew, FG19, Staff)

In similar vein, Roberto (FG5, Student) described the ideal student as 'an *inquisitive* person who would learn from different experiences, from different people, all the time', whilst Lottie (FG9, Staff) said 'for me an ideal student is one that's *curious*, one that stays curious all the time. Asks questions and has the drive to succeed, whatever that is'. Informed by these data, we are confident that item 8 coherently sets out a popular ideal of university students.

Being independent or self-directed (item 28)

Item 28 refers to the ideal student as an independent or self-directed learner, where students are able to make decisions for themselves and be autonomous in their approach to and practice in learning (see also Thomas et al. 2015). According to Tyson (FG18, Staff), the ideal student should be '*independent* and take responsibility for learning rather than being spoon fed it'. Similar views were expressed by students, some of whom listed independence as their most important attribute in an ideal student:

> I did say *independent*. So, having that *independence* in yourself, being able to do things without somebody else's opinion. Obviously, there are times when you do discuss things and you're like okay I see where you're coming from but to be able to *think about something by yourself* without something affecting it initially is quite important. (Reham, FG13, Student)

We acknowledge that there are potential crossovers here with item 4 (under *Diligence & Engagement*), especially with the keyword responsibility, because often, descriptions of being independent entails taking responsibility for one's own actions. Whilst item 4 also emphasises being professional, in the sense of maturity and sensibility, item 28 is more about autonomy and making one's own decisions, which we strongly believe merits a separate statement in our ideal student survey.

Being reflective or self-aware (item 31)

Another popular construction of the ideal student is the importance of being reflective or self-aware, which was adopted as a keyword in this whole dimension (i.e. *Reflection & Innovation*). In everyday language, a reflective person is typically someone who is thoughtful or thinks things through. For example, taking the time to think about something that has recently happened and perhaps asks themselves what, if any, different courses of action they could take if the situation arises again. Relatedly, the concept of self-awareness (Duval and Wicklund 1972) has been studied for many years and whilst it is beyond our scope to delve any deeper, the simple but sufficient meaning would be one's ability to understand or learn about oneself. Below, we have selected two excerpts to highlight the value of being reflective and self-aware:

> [The ideal student is] someone who is kind of *self-aware* in terms of their own abilities and knows what they have to do next time. (Doris, FG20, Student)

> A lot of the content that I produce for our programme requires the students to *reflect* on what they produce. So, to look back at the stuff that they've done and analyse, and think about, okay, what worked? What didn't work?

What can we do differently? What might improve it? So, I guess I'd like them to *reflect* on the work that they've produced. (David, FG10, Staff)

Being proactive and/or taking initiatives (item 36)

Being proactive or taking initiatives is a popular mention by staff and students in their descriptions of the ideal student, who are expected to take a lead and make things happen, rather than to wait or be reactive to the actions of others. Here, the ideal student is considered as someone 'who takes *initiative* in all aspects of their life, so their social life and other stuff, who's not passive' (Meggie, FG30, Student). Similarly, Sang (FG24, Student) conceived the ideal student to be '*proactively* seeking out what they want to do with their life because what you're gonna do in 3 or 4 years, after university you know? I don't think an ideal student would be a couch potato'. The reverse analogy of a 'couch potato' implies that the ideal student would be prepared (akin to item 6, under *Diligence & Engagement*), although more specifically in the context of taking actions, making things happen, through their proactiveness and self-initiations.

Being creative, innovative and/or divergent in thinking (item 37)

The characteristics of being creative, innovative and/or divergent in thinking are highlighted by some participants as an important feature of the ideal student, especially for those in disciplines that reward and celebrate creativity. A dictionary definition of being creative states, 'the use of the imagination or original ideas to create something' (Lexico.com), which is similar to the keywords of being innovative or divergent in thinking. According to one member of staff:

Creativity and *innovation*, as I said, for me means thinking outside the box, it's part of showing that you're kind of, on the ball and alive ... An ideal student adds something from inside themselves, about their experience, where they've come from, their background. And they take the stuff in, it somehow gets moved around, shifted, evaluated, prioritised, and when it comes out it's something new. And that's where I think *creativity*, and *innovation* is important. (Anto, FG16, Staff)

Here, the ability of students to create or generate something new as part of their educational journey may not necessarily be expected but it is certainly regarded as an ideal feature, in that it is a highly desirable and prized skillset. As another member of staff explains:

[The ideal student] should be exploring and engaging lecturers in really productive ways, rather than reproducing the same old stuff over and over again. I think this *creative* side is sometimes missing. That would be something that I really like to see students being *creative* with their own knowledge. (Tyson, FG18, Staff)

Acceptance of own weakness or room for improvement (item 44)

As an extension of being reflective (see item 31 earlier), item 44 specifies the capacity of students to be able accept their own weaknesses or admit that there is room for improvement. We found a spread of examples in the focus groups, within and beyond the brainstorming activity for ideal student characteristics, where students and staff deliberated on the importance of students to appreciate they are still a work in progress. For example, Roger (FG9, Staff) predicts that students 'are not going to get very far if they're not *willing to take things on board*'. The ideal student, for Callum (FG15, Staff), 'has this attitude … this kind of *growth mindset* … where they are able to *learn from their mistakes*' (for more details on growth mindset, see Dweck 2017). Furthermore, as Callum continues:

> The ability to attempt to answer or solve problems, are *willing to make mistakes*. They don't feel afraid that their reputation's going to be destroyed if they don't get a single question right during a lecture, or everyone looks at them because they picked the wrong structure of a chemical or something. (Callum, FG15, Staff)

Similarly, Andrew (FG19, Staff) said the ideal student will have the '*willingness to improve* and to *embrace feedback*', whilst Sian (FG19, Staff) said it is 'being able to *deal with failure* and accept it'. These views are consistent with our earlier work which found lecturers to construct the ideal student as those who are always improving and making progress throughout their degree journey (Wong and Chiu 2020).

Challenge instructions or existing knowledge/practices (item 48)

The final item under the dimension *Reflection & Innovation* was mostly inspired by our focus group participants who spoke about their different expectations and ideals of students in the different phases of higher education. More specifically, some participants highlighted that the ideal student at postgraduate, masters and doctoral levels might also include an ability to challenge instructions or existing knowledge and practices:

> If you're looking for someone at a PhD level, you're looking for someone that has that right attitude that they can *criticise*. They can approach the material in the field, in a specific manner. Not just good at replicating things or good at understanding things, necessarily. They could *challenge* you or the literature. (Callum, FG15, Staff)

To add more context, our focus here is on undergraduates but on occasions both students and staff make unprompted comparisons with postgraduates in their conversations, including our staff and postgraduate participants. In most cases, the ideal expectations of postgraduate students, when discussed, are not drastically different to those of undergraduates, albeit with a stronger emphasis on independence (item 28) as well as most items under the dimension

Diligence & Engagement. We included this item to explore the extent to which the ability to challenge instructions is ideal for undergraduate students.

Positive & Confident outlook

The fourth dimension of the ideal university student is *Positive & Confident outlook*, which refers to being positive, happy and confident. This dimension is made up of just two items and focuses on student optimism and a heathy mindset.

Being positive or happy (item 26)

There is a recognition by our participants, especially students, that the ideal student should champion the value of positivity or happiness, which is especially timely given the rise in concerns around university student welfare and wellbeing (Brown 2016). The emphasis on happiness, perhaps over and above the importance of attainment/grades, offers a slightly different perspective on the purpose and value of education, with the focus more on the experience and process of learning, rather than just the outcome of a degree certificate. For example:

> I feel like an ideal student should also be *happy* with themselves … If you're not enjoying what you're doing, then you're not doing it wholeheartedly. I feel like you become ideal when you actually *enjoy* what you're doing as well, because then it's like, even though you are putting in the effort, it feels like less of an effort. (Shelia, FG29, Student)

> Enjoy it, because *joy* is part of learning I believe. As long as they [students] find a *joy* in learning and as long as they don't see getting more knowledge as a pain, they will want to learn more. They will kind of integrate what they learn into their own lives. (Cara, FG9, Staff)

Similarly, others have also spoken about the importance of having a *'positive can-do attitude'* (Eva, FG18, Staff) and an optimistic mindset where the ideal students would be willing and happy to learn. Here, the ideal student would also 'need to appreciate their individual efforts and not forget the *positives*' (Suvi, FG13, Student). As such, it is important that the ideal student is generally positive and happy about their learning. An optimistic rather than a pessimistic learner.

Being confident (item 27)

The second and final item under the dimension *Positive & Confident outlook* is being confident, which is defined as 'a feeling of self-assurance arising from an appreciation of one's own abilities or qualities' (Lexico.com). In other words, the ideal student should be a confident person who is self-assured and poised about their ideas, opinions and learning strategies. The importance of confidence has been discussed as a scenario where students who lack confidence would be unable to fully participate or contribute in their learning. Below is an example of such a conversation (FG2, Students):

Sally: You have to be *confident* in your own ability to do the work, cos if not you're gonna keep second-guessing yourself saying, 'Oh, no. This is wrong'. You're not going to get anywhere. So, the ideal student must be *confident* in their work. Always be able to submit it. Just do it.
Rachel: I definitely agree. Yeah. You need to be *confident* in your own ability.

In other discussions, students spoke about how their past or current lack of confidence means they do not feel ready to identify themselves as an ideal student, even though it is something they are currently working towards. In a similar vein, some staff believed that part of their job as tutors is to help students to develop their confidence, which may be achieved through regular encouragement and practice because of the belief that 'the more you do something, the more you build *confidence*' (David, FG10, Staff). This is especially true for students such as Jean (FG7, Student), who said that 'with the course we're doing, we need a lot of *confidence*. So, us having practice, and having that *confidence* in practical, it'll help us to be the ideal student' (see also Sadowski et al. 2018). As a caution, one student reminds us that:

Overconfidence is probably a negative. Because it's going to push someone to think that they're better and then, they're not going to put in the work that they actually need to and that's not ideal. (Owen, FG1, Student)

As such, being confident is not all positive as overconfidence can have undesirable consequences. Indeed, being confident has also been placed in the list of least important (as well as most important) attributes in an ideal student. Similarly, some staff said they do not feel the ideal student needs to be confident at the beginning of their higher education journey because during their study, tutors will be able to develop students' confidence. Either way, it seems there is enough merit to have a statement about being confident as a characteristic that is important in an ideal student.

Supportive of Others

The fifth dimension, *Supportive of Others*, considers the importance of the ideal student to be collegial and helpful to others, such as being friendly, honest and trustworthy. As discussed below, it is composed of six items, with a focus around social skills and working with others.

Being friendly or approachable (item 29)

It was implied by some that the ideal student should be someone who is friendly or approachable, rather than self-centred or distant from their peers. For example,

Ben (FG7, student) spoke of the importance of being social and welcoming, advising that students should '*interact with all* of your classmates, but also establish friendships of course because I think that's quite healthy ... and it benefits you'. In contrast, some students spoke of their dismay towards fellow students who are high achievers but also seemingly egocentric (FG2, Students):

Sally: They aren't sociable. They don't talk to nobody. If you say 'Oh, hi', they're like, 'Hi'. You know that kind of rude like little cold shoulder.

Rachel: I know exactly what you mean by them being quite cold. But obviously every ideal student isn't like that, but just from my experience. People that are more dedicated and work aren't as *friendly* and *open*.

Sally: For some reason they get the good grades, which pisses me off. In life it's all about *being nice. Be nice* to people.

This exchange also supports the broader view that the ideal student should be a nice person, either as a friend or towards staff. The aim of this item is to gauge the extent to which being friendly and approachable is widely considered to be an important aspect of the ideal student.

Being supportive of others (item 32)

Being supportive of others highlights the importance of the ideal student to be considerate of those around them, especially fellow students. Being supportive of others can be seen as helping peers with their academic learning but can also be regarded in the broader context of social or personal relationships. Our data suggest that it is mostly about the latter, notably the role as a supportive and caring friend who is willing to listen, help, advise or just to be around if and when needed. For instance, one member staff saw the ideal student as someone who 'engages in the broader sense, positively with the rest of the class. So is more of a *supportive learner* as well' (Eric, FG11, Staff). This item, being supportive of others, has some overlap with the other items in this dimension, especially items 34 and 38, which are discussed below.

Being a good team player and/or working well with others (item 34)

Item 34 is a popular key skill that people tend to include in their CVs or résumés, and so it may be a surprise that it is not part of the dimension *Employability skills*, which is described later. From our survey outcome, this item on being a good team player fits more strongly, statistically, under this dimension, *Supportive of Others*. Although it is also related to the dimension of *Employability skills*, the relationship is not as 'strong'. Regardless of the dimension, the ability to be a good team player or working well with others is recognised in existing literature as a key skill that is expected of graduates (Oliver and Jorre de St. Jorre 2018; Osmani et al. 2017), as well as by our participants in the ideal student. As an example (FG18, Staff):

Malinda: Well, I've got *good team player* and all that encompasses, being empathetic, supportive, inclusive. All those things.
Interviewer: Good team player. That is very important for your discipline?
Malinda: I think life, in general. Work, in general. Yeah, I mean, research ... I think about research, you're often in *teams* ... Being able to understand that some people in the group might not work so well, so you're not excluding them. You're sort of trying to include people as well. That's what I mean by *good team player*.

Here, a good team player is one who tries to be inclusive and conduct themselves in a cooperative and collaborative manner when appropriate or required. In a different conversation, Jean (FG7, Student) included the keyword communication (see item 20, under *Employability skills*) as part of her description on the importance of teamwork:

Jean: The reason why I said *teamwork* is because most of our, like Mondays and Fridays are most practical. And we're always doing group work, and you always ...
Interviewer: Need to be in a team?
Jean: Yeah, so you need to know how to communicate in a *team*.

As can be seen, an item on being a good team player or working well with others helps us to appreciate the relative importance of collegiality in an ideal student when compared to the range of other characteristics.

Being a trustworthy individual (item 35)

Moving slightly into the realm of personal traits, this item is interested in the extent to which an individual is considered to be trustworthy, such as a dependable or reliable person. The phrase trustworthy individual can be interpreted in the sense of a confidant, as well as mutual trust where the ideal student would be expected to deliver what was agreed or promised. As Lorna (FG1, Student) explains:

You rely so much more heavily on group work that you need to be able to *trust* that your other peers are going to actually do the work, so I think we need to *trust* in each other that they're going to join in and do their part.

For a handful of staff, the notion of trust was expressed in the context of the staff–student relationship. According to Jofra (FG19, Staff), 'if you set a task or an assignment, I want the students, in a sense, to *trust me* that this will develop their cognitive abilities, their intellectual prowess. And I know that's quite hard for a student to do', especially at the beginning when students have little or no knowledge about their tutors. From the data, there is a case to be made that the ideal student may also be a trustworthy individual.

Contribute to discussions and/or learning of others (item 38)

In education and learning, students who actively contribute and participate in class or group discussions tend to benefit the most, especially those who may have also made a difference to the learning experiences of fellow students. Here, the ideal student is expected to make a meaningful contribution to the discussions or learnings of others. For example:

> I put *participating in class*, but especially if it's a discussion. Like listen and bring your ideas and listen to other people's ideas. So you are *participating fully*. (Vini, FG5, Student)

> We've already talked about how important teamwork is, so helping others when someone's not performing as well, perhaps. *Giving them feedback*. (Malinda, FG18, Staff)

We also had counterexamples from students who distanced themselves from being associated with the identity of the ideal student because, as in the case of Finlay (FG1, Student), 'I was like too shy to be the ideal student because I didn't like *participate enough* or ask questions and stuff'. As such, we are interested in the extent to which the ideal student ought to be someone who contributes to and participates in discussions or the learning of others.

An honest, moral or ethical person (item 39)

The last item in the dimension, *Supportive of Others*, is very much focused on the integrity of the individual as an honest, moral or ethical person. In other words, the ideal student should try and do the right thing, whatever that means within the circumstances and context. Similar to item 35 earlier, this characteristic probes into a personal trait. For some participants, the ideal student should have 'a good set of *moral values* and is judged by their peers and lecturers to be, you know, caring, compassionate and very helpful' (Roman, FG21, Student). Similarly, Eric (FG11, Staff) spoke of the importance of honesty, although alongside the keywords of responsibility (item 4), self-awareness (item 31) and room for improvement (item 44):

> [The ideal student is] open and *honest*, who can assume responsibility for their own learning, realises why they may not have achieved as well as they could, and has a functional and effective plan in place to help them back on track. (Eric, FG11, Staff)

In other words, the ideal student should be honest with themselves, with a realistic outlook and reflection on their current and future progress.

Academic skills

The sixth dimension, *Academic skills*, refers to the academic study skills that are typically valued and rewarded at university, such as critical thinking and skills in writing, statistics, presentation and research. It is made up of six items, some of which are more informed by existing literature.

Good critical thinking, analytical and/or problem-solving skills (item 12)

Consistent with our previous study, the importance of critical thinking is recognised as a key characteristic within the dimension of *Academic skills* (Wong and Chiu 2020). Expectations of students to be critical, analytical or skilled in problem-solving are relatively common in higher education discourses, which can broadly mean the ability to evaluate and scrutinise the information available or provided. For David (FG10, Staff), 'it's that free thought and ability to push back I guess'. Similarly, Teresa (FG15, Staff) defined critical thinking as 'having this kind of attitude to actually question the authorities in some sense, I think that's pretty critical'. Some staff also discussed their teaching pedagogies in support of critical thinking, analytical or problem-solving skills. For example:

> I guess you could call them *critical thinking* exercises, where I will question the thing as well on the slide and I will try not just put things in front of it. I do Semiconductor Physics. Sometimes you put a slide on there, and instead of just saying, 'This is the law, this is how it works', I tried to have discussions about the limitations, and actually what are the problems, and, in that, trying to get the idea of *critical thinking* and trying to not just be this sort of, 'Oh, I just take the information and I will just go with it'. (Kathy, FG17, Staff)

Whilst it was mostly staff who mentioned that the ideal student should have good critical thinking, analytical or problem-solving skills, it would be interesting to see how staff and students across disciplines and universities rate the relative importance of this item alongside other ideal student characteristics.

Good numeric, mathematical and/or statistical skills (item 13)

Item 13 queries the importance of the ideal student to have good numeric, mathematical or statistical skills. Admittedly, the only mention of the keywords here in our focus groups was under a discussion on the least important characteristics of an ideal student. However, we acknowledge that mathematical skills are often regarded as a core skill or subject in schools and educational systems around the world. For example, it is a key measure in influential and international assessment studies of young people in secondary/high schools, such as OECD's PISA, 'Programme for International Student Assessment' (see oecd.org/pisa) or TIMSS, 'Trends in International Mathematics and Science Study' (see timssandpirls.bc.edu). We thought it would be appropriate and interesting to explore how participants, especially across disciplines, might consider numeric, mathematical or statistical skills to be an important feature of the ideal student in higher education.

Good reading and/or writing skills (item 14)

Like the preceding item, the qualities of good reading or writing skills were partly inspired by the importance of reading in international assessments (i.e. OECD's PISA and PIRLS – 'Progress in International Reading Literacy Study', see timssandpirls.bc.edu). Our previous research on the academic success of non-traditional university students also highlighted the importance of reading skills, even though for some students this skill was enhanced by chance as part of their hobby (Wong 2018). We found that students with good reading and writing skills found it easier to articulate and convert their ideas and arguments into written text, especially for assignments. The importance of academic writing in an ideal student was also elaborated by a member of staff:

> I would also say essay *writing skills*. I mean, it sounds silly in some sense but when you have to write a project, you have to know how to do it ... It's absolutely crucial for writing a good research project or something like that. I think it's the lowest level of an ideal, sometimes, but it's some groundwork they have to do first, essentially, before they can do the more sophisticated. (Teresa, FG15, Staff)

The excerpt above infers that good writing skills would be a minimum expectation in an ideal student, and perhaps even too obvious ('*it sounds silly*'). However, it is important for us to acknowledge and spell out the breadth of student characteristics that are considered ideal. We want to avoid assumptions and ensure that these ideal characteristics are not taken for granted. As such, this item considers good reading or writing skills in the constructions of our respective ideal students.

Good presentation, speaking and/or communication skills (item 15)

Following items 13 and 14, this statement focuses on students' oral and verbal competences, including presentation skills. In short, the ideal student should be a good conversationalist who can communicate and convey information and ideas to their peers or tutors. For Anto (FG16, Staff), the ideal student:

> Would be someone with very good *communication skills*. They can draw people together; they can inspire people; people are confident to follow them. People like [Winston] Churchill after the war, he gave these great rhetorical speeches, you know, you have a leader.

Whilst being a good speaker may be a criterion for a good leader (see item 21 under *Employability skills*), there is recognition from our participants that good presentation or communication skills are generally beneficial for personal and professional relationships, especially the establishment of mutual trust (see item 35 under *Supportive of Others*) and confidence (see item 27 under *Positive & Confident outlook*). Existing research on graduate attributes also noted communications skills as a popular expected outcome for university students (Osmani et al. 2017).

Good digital and/or technology skills (item 16)

Exclusively informed by literature on graduate attributes (e.g. France et al. 2016), the emphasis on good digital or technology skills reflects the growing importance and expectations of university students to be digitally literate and competent. These may range from the basic use of popular programs such as *Microsoft Office* (including *Word, Excel, PowerPoint, Outlook* and so on) to perhaps more contemporary or sophisticated use of mobile apps, social media or specialised software. Much of the focus on the development of students' digital or technology skills appears to reflect the idea that these skills represent twenty-first century skills that are seemingly more future-proof, especially for jobs that may not even exist yet (Ipperciel and ElAtia 2014). We included this statement as a way to explore if institutional goals (as illuminated through graduate attributes) are also shared by staff and students.

Good research and/or inquiry skills (item 17)

The last item under the dimension *Academic skills* refers to good research or inquiry skills. Again, literature on graduate attributes found an increasingly number of universities to expect their students to have developed research literacy, which is primarily the ability to independently conceive, design and undertake research projects (France et al. 2016; Rust and Froud 2011). In many undergraduate degrees, typically in the final year, students will be expected to write up a dissertation, which is often an extended piece of writing that involves some form of research or inquiry into an area that is of interest to students. In our focus groups, the ideal student was suggested by some to be a potential or emerging researcher, especially for those in postgraduate study or research, although research skills, more broadly, are also recognised as a desirable trait for undergraduate students. According to Irene (FG7, Student), staff would generally expect the ideal student:

> To already have done some *research* on it [teaching topic], so you already know the pre-reading. They [tutors] just give us just something to look at, but if you want to know about it in-depth, you will have to do it yourself.

Whilst the application of research skills is interlinked here with the importance of students to be proactive (see item 36 under *Reflection & Innovation*), we believe item 17 offers a dedicated focus on the value of research or inquiry skills in an ideal student.

Employability skills

The seventh dimension, *Employability skills*, refers to employee or job skills that are typically valued by employers, including interpersonal, leadership and social skills, as well as work experience and extracurricular activities (Bridgstock 2009).

As with the previous dimension, some of the ideal student characteristics under this dimension are also informed by literature on graduate attributes (Normand and Anderson 2017), which tend to reflect the goals and aspirations of universities, rather than particular individuals. In particular, we are interested in the extent to which staff and students might share some of these institutional visions that are generally expected of graduates.

Good job searching or job application writing skills (item 19)

One of the key purposes of higher education is undoubtedly to prepare students for their future employment. In particular, the notion of career or job readiness has taken on increased meaning and implications in the last decade or so, especially in the UK (and more specifically in England) as universities are increasingly ranked and rated by the employment statistics of their graduates, in government-endorsed initiatives (e.g. TEF – 'Teaching Excellence and Student Outcomes Framework') as well as in national and international league tables (e.g. QS, The Guardian, Times Higher Education and many others). As part of career readiness, one of the key skills would arguably be for students to have good job searching or job application writing skills, which can encompass their understandings of what employers want, their awareness of self-branding and promotion, as well as the common skills in job hunting, such as CV or résumé writing (de Waal 2019).

There was some recognition by our participants that the ideal university student should 'have the transferable skills to get into employment' (Serena, FG4, Student). In a related vein, Tricia (FG11, Staff) acknowledges that some of the teaching by her colleagues have a 'focus on essential employment tasks … that might be more applied to the world of work', which supports the view that university staff are increasingly aware and conscious of the importance of embedding the training of work-related skills into their curriculums (Diver 2019). The ideal student, therefore, may also be expected to have good job searching or job application writing skills.

Good interpersonal and/or communication skills (item 20)

Within the context of transferable and employable skills, the importance of interpersonal or communication skills is very much a key attribute that employers tend to value in potential employees. In short, item 20 considers the ideal student as someone who has and maintains good relationships with people, from fellow students to university staff to the general public. We appreciate that the keyword communication was also featured in item 15 (under *Academic skills*), albeit more in the context of academic presentation and conversation. We also recognise that good interpersonal skills are usually an important ingredient for good teamwork, which is covered in item 34 (under *Supportive of Others*). As briefed above, tutors progressively find their role as subject experts to be extended to include supporting student development of work-related competencies such as interpersonal skills:

> I think we're increasingly being required to teach them [students] employabil-
> ity, to teach them to engage, to develop their *interpersonal skills*. In the
> classroom, I do feel more and more so that I have to get them to speak.
> (Lottie, FG9, Staff)

According to Ben (FG7, Student), a command of good interpersonal skills
enables students to 'interact with all of their classmates and … establish
friendships', which is 'quite healthy because the more friendships that you
form, it [can] benefit you' in the future. As discussed below, this characteristic
is very much interlinked with item 22, which focuses on social skills and networks. Here, our emphasis is more on the interpersonal skills and the ability
of the ideal student to establish and maintain good relationships with different
people.

Good leadership skills (item 21)

Whilst strong leadership skills are often a requirement for those in management or senior positions, the act of taking a lead or making a decision, such as
in small group work, can be a frequent occurrence for university students,
especially for those who have taken on additional roles and responsibilities.
Academically, there is a large field of literature on the concept of leadership
(Day 2000), which is sometimes discussed as leadership and management, and
the qualities associated with leadership can include many other skills. Using a
popular job and recruitment website as an example (indeed.com), the following
keywords are listed as examples of skills that make a strong leader: active lis-
tening, ability to teach and mentor, creativity, dependability, effective feedback,
empathy, flexibility, patience, positivity, reliability, risk-taking, team-building
and timely communication.

As can be seen, the descriptors associated with leadership skills can include
other characteristics as some of these keywords are also featured in our own
survey, albeit as separate and different items. In our focus groups, the keyword
leadership was only mentioned in a few instances, typically in passing alongside other traits but without further elaborations. Our decision to include good
leadership skills as part of the ideal student survey was also supported by literature on graduate attributes, which noted leadership as one of the key skills
that graduates should have developed (Osmani et al. 2017).

Good social skills and/or with wide social networks (item 22)

Item 22 is interested in the attribute of social skills, especially those with a wide
social network. By social skills we mean the ability to easily socialise and
immerse into different social groupings, akin to the slang term of a social but-
terfly. The focus on social skills and networks can be seen in parallel with item
20 (on good interpersonal or communication skills), with the emphasis here
more on the breadth and depth of networks and contacts, which is similar to
Putnam's (2000) concept of bridging and bonding social capital. In our focus

groups, there was some recognition that the ideal student should be socially competent:

> You want to exit uni with a working *network of people* that you can reach out to in the future and be like, 'oh I know you, I knew you once upon a time. We can be good business friends or something'. So, in that regard, the ideal student cannot only be a one-dimensional academic character. And they have to have some element of *sociability* or some base of a *social network*. (Joshua, FG33, Student)

As can be seen, the ideal student ought to have good social skills or a wide social network, especially in preparation for life after university. As a side note, Joshua referenced the value of social networks, which brings to mind the popular saying: 'it's not what you know but who you know'. From a sociological and critical perspective, the concept of social capital, as described by Joshua, plays a key role in the production and reproduction of social inequality (Bourdieu 1986). In short, whilst individuals can train, develop and practise their social skills, we must recognise that cultural and structural barriers will mean that certain social groups are better, or worse, prepared and supported in the development of these skills. Frankly, we can even apply this view to most if not all items in our survey, in that the embodiment of these characteristics could arguably be classed. We discuss the role of social identities in the constructions of the ideal student in Chapter 7.

Good cross-cultural awareness and/or appreciation of global diversity (item 23)

Expectations that the ideal student as someone who has good cross-cultural awareness or appreciation of global diversity are primarily informed by literature on graduate attributes (Oliver and Jorre de St. Jorre 2018). Here, we take note of the growing aspirations of universities for their students to be global citizens, with an understanding and consciousness of global issues, affairs and economies (Harris 2005; Ipperciel and ElAtia 2014). According to Rust and Froud (2011), a global citizen would value human diversity and demonstrate cross-cultural awareness, including an appreciation of different cultural perspectives and practices. Similar views were implied in our focus group activities, where one student wrote that it is important for the ideal student 'to look beyond your small community and learn about what's going on outside of uni or your immediate environment' (Fala, FG24, Student), and a member of staff commented on the 'ability to connect what they learn to other parts of their lives' (Roger, FG9, Staff). Thus, we included this item to explore the extent to which the ideal university student ought to have good cross-cultural awareness or appreciation of global diversity.

Good balance between academic or social activities (item 24)

Several participants, particularly students, imagined that the ideal student should be able to maintain a good balance between academic study and social activities. The emphasis on a healthy work–life balance is particularly relevant for students, especially with the rise in concerns about mental health and well-being at university (see also item 26 under *Positive & Confident outlook*, where discussions of the keywords positive and happy also referred to student welfare). The following excerpt exemplifies the importance of the ideal student to be a balanced individual (FG32, Student):

Robina: [The ideal student] should be considered in different aspects, not only studying, but how they *manage their free time* with studying as well ... like, you do sports, you take care of your body overall.

Yu: I think of a student who is very *all-rounded*, not only excels in academics but maybe has like roles in the school as well ... they're able to *balance* their life in all aspects.

Several others also spoke about the importance of the ideal student to be holistic and all-rounded, especially between the demands of academic studies and personal life, including part-time employment for some. For Shakira (FG23, student), a successful work–life balance requires a committed management of time (see item 18 under *Organisation & Discipline*) 'for the rest of your life', because of the need to balance between 'your family and your life and your work life, and time for yourself and if you have kids, time for your kids, for your husband, wife. So, I think it's essential for life basically'. Based on this item, we considered an ideal student ought to be someone with a good balance between academic and social activities.

Participation in extracurricular activities (societies or clubs) (item 45)

Participation in extracurricular activities is an important discussion point in some sociology of education literature, especially for its contributions to social inequality and reproduction (Bathmaker et al. 2013). In short, some students, especially those from disadvantaged or non-traditional backgrounds, may not be able to afford to spend time doing extracurricular activities, as that time could instead be spent on making money doing part-time jobs. By extracurricular, we mean activities that are outside of the formal curriculum, such as lectures, labs, seminars or tutorials. At university, extracurricular activities would typically involve the student union, especially student-led societies and clubs, including sports. These engagements are often used as indicators of esteem in CVs and employment applications. Other forms of valued-added activities include participation in optional or external events, such as those related to careers as well as open lectures or discussion forums.

The importance of students participating in extracurricular activities is sometimes mentioned alongside achieving a good work–life balance, as discussed above (item 24). Here, some students considered extracurricular activities as a way to help them better balance the pressures of study (FG26, Students):

Kyle: I prefer to have an equal balance of studying and *extracurricular* just because studying too much I would feel stresses me out more than it helps. And my extracurriculars do ... what's it? They're for me as like a way of destressing and in that way, I feel like it benefits me more than, yes.

Ilan: Like attend a club or society.

Similarly, Gola (FG25, Student) said that 'you have Wednesday off because Wednesday afternoon is off because work–life balance is important, so you'll be able to join societies'. Here, we note that undergraduates in most UK universities, at least for those in our study, tend to have Wednesday afternoons free from teaching to encourage participation in wider university activities. In sum, we included this item on the ideal student survey to ascertain the relative importance of extracurricular participation.

Participate in work experience, placement or volunteering during university (item 49)

The last item under the dimension *Employability skills* focuses on the ideal student as someone who participates in work experience, placement or volunteering during university. Like item 45 above, we are interested in the value-added activities that students could take part in during university, with the focus here on experiences of real-life work, which are typically gained through placement or volunteer opportunities. As with the preceding item, the ability of students to participate in these activities is not based solely on individual attitude and aptitude – we must also recognise social and structural barriers, especially for students with limited resources or additional responsibilities. In focus group discussions, the value of work experience as preparation for employment is increasingly recognised, or perhaps even expected in an ideal student. For example:

> I think there should be a level of engagement with the world, of the real world, *work experience* or being *volunteer* work. That should be seen as part of your education ... I'm not saying you have to get a job where you come to class the next morning and you're tired. (Stefan, FG12, Staff)

> The other day I was sitting at the back of a lecture and I'm like, you know what? Even if I'm the worst person here, I'm the worst person amongst all of the best. So, essentially like how people have a *year abroad for work*. Because we always have access to [an internal work experience programme], throughout the four years we're having that *work experience*. So, that's really good. (Shelia, FG29, Student)

As can be seen, experience of work is a valuable and even desirable student attribute, especially in the context of employability and CV-building (Helyer and Lee 2014). Hence, this item captures the extent to which the ideal student participates in work experience, placement or volunteering during university.

Intelligence & Strategic approach

The eighth and final dimension, *Intelligence & Strategic approach*, refers to the ideal student as someone who is academically smart, capable and high achieving, as well as with a plan for the future. It is made up of seven items, each of which is described below.

Being a high achiever and/or has top grades (item 25)

An attribute that is often mentioned in discussions about the ideal student is academic attainment, such as being a high achiever or has top grades. In our earlier study with social science lecturers, we found students' attainment to be less relevant in their constructions of the ideal university student (Wong and Chiu 2020), which is a perspective also shared by some of our focus group participants. Predictably, we also had individuals who considered academic outcome and performance to be inextricably linked to the identity of the ideal student.

For those who supported the importance of high achievement, there is recognition that '*academic credentials* and *grades* … are the first things I think of … in an ideal student' (Doris, FG20, Student). So much as that for students such as Guy (FG3, Student), it was 'automatically assume[d] that the ideal student … has the *top grade*'. Furthermore, academic outcome may be particularly important for international students, who often pays 'crazy fees to be here', which can mean 'not *getting good grades* kinda just isn't an option' (Emile, FG22, Student).

However, there were many counterstatements that questioned the importance of the ideal student to be a high achiever. Teresa (FG15, Staff), for instance, emphasised that '*academic performance* is not as crucial as the right attitude. I just wanted to say that the *grades* don't define the ideal student'. Similar to item 33 (see later), a student will not be ideal, even for 'someone with a top grade, like 98 per cent … if they were disrespectful, very challenging or never attend lectures' (Reham, FG13, Student), which are covered in items 3 (under *Diligence & Engagement*) and 11 (under *Organisation & Discipline*).

In short, there appears to be an ambiguous relationship between the ideal student and academic outcome, especially since the keywords associated with being a high achiever or has top grades were considered by our participants to be among both the most as well as the least important characteristics of an ideal student.

Being modest, low-profile or quiet (item 30)

For this item, we are interested in the extent to which being quiet, low-profile or modest is considered to be a desirable trait in an ideal university student, which is also a personality trait. On the one hand, some students have speculated that staff would construct 'an ideal student as just a quiet student' (Mia, FG4, Student), especially 'when the teacher is talking and we're supposed to be quiet'

(Natasha, FG6, Student). As will be elaborated in Chapter 5, there are differences in how students construct their own ideal student and how students think staff construct the ideal student. On the other hand, staff and students also spoke about how the ideal student should be anything but quiet or low-profile:

> Thinking of what some people want in tutorials, in my department, is they like students who are *very vocal* and *very chatty* ... They don't want students to be *quiet*. (Eva, FG18, Staff)

> To be engaged more, preferably answers questions or ask questions *rather than staying quiet*. (Kyle, FG24, Student)

The excerpts above suggest that being quiet is most definitely not an ideal characteristic expected of university students. With these competing views, we believe an item that seeks the relative importance of the ideal student as someone who is modest, low-profile or quiet will provide us with a quantifiable outcome.

Being intelligent, smart or clever (item 33)

The idea of the ideal student as someone who is intelligent, smart or clever is an attractive proposition, as these keywords were frequently mentioned in discussions about ideal student characteristics, even though these drew opposing views and perspectives. Unsurprisingly, some participants, especially students, admitted that one of the first things that comes to mind about the ideal student is their exceptional academic ability, who are often a standout person with a natural and effortless talent. For example, Jinnie (FG21, Student) admitted that:

> When I hear the word ideal student, it kind of gives me the sense that the person is like *exceptional* ... multi-talented, maybe like has won some awards and then, the President of some society and has good grades, so that's what I kind of picture.

However, we also found a number of comments and counterexamples that queried the importance of intelligence in an ideal student. Jane (FG12, Student), for instance, explained that she 'put academic [ability] as the least important to me, just because if you have someone that is really *clever*, but they're not motivated and they're not driven, then they're not really the ideal student'. In other words, Jane believes that being an ideal student has more to do with enthusiasm, dedication and attitude (see items 1, 2 and 5 under *Diligence & Engagement*) than intelligence. Similar views were also mentioned by staff, who spoke about the dangers of smart students being big-headed:

> There are some people I think can be very, very *smart*, but can almost be a little bit abrasive and arrogant with that, and ... I would far rather teach someone who had less *ability* but was engaging in a positive way and wanting to learn. (Eva, FG18, Staff)

The darker side to being clever can also be seen in how students prepare for their assignments. Kathy (FG17, Staff) explained that with standardised exams, some intelligent students can be particularly strategic and therefore can 'conserve their energy and apply minimal effort' to pass, especially for assessments of rote learning. For Kathy, students who adopt such a strategic approach to their education are not, for her at least, considered to be ideal students because 'I would want to see students ... to actually figure out how the things works'. Here, perhaps, intelligence alone is insufficient as the ideal student ought to be able to demonstrate their attitude and effort in the learning process (see also item 10 under *Diligence & Engagement*). Whilst the relative importance of being intelligent, smart or clever is unclear for the idea of an ideal student, these keywords were certainly topical in our discussions.

Prior knowledge or experience in the discipline (item 40)

Unlike most statements in this chapter, item 40 was inspired and informed by keywords that were prominently listed as the least important attributes of an ideal student. The importance of prior knowledge or experience in the discipline was only mentioned twice, when it was felt that the ideal student should have some 'awareness of their subject area' (Oliver, FG10, Staff) or 'have enough academic knowledge for the field which they focus on' (Wing, FG13, Student). All other comments related to prior experiences were discussed in the context of being unimportant and insignificant, especially for social science and arts & humanities staff, where some have considered it to be their role and responsibility to educate and equip students with subject knowledge throughout their degree. In other words, if students are accepted into their course, then there are no further expectations or requirements in terms of prior knowledge and experience.

Yet, we note that the entry criteria for some disciplines, especially Science, Technology, Engineering and Mathematics (STEM) degrees, often have particular subject requirements as a prerequisite. For example, most engineering degrees require students to have a strong mathematics qualification at A-level (or equivalent). With this in mind, it is not unreasonable to anticipate that staff from the natural and applied sciences might expect their students to have some prior knowledge in their respective disciplines. Whilst the topic of prior knowledge or experience in the discipline did not really emerge in the focus groups with our STEM staff, we note that such expectations are more likely for postgraduate study (see Chapter 7, 'Perceptions of age').

Someone with a strong belief in themselves and/or single-minded (item 43)

Item 43 considers the extent to which the ideal student is someone with a strong belief in themselves, or even single-minded. As a personality trait, individuals with a strong self-belief are likely to be confident about their abilities (see item 27 under *Positive & Confident outlook*), although our emphasis here is more about the self-assurance of their own beliefs and visions. We included the key-word single-minded here to highlight the associated values of dedication and resilience (see item 2 under *Diligence & Engagement*), particularly the focus and attention that may be needed to achieve specific aims or outcomes.

This item on self-belief is also inspired by the work of renowned psychologist, Albert Bandura (1982), who explored the concept of self-efficacy. In our basic interpretation, self-efficacy refers to the confidence that individuals have in their own ability, akin to the phrase, *believe in yourself*. The importance of having a strong belief in oneself is also a popular attribute that is celebrated in entrepreneur or business success guides, which brings us to include it as an item for consideration in the construction of the ideal student. We also wonder if students who are single-minded or with a strong belief might be more desirable in particular disciplines.

Has plans or thoughts on post-degree pathways (Item 47)

For this item, the ideal student is seen as someone who has plans or thoughts on post-degree pathways. In other words, we query if the ideal student should be prepared or have a strategy in place for life after university. The ability to plan for the future can be seen as part of their career readiness, especially preparation for employment or postgraduate studies. As such, there are some obvious associations with the dimension *Employability skills*, although item 47 is more than just about employment. Rather, the focus here is on an individual's strategy and their abilities to imagine and work towards viable future post-degree study. This ability to plan and strategies for the self was also mentioned in existing literature as a desirable characteristic for university students (Llamas 2006; Thinyane 2013). Some focus group participants, especially staff, shared these concerns, as illustrated in the extended excerpt below:

> I see people who are floundering at working out what they're doing there. If you don't have a story to tell yourself by the final year, I really fear for them … I think in that sense, reality does play a part in that. When they look outside of the institution and they're trying to find that fit, where they will potentially sit, or where their careers might take them, it's a struggle … I expect [the ideal student] to have a basic understanding of what the programme will give to them, what they're going to get out of it, what the outcome to doing this programme will be. At the very basic level, it's not to say they have their career set in stone, but I want to have thought about if I do this, this is what I'm gonna get out of it. (David, FG10, Staff)

Although David stressed that the planning of a specific career pathway is not what he meant, because 'I don't need them [students] to necessarily have that binding definition of what they want to do', he was keen for students to have taken the time to think and plan about their futures, with a broad understanding of the range of career possibilities afforded by their degree specialisms. In short, item 47 asks whether the ideal student should have plans or thoughts on post-degree pathways.

Presentable or professional appearance (well-dressed, 'smart') (item 50)

The last item under the dimension *Intelligence & Strategic approach* refers to the ideal student as someone who is presentable or professional in appearance, notably in the sense of being well-dressed or 'smart' – which is sometimes denoted as being clean, tidy or well-groomed. As with item 40, we also took inspiration from our focus group activity keywords that appeared in the list of the least important characteristics of an ideal student, although the keyword appearance was mostly interpreted by participants in the context of social identity, especially gender and ethnicity. In other words, the ideal student should not be constructed as specific or biased towards any groups (see Chapter 7). We reiterate that our focus on appearance is more about the ways that students dress and present themselves aesthetically, which is why we included the examples of well-dressed and 'smart' in brackets as part of the item (to reduce potential confusion with item 4, under *Diligence & Engagement*, which shares the keyword professional in the statement, although explicitly in the context of learning).

Some staff said that an increasing part of their role is to prepare and equip students for work and employment, where 'we try to show them time to time … how they *present themselves* in public spaces, in *professional* environments' (Cara, FG9, Staff). Another staff from the same focus group also felt that she has 'to get them to speak, how to *look more professional*' (Lottie, FG9, Staff) as training for life after university. Lottie also spoke about her perceptions of how people from different disciplines tend to dress:

> Social science is a very, kind of we wear jeans, smart casual. Whereas the business school, you could even see the business school students going along with a briefcase. The art students are all pink hair, you know, piercings. Whereas health and bio students, I don't know. (Lottie, FG9, Staff)

From a curiosity perspective, it would be interesting to explore if there are any patterns in the way the ideal student is seen as someone who is presentable or projects a professional appearance.

Honourable mentions

So far, we have described each of the items that made it into the ideal student survey. To recap, these items on ideal student characteristics were predominantly inspired and informed by our focus group activities, although we also considered relevant existing literature. Of the 795 keywords that were brain-stormed by staff and students, the vast majority were coded and used, directly or indirectly, within the final 50 items. However, conscious of the question-naire's length, not every keyword was developed into an item for the final sur-vey. We would therefore like to share some of the keywords that were not included as a survey item, but could potentially be considered, especially in future iterations and development of the ideal student survey.

Most of the keywords that did not make it into the survey were seen as among the least important characteristics of an ideal student, such as being competitive, ambitious, goal-oriented and pragmatic (although may have inspired other items, such as item 43). Others were mentioned only once, often without much deeper description or elaboration, such as 'having fun', 'being realistic' or developing 'transferable skills'. One student, Nasreen (FG20, Stu-dent), spoke of the importance of 'not just spending countless hours at the library because sometimes you can find more effective ways to do things ... so working smart'. Informed by this excerpt, we included an item called 'work smarter, rather than harder' in our original survey. However, the statistical analysis found this item to be an outlier that did not situate in any one of the eight dimensions and so we removed it to enable a stronger set of 50 items for further analyses in Chapters 5, 6 and 7.

Whilst not explicitly mentioned in the focus group activities, we feel, more in hindsight, that the keywords of emotional intelligence or mental wellbeing could be a specific survey item here, perhaps seen as an extension to the dimen-sion *Positive & Confident outlook* or *Reflection & Innovation*. We also received helpful comments and suggestions in the open-ended aspects of the survey (see Appendix 1 for our post-survey reflections).

Summary

In this chapter we presented eight dimensions of the ideal university student, which emerged from an analysis of 50 items that we developed to describe the range of ideal characteristics in university students. We provided a description of each survey item, with a focus on the empirical evidence which informed our decisions, supported by existing literature where relevant. Table 4.1 pro-vides a brief description of each dimension and these are explored further in Chapters 5, 6 and 7.

Table 4.1   The eight dimensions of the ideal university student

Dimension	Brief description
Diligence & Engagement	Strong work ethic and positive learning attitude
Organisation & Discipline	Being efficient, punctual and procedural
Reflection & Innovation	Thoughtful and proactive about decisions and ideas
Positive & Confident outlook	Being positive, happy and confident
Supportive of Others	Being collegial and helpful to others
Academic skills	Study skills typically rewarded by lecturers
Employability skills	Employable skills typically valued by employers
Intelligence & Strategic approach	Someone who is clever, focused and capable

5

The ideal student as perceived by staff and students

In this chapter, we investigate how characteristics of the ideal student are described and discussed by university staff and students as we strive to better understand how different stakeholders conceptualise their desirable expectations of university students.

With the prominence of the student-as-consumer discourse, recent research has focused on what universities and staff can do to support students, rather than the views and experiences of staff amid these changes (Bunce et al. 2017). Existing research on university staff has tended to focus on their reflections of teaching practices or excellence (Uiboleht et al. 2016; Wood and Su 2017). The role of lecturers is fundamental in the student learning experience, with responsibilities that typically include the design, teaching and assessment of subject courses to the standards and expectations of higher education. University students are therefore expected to produce work that is appropriate to the level of their study and lecturers will inevitably form ideas and expectations of their students, which are underexplored. By the same token, students will also have expectations of themselves as well as their fellow students. It is equally important to understand how students construct the ideal student and how these perceptions may or may not align with the expectations of their tutors.

To begin where we left off in Chapter 4 – which described the items in the ideal student survey – with an overview of the eight dimensions of the ideal student and how these are rated and ranked by staff and students. We focus on their similarities and differences and highlight potential tensions that may arise from their respective roles and expectations. After the statistics, we explore how attributes of the ideal student are perceived and described by staff and students. Here, we are also interested in what students think lecturers expect of them, which offers an additional insight into the perceived expectations of university students. Note, most of the statistics reported in this chapter also formed part of a research paper (Wong et al. in review).

The ideal student survey dimensions

We start with a descriptive overview of the survey outcome. As detailed in Appendix 1, the ideal student survey was completed by 1,043 staff and students and our analyses revealed eight dimensions based on 50 questionnaire items that attempt to capture the breadth of ideal student characteristics (see also Appendix 2 and Chapter 4).

Table 5.1 presents the ideal student dimensions as ranked by staff and students based on their respective means. We used a 5-point Likert scale, where 1 = *not important* and 5 = *very important* (see also Table A1.4 in Appendix 1 for the overall mean and standard deviation, SD). Differences between the ratings of staff and students were all found to be statistically significant (Sig(2-tailed)), with an alpha of .006 using the Bonferroni correction for multiple tests, and so we include the effect size (Cohen's *d*) to underscore the magnitude of this difference (see Appendix 1, 'survey analysis' for more details). Here, an effect size of 0.2 is generally considered to be small, 0.5 medium and above 0.8 large (Cohen 1988).

As shown in Table 5.1, the most highly rated dimension is *Diligence & Engagement*, which is by far the most important for staff and students alike. As explained in Chapter 4, this dimension comprises nine items that broadly capture students' learning attitude and work ethic, such as enthusiasm, dedication and effort. For students, not only is it their top dimension, their rating for this dimension is also the highest of all dimensions between students and staff. In short, both staff and students viewed *Diligence & Engagement* as the most important aspect of an ideal student.

The second dimension is *Organisation & Discipline*, which includes being organised, prepared, punctual and procedural/rule-following. It is the second overall highest dimension, ranked 3rd by staff and 2nd by students.

The third dimension is *Reflection & Innovation*, ranked by staff in 3rd and students in 4th place. This dimension considers the ability of students to be thoughtful about the choices and decisions they make, as well as their initiative to be proactive or creative about their ideas and thinking.

The fourth dimension is *Positive & Confident outlook*, which refers to being positive, happy and confident. This dimension focuses on student optimism and a heathy mindset. With student mental health and wellbeing an increasing priority for higher education (OfS 2019; Universities UK 2015), our student participants ranked this dimension in 3rd place, but only 6th by staff. In other words, being confident and optimistic does not seem to be as important for staff as for students in their constructions of the ideal student.

The fifth dimension is *Supportive of Others*. It was rated in 5th place by both staff and students. This dimension considers the importance of being collegial and helpful to others, including teamwork, trustworthiness and honesty.

The sixth dimension, *Academic skills*, refers to the study skills that are typically valued and rewarded at university, such as critical thinking and academic skills in writing, statistics, presentation and research. It was ranked in 4th place by staff and 6th place by students, although we note that the means in 4th, 5th and 6th place display marginal differences, especially for students. Furthermore, it may be lower ranked for students but their mean for this dimension is still higher than the rating by staff.

The seventh dimension, *Employability skills*, whilst ranked by both staff and students in 7th place, students outscored staff by over half a point.

Table 5.1 Staff vs. students on dimensions of the ideal university student

Dimension	Staff mean (SD) [rank]	Student mean (SD) [rank]	Mann–Whitney U	Sig (2-tailed)	Effect size (Cohen's d)
Diligence & Engagement	4.213 (.491) [1]	4.299 (.516) [1]	93518.0	.008	.17
Organisation & Discipline	3.880 (.637) [3]	4.165 (.653) [2]	78636.0	<.001*	.44
Reflection & Innovation	3.984 (.546) [2]	4.091 (.611) [4]	96058.5	.007	.17
Positive & Confident outlook	3.515 (.932) [6]	4.105 (.892) [3]	67116.0	<.001*	.64
Supportive of Others	3.677 (.729) [5]	3.990 (.791) [5]	79942.5	<.001*	.42
Academic skills	3.769 (.650) [4]	3.915 (.679) [6]	94499.5	.002*	.19
Employability skills	3.054 (.819) [7]	3.621 (.811) [7]	66954.5	<.001*	.62
Intelligence & Strategic approach	2.265 (.743) [8]	3.064 (.906) [8]	54238.0	<.001*	.86

* Significant difference at Bonferroni-adjusted alpha value (.006).

This dimension refers to employable skills that are typically valued by employers, including communication, leadership and social skills, as well as work experience and extracurricular activities. Most of the ideal student characteristics under *Employability skills* are primarily informed by literature on graduate attributes (e.g. Normand and Anderson 2017), which tend to reflect the goals and aspirations of universities. However, such a relative lack of importance among staff merits further investigation, especially the potential mismatch between staff and their institutions on the ideal student.

The eighth and final dimension is *Intelligence & Strategic approach*. This dimension refers to students who are academically smart, capable and high achieving, as well as having plans for the future. Whilst ranked last by both staff and students, the difference in means is the largest on any dimension, at over three-quarters of a point. In other words, this dimension is not particularly important for staff and only moderately important for students. As discussed later in the chapter, although it is the lowest rated dimension, our students still see it as a relevant and important dimension of the ideal student, which is also reflected in the overall mean.

Across all eight dimensions, students rated each dimension as more important than staff did (i.e. higher means). The largest mean and effect size differences are *Positive & Confident outlook*, *Employability skills* and *Intelligence & Strategic approach*, even though the latter two were both ranked 7th and 8th by staff and students. We discuss these in more details below. A granular breakdown of how staff and students responded to the individual survey items can be found in Appendix 3 (Table A3.2).

Staff vs. students: Positive & Confident outlook

The dimension *Positive & Confident outlook* saw the largest ranking difference (3 ranks apart, 6th for staff and 3rd for students, see Table 5.1), as well as the second largest effect size of the staff–student comparisons (Cohen's d = .64, so the effect size is considered to be medium, see earlier). Compared to staff, students highlight the importance of personal welfare in the ideal student. Being happy, confident and positive *during* university education appears to be highly regarded by students, perhaps in recognition of the awaiting pressures *after* their higher education, especially financial debt and employment (Esson and Ertl 2016). For students, it would seem ideal if undergraduates could also enjoy and be satisfied about their education.

Another explanation may be age gap. Undergraduate students, who are typically younger than staff, represent a different generation (e.g. 'generation Z') that has a stronger focus on happiness and wellbeing (Twenge et al. 2016). Indeed, we note that confidence and happiness are also key focus areas in recent efforts to promote better student mental health and wellbeing (HEFCE 2015; Laidlaw et al. 2016), especially as student demands for mental health services and counselling have reportedly increased in recent years (The Guardian 2016). Student welfare, including the provision of counselling services, is now a policy priority in UK higher education (OfS 2019).

The discrepancy between staff and students on the dimension *Positive & Confident outlook* highlights a potential difference in their respective perceptions and priorities around student welfare. In their Higher Education Academy report, Houghton and Anderson (2017) recommended the development of student mental wellbeing to be embedded in the mainstream curriculum to improve student learning, success and satisfaction, rather than as a separate responsibility for a dedicated, usually centralised, support team/service. If we wish to promote staff's perceptions on the importance of students to have a *Positive & Confident outlook*, especially for lecturers, then it might be beneficial for staff professional development and training to have a focus on the potential roles that staff can take on to support the welfare of students (e.g. coach, mentor and personal tutor).

Staff vs. students: Employability skills

Whilst the dimension *Employability skills* was ranked 7th by both staff and students (see Table 5.1), the difference in their mean rating was over half a point, with the third largest effect size ($d =. 62$). Here, students are more likely to value the importance of employable skills than staff in the ideal student. We speculate that the relative lower ratings by staff on this dimension may reflect their assumed roles and purposes, which are likely to be as specialist educators in their own teaching and research discipline. In other words, the responsibilities of lecturers – the overwhelming majority of our staff respondents – are not traditionally associated with careers advice and preparation, which are typically the responsibilities of a separate career service (Bradley et al. 2019; Habermas and Blazek 1987; Speight et al. 2013).

In their study of student readiness for graduate employment, Jorre de St. Jorre and Oliver (2018) called for a greater shift of degree programmes towards 'assessment for employability', which aligns with the concept and objective of 'authentic assessments' (Sotiriadou et al. 2019) where assignments are based on *real-life* problems and situations. Our findings would seem to support this call if we wish to bridge the gap in expectations between staff and students on the importance of *Employability skills* for university students. Furthermore, as universities are increasingly measured, advertised and ranked by the employment statistics of their graduates, it is important for institutions to ensure that their priorities in developing students' employability skills are sufficiently aligned with, and shared by, their staff. It is therefore worth while to consider how staff can help students to appreciate the transferable skills gained from their degree course, as these skills are not always recognised by students (Times Higher Education 2019).

Staff vs. students: Intelligence & Strategic approach

The dimension *Intelligence & Strategic approach* is ranked bottom and rated lowest by staff and students (see Table 5.1), despite having the largest mean difference (0.7986) and effect size ($d = .86$). In particular, staff are less likely than students to consider high achievement (item 25 in the ideal student survey) to be an important aspect in an ideal student (see also Table A3.2 in Appendix 3, with a difference in mean rating of 0.94). The apparently minor importance of student grades or outcomes was previously reported in our research on social science lecturers (Wong and Chiu 2020) and thus the survey outcome is consistent with this view. There is also a notable gap within the staff ratings as the means between the 8th and 7th ranked dimensions also had over three-quarters of a point difference (see Table 5.1), which reiterates the message that as far as staff are concerned, *Intelligence & Strategic approach* is the least important dimension in their views of the ideal student. We revisit this later in the chapter.

Whilst *Intelligence & Strategic approach* is also the lowest rated dimension for students and over half a point lower than their 7th dimension, the large mean difference between staff and students (0.7986) highlights a potential mismatch of views on what is considered as desirable and ideal for university students. It should not be surprising that students value academic outcome. After all, their experiences of higher education are predominantly recognised in the form of a degree certificate, especially by employers, which highlights their academic achievement in a discipline. Since getting a good degree often has implications for future employment or further studies, it would be an understandable feature to include in students' perceptions of the ideal student.

To better appreciate the views and opinions of staff and students, we need qualitative data and so for the remainder of this chapter, we explore their descriptions and discussions of ideal university student characteristics. In Chapter 3, we explored their concerns about the concept of ideal itself, as well as the potentials and opportunities. Below, our focus is on how staff and students talked about the different features of the ideal student. These perspectives also informed the development of the ideal student survey (see Chapter 4 and Appendix 1).

How do staff describe the ideal student?

When we surveyed our data and coding for the range of ideal student characteristics that were mentioned by staff alone, certain keywords and codes stood out, at least in terms of how often we categorised their focus group excerpts into those codes. Although these coding frequencies have limited meaning, it provides us with a starting point and an indication of the ideal student characteristics that appear to have generated the most references and discussions.

As such, the most popular code for describing the characteristics of the ideal student was around curiosity, which corresponds to item 8 in the ideal student survey (see Chapter 4), followed by being reflective (item 31), motivated (item 1), respectful (item 3) and trying their best (item 10). These top five codes, and their associated survey items, were all under the dimensions of *Diligent & Engagement* and *Reflection & Innovation* – the top two rated dimensions by staff (see Table 5.1). Whilst Chapter 4 has already described each individual survey item, our emphasis here is on the views of staff and how closely interrelated these different characteristics can be when staff unpack their ideas and expectations of the ideal student.

Several staff spoke passionately about the importance of curiosity in an ideal student. For example, Lottie (FG9, Staff) said 'an ideal student for me isn't one that's perfect in getting a first [class degree], it's staying curious ... if you're always inquiring, you've got an inquiring mind'. Whilst curiosity is situated in item 8 (Curious, inquisitive and/or open-minded about learning) of the survey, we find that staff often describe features of the ideal student in a fluid and holistic way, where they use keywords that can also be the foundations of other items in the survey. For instance, a curious ideal student has been described as someone who also 'keeps questioning and challenging' (Gloria, FG8, Staff), which also aligns with item 48 (Challenge instructions or existing knowledge/practices) in the survey. Similarly, curiosity has been described alongside creativity, which would be item 37 (Being creative, innovative and/or divergent in thinking). Anto (FG16, Staff) described the ideal student as 'naturally curious and they just want to find the answers to things', which requires them to 'show a sort of a spark of interest and imagination'. Tyson (FG18, Staff) specified that the ideal student should be 'exploring and engaging in really productive ways, rather than reproducing the same old stuff again'. This also seems to suggest the importance of active learning where an ideal student would participate and interact with their learning actively, taking ownership of their learning process. As such, the qualitative meaning of being curious is not just about curiosity but can also include other related characteristics such as creativity and challenging existing knowledge (Kaufman and Sternberg 2010).

For staff, the ability to reflect seems to be a prized characteristic in an ideal student (see item 31 of survey, Being reflective or self-aware). A reflective student is believed to have 'the ability to ask meaningful questions that can help them grow and develop their knowledge' (Eric, FG11, Staff). For David (FG10, Staff), it is imperative for the reflective ideal student to question 'what worked? What didn't work? What can I do differently? And what might improve it?' when thinking about their progress and accomplishments. Through reflection, some staff felt students will also develop their critical skills (item 12, Good critical thinking, analytical and/or problem-solving skills) as well as respect and 'tolerance of other views' (Gloria, FG8, Staff), which is captured in items 3 and 8 (on respectful and being open-minded about learning). At least two other survey items were inspired by or discussed alongside the keyword reflection, such as 'a willingness to improve and embrace feedback' (Andrew, FG19, Staff), which aligns with item 44 (Acceptance of own weakness or room for improvement), and the importance of 'seeking help early ... if they notice something is going wrong' (Teresa, FG15, Staff), which aligns with item 41 (Seek support when needed).

It is also not surprising that being motivated (item 1, Enthusiastic, passionate, engaged and/or motivated in learning) and respectful (item 3, Disciplined, diligent and/or respectful in learning) are amongst the most popular characteristics in staff discussions about the ideal student. Whilst the word motivation was used interchangeably alongside enthusiasm, passion and engagement (see Chapter 4), these keywords were also often used as precursors to describe other potential characteristics of the ideal student. Ayra (FG8, Staff), for instance, imagined the ideal student to be motivated individuals who are 'committed, willing to learn and hardworking, with organisation and planning skills'. From this short excerpt alone, there are new keywords that can be aligned with item 2 (Dedicated, focused and/or determined in learning), item 7 (Hard-working and/or studious in learning) and item 18 (Good organisational or time management skills) of the survey. Similarly, a respectful ideal student is also expected by some staff to be punctual (item 11, Good attendance and/or punctuality) and organised (item 18, see above). In short, discussions of the ideal student as someone who is motivated and respectful can often include other characteristics of the ideal student, most of which are within the dimension of *Diligence & Engagement*, although some can be grouped under *Organisation & Discipline*, which again highlight the interconnectedness of ideal student characteristics (the 3rd highest rated dimension for staff, see Table 5.1 and Appendix 1, Table A1.6).

The importance of effort over outcome completes the 'top five' most popular topics for staff, as many seem to appreciate students who try their best (item 10, Always trying their best in learning). For instance, Stacey (FG14, Staff) said 'my ideal student is someone who wants to engage with being a student ... be the best person they can and get the best marks they can, whatever those marks are' (see also item 35, Being a high achiever and/or has top grades). The emphasis on effort, and therefore attitude, also prompted some staff to stress that their ideal student ought to be students 'who want to be here ... ready to engage, ready to ask' (Tricia, FG11, Staff), 'willing to learn' (Andrew, FG19, Staff) and ultimately, 'they want to be a student' (Flora, FG14, Staff). These excerpts align with other characteristics in the dimension *Diligence & Engagement*, notably item 5 (Good attitude, willingness and/or behaviour in learning), item 7 (Hard-working and/or studious in learning) and item 9 (Do more than required and/or go the extra mile in learning). The views of Flora, and others like her, may reflect growing concerns on the part of staff that students are increasingly pragmatic about their degree education, overlooking the holistic aims of higher education (Molesworth et al. 2009).

We conclude this subsection with a focus on what staff think are the least important characteristics in an ideal student. In the development of the ideal student survey, these keywords were also used to inspire and inform the breadth of ideal student characteristics, some of which were included in the survey to attest their relative importance. The three standout codes for staff on the least significant traits were students' prior knowledge (item 40, Prior knowledge or experience in the discipline), attainment (item 35, see earlier) and innate ability (item 33, Being intelligent, smart or clever) – all of which are in the lowest rated dimension, *Intelligence & Strategic approach* (see also Appendix 3, Table A3.2). For example, Ayra (FG8, Staff) explained that 'it can be harder to undo assumptions' if students are overcommitted in their prior/existing knowledge and ideas, which may curtail their abilities to be curious or open-minded about learning (item 8). Under these circumstances, staff would need to work harder to 'instil a new way of looking' and thinking for their students. Perhaps the value of prior knowledge is more applicable for postgraduate students, which is beyond the scope of this study.

A number of other staff spoke about the unimportance of 'excellent grades' (Tyson, FG18, Staff) in an ideal student. Sian (FG19, Staff) said that 'I wish students were more focused on the whole process and not what comes out at the end'. Similarly, staff also played down the significance of intelligence and instead emphasised student progress and growth (item 44, see earlier) as idealistic (Wong and Chiu 2020). The emphasis on the learning process seems to align with the popular concept of growth mindset (Dweck 2017), which positions learners as reflective and progressing individuals who appreciate continuous learning and lifelong education. Arguably, the relative unimportance of academic grade and intelligence in an ideal student would reflect the view that these qualities are malleable and can be developed through education and experience.

For staff, their qualitative discussions about the ideal student align with the ideal student survey outcomes, with the popular themes and keywords very much in sync with the highest ranked dimensions. Whilst their descriptions are often fluid, with multiple interrelated keywords relevant to other characteristics, the overall picture appears consistent in both the focus groups and survey. The ideal student, according to staff, is therefore signified by the dimensions of *Diligence & Engagement* and *Reflection & Innovation*.

How do students describe the ideal student?

Amongst students, their most popular attributes when discussing characteristics of the ideal student were about going the extra mile (item 9), being well-rounded or balanced (item 24), a high-achiever (item 35), enthusiastic and motivated (item 1) and reflective (item 31). The associated survey items for students' top five attributes are spread across four dimensions of the ideal student survey outcomes, namely the top-rated *Diligence & Engagement*, 4th rated *Reflection & Innovation*, 7th rated *Employability skills* and the lowest-rated *Intelligence & Strategic approach* (see Table 5.1).

For students, the importance of doing more than expected was the most popular topic. Many students described the ideal student as someone who 'does additional reading' (Lorna, FG1, Student), 'do things off your own back ... outside the classroom' (Guy, FG3, Student) or simply just 'go the extra mile to learn more about it, to gain knowledge about it' (Kyle, FG26, Student), which might include 'having a conversation with the lecturer after class' (Alana, FG12, Student) and 'doing further research' by yourself (Shelia, FG29, Student). These descriptions are represented in item 9 (Do more than required and/or go the extra mile in learning) of the survey. As with staff conversations, several interrelated keywords were also expressed alongside going the extra mile, some of which form the basis of other items in the ideal student survey. For example, the practice of doing more than required is often raised alongside a good work ethic and being studious, as captured in item 7 (Hard-working and/or studious in learning), as well as being focused (item 2, Dedicated, focused and/or determined in learning) and willing to learn (item 5, Good attitude, willingness and/or behaviour in learning). These keywords and associated survey items are all under the dimension *Diligence & Engagement*, including, of course, the characteristic of going the extra mile.

The capacity to strike a balance between academic and social life was the next most popular theme in students' discussions of the ideal student. Operationalised as item 24 (Good balance between academic or social activities) in the survey, students seem to appreciate the value of personal time in addition to study. Elise (FG4, Student), for example, believed that the ideal student should achieve a balance where they could 'enjoy their life ... whilst doing well in a course ... [and] knowing when you need to give yourself a break'. In other words, the ideal student is 'someone [who] can balance between social activities and academic work' (Kelly, FG32, Student). For some this meant the ideal student ought to be able to 'have fun, have friends, have vacations' (Diana, FG12, Student), with 'a good social life' (Alisha, FG24, Student). At university, the balance between study and social life is often achieved through joining sports clubs or societies (item 45, Participation in extracurricular activities – societies or clubs), which is typically seen as part of the holistic university experience (Hughes and Smail 2015). Jinnie (FG21, Student) argued that 'an ideal student is someone who has a balanced academic, extracurricular and personal development'. The latter form of balance is also about 'being happy and satisfied with your life ... having a healthy mindset', which aligns with item 26 (Being positive or happy) in the survey. Relatedly, for students such as Wanda (FG5, Student), achieving balance can also refer to family commitments and the ability to manage different priorities and demands, which links to item 18 (Good organisational or time management skills). The breadth of keywords and associated survey items suggest that at least three dimensions of the ideal student (*Employability skills*, *Positive & Confident outlook* and *Organisation & Discipline*) are relevant in understanding students' broad interpretation of a balanced ideal student.

Whilst it was considered by staff to be an insignificant attribute in an ideal student, academic attainment was a hotly debated topic by students, with competing views and perspectives where being a high achiever (item 35, Being a high achiever and/or has top grades) was popularly discussed as the most *and* the least important ideal student characteristic. In the early moments of the focus groups, some students felt high attainment was a key marker of an ideal student because academic outcome was assumed to be desirable. The ideal student was therefore synonymous with a high achiever. As Guy (FG3, Student) and several others agreed, 'stereotypically, you would think ideal student, top marks'. Here, the ideal student would be 'better than average' (Suvi, FG13, Student), which includes 'being smart ... like a genius' (Xin, FG13, Student) – or item 33 (Being intelligent, smart or clever) in the survey, which is also in the dimension *Intelligence & Strategic approach*. With a broader description, Dior

(FG23, Student) argued that being a high achiever is often 'a result of … being disciplined, having good time management and being self-motivated', which align with items 3, 18 and 1 (see earlier) of the survey. Whilst these associated characteristics are generally seen as important attributes in an ideal student, not all students agreed that top academic grades are essential. In fact, students quite often adjusted their viewpoints on the role of attainment in the latter parts of their focus groups, having a greater appreciation of other ideal characteristics and an acknowledgement that attainment alone is an insufficient marker of the ideal student.

For instance, Gabriel (FG22, Student) agreed that the ideal student should be 'very strong in academics, but they're also able to balance their life in all aspects, not just be good at one thing, they'd be good at everything'. Here, the importance of balance is mentioned again. Other students were also conscious of the negative attributes typically associated with high achievers, especially arrogance. Reham (FG13, Student) explained that 'some people can be so academically gifted [where they can achieve] without any effort being put in it … but they could be very challenging [to work with], sort of very disrespectful and never attend lectures'. As such, students who display these undesirable characteristics, even if high achievers, would not be recognised as ideal students because there are other, more important characteristics of an ideal student, which is consistent with the survey outcome.

As mentioned already, like staff, students also discussed the importance of motivation (item 1) and reflection (item 31) as key attributes of an ideal student. Here, students articulated similar views and associated keywords as their staff counterparts, and so we will avoid repetition. As a reminder, these keywords and associated survey items correspond to the dimensions of *Diligence & Engagement* and *Reflection & Innovation* – ranked 1st and 4th by students (see Table 5.1), with mean scores > 4, meaning that these features are considered important in an ideal student.

Of the least important characteristics, students spoke of attainment (item 35), as already mentioned, alongside confidence and sociability. We focus on the latter two attributes as these were only mentioned by students and not staff. Being confident was item 27 in the ideal student survey and it is typically a desirable trait, although the student discussions here were mostly concerned with those who are too confident, which 'is probably a negative because it's going to push someone to think that they're better and then they're not going to put in the work that they actually need' (Owen, FG1, Student). The other least important attribute is sociability, which again is normally a positive characteristic. In the ideal student survey, this is best represented by item 22 (Good social skills and/or with wide social networks), part of the *Employability skills* dimension. Some students argued that 'you don't have to be very outgoing, like going out and drinking … to be an ideal student' (Holly, FG1, Student), which is a specific interpretation of sociability. Others, perhaps jokingly, claimed that the ideal student 'won't have much of a social life because they'd be in the library like 24/7' (Rachel, FG2, Student) and are therefore 'more dedicated to work, but aren't as friendly and open' (Sally, FG2, Student). Here, being friendly or approachable may not be considered a priority for the emerging ideal student, but some argued that being 'too cold or distant' (Anna, FG6, Student) is equally undesirable. As such, these so-called least important traits can also be regarded as important, if it is in moderation and balanced – as in the case of confidence and sociability.

What do students think staff expect of them?

The final section of the chapter looks at what students think staff expect of them in higher education, which is partially inspired and informed by theories of social identity (see Chapter 2). Our interest in students' perceptions of others (e.g. staff) can offer a different perspective on how the ideal student is envisioned, as students' ability to associate with the ideal student identity is often shaped through recognition by self and by others (which we discuss more in Chapter 8). By exploring what students think is ideally expected of them, especially by staff, we gain further insights into their thoughts about the key characteristics of the ideal student and their observations of their role as university students.

It is widely assumed by students that staff prefer students who are passionate, motivated and engaged in their degree of study. These characteristics are captured in item 1 of the ideal student survey, which is the highest rated individual item by both staff and students (see Appendix 3, Tables A3.1 and A3.2). Elon (FG23, Student), for example, is convinced that 'any lecturer or professor would be thrilled if their students were to come close to their level of passion or interest in their field'. Similarly, students believed staff would also prefer learners who are enthusiastic and 'genuinely interested … around the topic' (Shelia, FG29, Student), especially 'people who engage with them and ask the questions or speak out during lectures and then come and see them later' (Joshua, FG33, Student) – which are partially represented in item 38 (Contribute to discussions and/or learning of others) of the survey. These views are consistent with what staff actually said they expect of students, as discussed earlier.

A small number of students suspected that lecturers would only be interested in their grades and outcomes (item 35, see earlier) because it is a quantifiable metric that could be used as an indicator of their teaching quality and ability (Giraleas 2019). As Holly (FG1, Student) said, 'for a teacher, the ideal student is obviously getting the grades because it's then showing that they're a good teacher because their kids are getting the grades'. However, most other students reckoned that staff are more concerned about their efforts (item 10, see earlier). Michael (FG30, Student), for instance, felt that some lecturers are 'like a performer and they don't actually care about what we get as grades; they want a receptive audience to what they're doing'. In other words, staff are believed to be more interested in the efforts and responses of their students, rather than academic outcome. Relatedly, Shelia (FG29, Student) shared that 'our lecturers are always like, it's okay if you flop in first year. They've never said you need to get good grades. They're always like, don't worry if you fail, we'll give you some extra help'. For students such as Shelia, these reassurances were enough to convince her that high achievement, at least in the first year, was not expected of students by staff. Again, consistent with student perceptions, staff rated student attainment as one of the least important characteristics, whilst student effort, grouped under *Diligence & Engagement*, was the highest rated dimension in the ideal student survey (see Table 5.1).

Most students accept that some characteristics of the ideal student may be universally shared but also point out that expectations of students can vary between staff, which may reflect their specific disciplines (see Chapter 6) as well as individual priorities and personalities. Jamal (FG29, Student) distinguished two types of tutor – lecturer and researcher. Here, the lecturer is often 'very nurturing ... and he or she actually wants you to learn and grow, then they would place emphasis on your learning', whereas the researcher would typically be 'just doing their day job, just here to teach this module, don't ask so many questions, [they] want to do research'. Dependent on the priorities and roles of the tutor, students felt that expectations of them can vary. According to Elon (FG23, Student), 'I sometimes get two lecturers saying completely different things, like, it's just bizarrely different', and gave an example of a written work that is praised by one tutor but criticised by the other. Similar inconsistencies were also suggested around student punctuality (item 11, Good attendance and/or punctuality), from strict to relaxed attitudes. As Net (FG21, Student) recalled, 'some lecturers rather you not waste time and just *Panopto* at home [view online recording], but others rather you come to class, even if you're late'.

Lastly, there was an interesting conversation about differences in expectations between younger and older staff, with the latter constructed by students as more authoritative or traditional in their approach and therefore having higher or stricter expectations of students. Another student, in a different discussion, also spoke about differences between experienced and less experienced lecturers, with the former more likely to 'know what is important ... and what is supplementary' (Fala, FG24, Student) for students to learn. The suggestion here is that experienced staff are more likely to have realistic expectations of students than their less experienced counterparts, which is an area that merits further research. Our ideal student survey did seek information about staff teaching experiences, but their lower response rate meant statistical analyses were limited.

Summary

In this chapter, we have presented the views of staff and students in relation to the ideal student. We examined their responses to the ideal student survey and found, in general, that the relative importance of the eight dimensions of the ideal student is similar.

Notable differences, by overall ranks or mean ratings, were discussed further, namely the dimensions of *Positive & Confident outlook, Employability skills* and *Intelligence & Strategic approach.* We also explored the qualitative views of staff and students, with a focus on their discussions and descriptions of ideal student characteristics. We highlighted the fluidity and interconnectedness of the keywords used to characterise the ideal student.

The final part of the chapter offered additional insights into what students think staff expect of them, which further contributes to our overall understanding of the ideal student from the perspectives of staff and students. Whilst students generally expect staff to prefer motivated learners, their views were diverse and inconsistent, which further highlights the importance of mutual recognition. The next chapter will explore differences by institution types and disciplines.

6 | The ideal student by university type and discipline

In the UK, universities can broadly be categorised as *pre-92* or *post-92*, which refers to whether their status as a university (with degree awarding powers) was granted before or after the year 1992 – as part of an expansion of higher education institutions in light of the government's Further and Higher Education Act 1992. Pre-92 universities are typically considered to be more research-oriented ($n = 48$, see Tight 2011), some of which – a self-selected subgroup called the *Russell Group* (currently with 24 institutions) – are considered to be the 'elite' or 'leading' UK universities. Post-92 universities are mostly former polytechnics, with a history of being more teaching-oriented and often seen as less 'prestigious', especially in national or international league tables. Globally, different categories or groups have been created to distinguish the elite or top institutions from the rest (e.g. *C9 League* in China, *Group of Eight* in Australia, *Ivy League* in the US, *RU11* in Japan and *U15* in Canada and Germany, respectively).

Although individual institutions are different in their own ways, they also share similarities, even though these may not always be obvious. This chapter, therefore, is interested in the ways the ideal student is perceived by participants from different types of university. The same principle applies to subject disciplines, as expectations of students can be influenced by the field of work or study. As such, we address whether there are any notable differences in constructions of the ideal student between respondents from pre-92 and post-92 universities. Similarly, what about participants from the natural and applied sciences (e.g. STEM – Science, Technology, Engineering and Mathematics) compared with those from the arts, humanities and social sciences (e.g. SHAPE – Social Sciences, Humanities and the Arts for People and the Economy, see thisisshape.org.uk). An understanding of these potential disparities can provide us with a deeper insight into how desirable student characteristics are viewed, valued and appraised across university types and disciplines. Data from both the ideal student survey and focus groups are used in this chapter.

Differences by university type

As discussed in Chapters 1 and 2, we know that student experiences and their sense of belonging can vary significantly between pre-92 and post-92 universities, especially those from non-traditional backgrounds, who tend to struggle more in pre-92 or elite institutions (Reay et al. 2010). The potential mismatch in values, practices, dispositions and expectations between students and their universities can generate inequalities in student experiences and outcomes. Whilst universities may communicate their expectations and ideals of students through graduate attributes (see Chapter 2), the extent to which these institutional ideals are shared or even recognised by staff and students is unclear (de la Harpe and David 2012). Our approach to understanding how the ideal student may be constructed differently across institutions is through the lens of staff and students from pre-92 and post-92 universities. Of course, participants can be mobile, especially staff, with experiences of studying or working in both university types (see also Chapter 3, the excerpt from Angel on p. 26).

Below, we report on the ideal student survey as we compare the views of respondents from pre-92 and post-92 universities. Although we are aware that the current affiliations of our respondents can and do change, we feel that their perspectives – at the point of participation – can still be a useful proxy that potentially reflects the ethos of their respective institutions. After all, the environment in which we work, or study, is likely to have some influence on our views and perceptions of what is ideal and desirable of students at our own university.

The ideal student survey: Comparisons between pre-92 and post-92 universities

We begin with a focus on how the dimensions of the ideal student survey were rated by respondents from pre-92 and post-92 universities. Participants were asked to associate with a UK university from a predefined list, with the option of an open-ended response to account for any oversights and non-UK universities. We also included a categorical question for university type and these responses were all manually cross-checked and corrected as we grouped our participants into *pre-92* ($n = 612$, 59%) and *post-92* ($n = 409$, 39%) respondents, with two missing or unclassifiable (e.g. international institutions) – these were omitted from the analysis.

According to Table 6.1, which highlights the differences between pre-92 and post-92 participants, their ratings in the ideal student survey are generally similar, with only one statistically significant difference. The dimension *Organisation & Discipline* was rated more importantly by post-92 participants than their pre-92 counterparts, although the strength (effect size) of this difference is considered weak ($d = .23$; see Cohen 1988 and Chapter 5). Differences in order of ranking are also minimal.

The intersectional analysis found post-92 university staff ($n = 163$) to rate higher than pre-92 university staff ($n = 139$) for all dimensions, but again with only one statistically significant difference, this time for the dimension *Employability skills*. The effect size is higher but is still considered small ($d = .32$). We speculate that *Employability skills* may be higher on the agendas of post-92 universities and their staff, in recognition that their students may be

Table 6.1 Effects of university type on dimensions of the ideal university student

Dimension	Pre-92 (SD)	Post-92 (SD)	Mann–Whitney U	Sig (2-tailed)	Effect size (Cohen's d)
Diligence & Engagement	4.239 (.527)	4.324 (.480)	112545.0	.028	.17
Organisation & Discipline	4.011 (.683)	4.179 (.625)	107540.0	.000*	.26
Reflection & Innovation	4.063 (.601)	4.045 (.590)	122453.5	.558	.03
Positive & Confident outlook	3.965 (.960)	3.863 (.931)	117488.5	.025	.11
Supportive of Others	3.887 (.806)	3.902 (.766)	126539.5	.975	.02
Academic skills	3.858 (.677)	3.889 (.671)	121875.0	.387	.05
Employability skills	3.425 (.882)	3.489 (.808)	121802.0	.380	.08
Intelligence & Strategic approach	2.805 (.899)	2.849 (.992)	124283.5	.605	.00

* Significant difference at Bonferroni-adjusted alpha value (.006).

at a relative disadvantage in the job market due to the added value of a degree certificate from pre-92 institutions, especially those historically seen as a top or elite university (see Wakeling and Savage 2015). Also, as mostly former polytechnics, post-92 universities are historically more oriented towards job training and preparation.

For students, those from post-92 universities (n = 246) gave higher ratings than their pre-92 counterparts (n = 473) to seven dimensions of the ideal student survey, with three statistically significant comparisons: *Diligence & Engagement* (d = .26), *Intelligence & Strategic approach* (d = .28) and *Organisation & Discipline* (d = .40) – although all had small effect sizes. Nonetheless, for post-92 university students, the characteristics of these three dimensions are comparatively more important in their vision and identification of the ideal student. For the dimension *Intelligence & Strategic approach*, we wondered if the lower ratings by pre-92 university students might reflect the higher entry requirements typical of their institutions. In other words, it is perhaps assumed by students that their peers in pre-92 universities are likely to be more adept on the dimension *Intelligence & Strategic approach*, as part of their admittance to university. In contrast, this dimension may need to be validated in post-92 universities, where students need to demonstrate their ability through academic attainment and aptitude.

From the ideal student survey, variations by university type are largely insignificant, with small effect sizes for the few statistically significant comparisons, including analyses that separated staff and students by pre-92 and post-92 universities. To better appreciate the differences between how the ideal student might be conceived differently across universities, we need to draw on qualitative data and unpack these views and perspectives through the lens of university type. Below, we separate our participants by university type to highlight issues that appear more prevalent or distinctive to pre-92 university (23 focus groups) and post-92 university (10 focus groups) participants. As with the survey outcome, there appears to be more similarities than differences in their discussions about the ideal student, from the concept itself (see Chapter 3) to the range of possible student characteristics (especially the importance of motivation, diligence, going the extra mile and seeking help, which correspond to items 1, 3, 9 and 41 in the ideal student survey; see Chapter 4).

Pre-92 universities: The normalcy of achievement?

In conversations with pre-92 university participants, one of the most popular topics seems to be the view that the ideal student should be someone who can attain high grades and 'comes across as an intellectual' (Jofra, FG19, Staff), as well as achieving a 'balance between social activities and academics' (Kelly, FG32, Student) without 'feeling like they're behind or stressed or anything' (Jake, FG28, Student). These descriptions and keywords, particularly prominent in student discussions, seem to align with items 25, 33 and 24 in the ideal student survey (see Chapter 4). In other words, the ideal student is thought to be someone who is holistically and effortlessly brilliant, with strong academic outcomes but also participates in social activities. Interestingly, the accomplishment of good grades is regarded by some as an institutional norm, particularly those from elite universities. As Nasreen (FG20, Student) explains:

> I felt like since coming here, is that's kind of, [having a 2:1] is not anything special, it's just like kind of the requirement to have good grades. And then on top of that you have to be doing things because everyone kind of has good grades anyway.

Nasreen's reference to her university implies that expectations or requirements of students are likely to vary across institutions, which can shape our perceptions and understandings of what it means to be a desirable student within an institution. Indeed, due to the competitive environment, academic excellence is interpreted by students like Nasreen to be the normal or even minimal expectation at her university (see also Cameron 2019).

Of course, not everyone from pre-92 universities agrees with the importance of academic grade. There are also voices which emphasise the importance of attitude and effort, more so than outcome (see items 5 and 10). Teresa (FG15, Staff), for instance, said that 'academic performance is not as crucial as the right attitude', whilst Nivaan (FG23, Student) accepts that 'you're here to learn so if I'm having bad grades, it's fine as well because I'm learning from it' (see item 44). However, although some students from pre-92 universities expressed these views, they were more generally prominent amongst those in post-92 institutions.

Post-92 universities: Process over outcome?

In post-92 universities, the importance of learning attitude and mindset (see item 5) is one of the prominent themes in discussions about the ideal student. Here, there seems to be a common recognition that the process of learning is just as important, if not more so, than the outcome. As such, the ideal student 'don't give up and they still keep going' (Lottie, FG9, Staff, see also item 2). According to Roberto (FG4, Student):

> I wouldn't say that the ideal student gets top grades always because part of being an ideal student would be learning from your mistakes ... I think knowing where you've gone wrong is a great place to be able to strive for the best.

For Lottie, Roberto and some other post-92 participants, the ideal student would have the capacity to keep trying and to better their performance through learning from mistakes (see items 10 and 44).

Unlike their pre-92 counterparts, participants from post-92 universities rarely spoke about institutional expectations (e.g. good grades as normalcy). Rather, their attention seems to be on the challenges posed by individual external commitments. Several post-92 university students, for example, discussed their difficulties and responsibilities outside of academia, especially those whose role included being the main carer or breadwinner (see also Chapter 7, 'Perceptions of age'). As such, the ideal student is perceived as someone 'who doesn't have responsibilities, or family to look after, or jobs to be concerned with. It's someone who can only concentrate on university, and that's the way they've become the ideal' (Muna, FG5, Student). Here, participants acknowledge that life can sometimes get in the way of being an ideal student, with competing demands as students juggle between different priorities. Carefree students are therefore more primed to be an ideal student than those laden with other obligations. Arguably, the concept of balance is also relevant here, although not necessarily between academic and social/extracurricular activities (see item 24), but more about managing the demands of personal as well as academic life.

It is telling that the above narratives are largely absent in pre-92 focus groups. Perhaps these issues are less common for pre-92 students. After all, post-92 universities tend to attract a more diverse student population, including those from non-traditional (and especially mature) backgrounds. In sum, there appears to be a qualitative difference in how the ideal student is discussed and constructed by university type, despite negligible differences in the ideal student survey. The ideal pre-92 university student appears to be an all-rounded high achiever, which can also reflect institutional expectations. The ideal post-92 university student, on the other hand, seems to value effort and progress, as well as a commitment to being a university student (see Bekhradnia 2012). The differences here also made us wonder about the extent to which students can meet their perceived expectations, especially the good grades that are anticipated in some pre-92 institutions. In Chapter 8, we discuss how students identify and associate with the ideal student identity.

Differences by discipline

Previous research has suggested that perceptions of the ideal student can vary by discipline, especially in specialist subjects where students may be expected to have a particular mindset or specific skillset. For example, on computer science degrees, Thinyane (2013) found lecturers in South Africa to rate self-efficacy, abstract thinking, creativity, computer playfulness and problem-solving as desirable features of their ideal student. In medical science, O'Brien et al. (2016) reported that proactive and self-directed students are highly rated by supervisors in the US, alongside academic ability, personal commitment, professionalism and discipline-specific attributes such as caring for patients. Similar findings were noted by Abdulghani et al. (2014) in the Saudi Arabian context from the perspective of medical students.

Whilst certain characteristics may be particularly valued in specific disciplines, Thunborg et al. (2012) concluded that academic skills, abilities and attainment were most desirable of university students in Sweden. Their study was conducted with lecturers and students from biomedicine, chemistry, engineering, physiotherapy and social work, which, like the abovementioned studies, are predominantly within the STEM disciplines (except for social work). With that in mind, we want to explore how the ideal student is perceived in different disciplines, in STEM (Science, Technology, Engineering and Mathematics) and SHAPE (Social Sciences, Humanities and the Arts for People and the Economy) disciplines, and we begin with the survey outcomes before we explore our qualitative data.

The ideal student survey: Comparisons between STEM and SHAPE disciplines

In the ideal student survey, the disciplinary background of respondents was requested through an open-ended as well as a categorical question, with the broad disciplines of the *applied sciences, natural sciences, social sciences* and *arts & humanities* as the four main options. The fifth choice, *none of the above*, was chosen by a small number (2; see Table A1.3 in Appendix 1), notably by staff from the professional services or support teams. Our initial aim was to explore how respondents from these four broad disciplines rated the characteristics of the ideal student. However, due to low numbers of respondents from the applied sciences and arts & humanities, and for ease of comparison, we decided to merge the applied ($n = 204$) and natural sciences ($n = 285$) to form a new category of *STEM* disciplines ($n = 489$, 47%). Likewise, arts & humanities ($n = 173$) was combined with the social sciences ($n = 359$) into *SHAPE* disciplines ($n = 532$, 51%).

In Table 6.2, the ratings and rankings of the eight dimensions of the ideal student are listed by discipline category. Generally, respondents from STEM disciplines gave a higher mean score than their SHAPE counterparts (with two exceptions but those differences are minor). There were three statistically significant comparisons, namely the dimensions *Positive & Confident outlook*, *Academic skills* and *Intelligence & Strategic approach* – all of which were rated to be more important by those in STEM disciplines.

The largest mean difference is for the dimension *Positive & Confident outlook*. Although the effect size is considered small ($d = .32$; see Chapter 5), it is interesting that being confident and positive is rated (relatively speaking) to be more important in STEM than in SHAPE subjects. We speculate that perhaps being confident would reflect the certitudes and certainties that are desired of students in STEM disciplines. Comparisons for the dimensions, *Academic skills* and *Intelligence & Strategic approach*, were both statistically significant but again, their effect sizes were small ($d = .22$ and $d = .23$ respectively). Both STEM and SHAPE respondents ranked these dimensions in 5th and 8th place. It is perhaps not surprising that the dimension *Intelligence & Strategic approach* was rated higher by STEM respondents, as popular stereotypes tend to portray STEM subjects as hard and difficult, and therefore students ought to be more competent, although overall, the mean rating on this dimension was relatively low (DeWitt et al. 2013; Wong 2012).

Table 6.2 Effects of discipline on dimensions of the ideal university student

Dimension	STEM (SD)	SHAPE (SD)	Mann–Whitney U	Sig (2-tailed)	Effect size (Cohen's d)
Diligence & Engagement	4.251 (.517)	4.296 (.508)	117690.0	.178	.09
Organisation & Discipline	4.065 (.669)	4.094 (.669)	124437.0	.542	.04
Reflection & Innovation	4.082 (.589)	4.035 (.604)	122181.0	.317	.08
Positive & Confident outlook	4.076 (.857)	3.777 (1.008)	107500.5	.000*	.32
Supportive of Others	3.932 (.793)	3.859 (.788)	119986.5	.090	.09
Academic skills	3.952 (.666)	3.805 (.679)	111433.5	.001*	.22
Employability skills	3.479 (.858)	3.439 (.854)	122744.5	.321	.06
Intelligence & Strategic approach	2.948 (.886)	2.730 (.966)	108738.0	.000*	.23

* Significant difference at Bonferroni-adjusted alpha value (.006).

Further analysis also found the difference between staff from STEM (n = 89, M = 2.498, SD = .805) and SHAPE (n = 196, M = 2.167, SD = .706) disciplines to have increased (compared with the overall sample) for the dimension *Intelligence & Strategic approach*, with a larger effect size of d = .37 (with U = 6636.5, p = .001, compared to d = .23 for staff and students combined in Table 6.2). In relative terms, this means intelligence and attainment are more important for STEM staff than for SHAPE staff in their constructions of the ideal student. Within the staff analysis, statistical significance was also found for the dimensions *Positive & Confident outlook* and *Supportive of Others*, both of which were rated higher by STEM staff. Here, the surprise may be the relative importance of *Supportive of Others* for STEM staff. Given the attributes of teamwork and sociability are often the emblems of the social sciences and arts & humanities (i.e. SHAPE disciplines), the higher ratings for *Supportive of Others* by STEM staff highlight the importance of collegiality in an ideal STEM undergraduate – a quality which may not always be highlighted to young people by wider media discourses and stereotypes (Tan et al. 2017).

Within students, there were no consistent directions of difference between the ratings of STEM (n = 399) and SHAPE (n = 321) students, with only one statistically significant comparison (U = 53706.5, p = .001) on the dimension *Organisation & Discipline*, where SHAPE students rated higher (M = 4.251, SD = .640) than STEM students (M = 4.095, SD = .659), but the effect size (d = .26) again is small.

From the ideal student survey, differences by discipline are minimal and modest, with some statistically significant outcomes but their magnitudes (i.e. effect sizes) are small, which means we ought to be cautious about any claims that can be made about these relationships. As with the earlier section, our attention is now on the focus groups as we explore how the ideal student is qualitatively discussed through the lens of disciplinary difference. Here, our analyses can revert to the four broad disciplines to reflect the recruitment strategy where each broad discipline is represented by at least five focus groups (see Appendix 1). Below, we summarise their most popular topics, with a focus on their distinctions because most discussions about the ideal student are not unique or specific to a discipline, but are popular across all disciplines (e.g. the importance of enthusiasm, hard work and organisation, which are captured in items 1, 7 and 18 in the ideal student survey; see Chapter 4). We also want to acknowledge that most participants in the natural and applied sciences were from pre-92 universities (see Appendix 1, Table A1.1), which may explain some of their similarities.

The natural sciences

Within the natural sciences (11 focus groups, see Appendix 1, Table A1.2 for more details), one of the most popular topics is the importance of the ideal student to strike a balance between academic and social life (see item 24, Chapter 4), which was also a prominent theme for those in pre-92 universities (see earlier) and students more generally (see Chapter 5, 'How do students describe the ideal student?'). According to Tyson (FG18, Staff), the ideal student should be 'having a social life, going out to the pub, joining a society, whatever. Just not doing degree-related work [all the time]'. The emphasis on balance within the natural sciences may reflect or be a response to the popular stereotypes of the natural sciences as a discipline dominated by laborious work, long working days and minimal social life (DeWitt et al. 2013; Masnick et al. 2010).

Another popular theme is the importance of being curious, open-minded (see item 8) and creative (see item 37). Participants in the natural sciences seem to particularly value students who are inquisitive, with 'originality and flair' (Anto, FG16, Staff), as well as those with intrinsic interests and motivation (see item 1) in the discipline. In other words, the natural sciences seem to especially appreciate students who are genuinely driven by passion, rather than a financial return or symbolic reward (see also d'Aguiar and Harrison 2016; Maltese and Tai 2011).

The third popular theme is the desire for students to have 'realistic expectations and understandings of themselves' (Maria, FG18, Staff), which can include being reflective (see item 31) and knowing their strengths and weaknesses (see item 44). The keywords and associated survey items are all part of the dimension *Reflection & Innovation*, which suggest that the ideal natural science student is someone who 'understands [themselves] and then understand what [they] need to improve on' (Shirley, FG20, Student).

A number of other characteristics were also discussed but the three aforementioned themes were the more popular topics for our natural science participants. As such, the characteristics of balanced, curious, creative and reflective seem particularly relevant in an ideal natural science student.

The applied sciences

Participants in the applied sciences (11 focus groups) discussed their ideal student in a similar way to those in the natural sciences, which is unsurprising given the close relationship between these two broad disciplines, as represented in the popular STEM acronym.

From the qualitative analysis, whilst the importance of work–life balance is also frequently mentioned, some of these discussions have morphed into another popular and more distinctive theme, namely academic ability, competence and attainment (see items 25 and 33, part of *Intelligence & Strategic approach*). Several applied science participants, especially students, talked about the ideal student as 'getting the best grades' (Santosh, FG27, Student) and 'is successful in a range of things' (Chloe, FG22, Student). Although the dimension *Intelligence & Strategic approach* was collectively rated in the survey as the least important (see Tables 5.1 and 6.1), applied science staff and students actually rated this dimension higher than their respective counterparts. In fact, applied science students were the subgroup with the highest mean ($n = 157$, M = 3.192, SD = .907) for this dimension. In relative terms, it seems that academic aptitude is an important characteristic of the ideal applied science student.

Although only mentioned in one focus group, amongst students in an applied health science degree, the importance of professionalism was discussed, especially in work placements where there are interactions with real clients or patients (see also O'Brien et al. 2016 in the context of medical students). As Ben (FG7, Student) recalled, 'we weren't allowed making any comments towards anyone … you can't even joke about yourself'. The characteristics of this professionalism are partially captured in items 4 and 50 (see Chapter 4) but there are nuances, which reminds us that some disciplines may demand or expect their students to embody particular qualities.

The social sciences

In the social sciences (6 focus groups), the ideal student is popularly discussed and described through the characteristics of dedication (see item 2), independence (see item 28) and critical thinking (see item 12), with the latter considered by some to be a standout feature of the social sciences. For instance, the ideal social science student ought to be 'questioning everything … that's [been] given to you … [which] kind of leads to critical thinking' (Xin, FG13, Student). Xin also suspected that STEM students, by comparison, may be more attuned to follow – rather than to question – disciplinary knowledge and instructions.

The ability to critique, nonetheless, is often intertwined with open-mindedness (see item 8), which is a popular attribute as mentioned earlier in the natural sciences. Social science participants appear to construct students in STEM disciplines as typically more serious, whereas those in the social sciences would be more casual, although in business degrees, dress code, especially in professional appearance (see item 50), may be particularly valued. Our data is limited regarding the possible differences *within* the social sciences, but it seems that as a broad discipline, the ideal social science student would be critical, independent and committed.

The arts & humanities

Participants in the arts & humanities (5 focus groups) expressed similar views to those in the social sciences and in our survey analysis, these two broad disciplines were grouped as the SHAPE disciplines. In addition to expectations of the ideal student as someone who is engaged (see item 1), diligent (see item 3), prepared (see item 6) and punctual (see item 11), the importance of studiousness (see item 7) was also popular. In the arts & humanities, it is acceptable for the ideal student to begin with a lack of knowledge or understanding, as long as these shortcomings are compensated through hard work, determination (see item 2) and a willingness to learn (see item 5).

As with the social sciences, there appears to be particular expectations of students *within* the arts & humanities. For example, Jane (FG12, Student) mentioned that 'with dance, they always encourage us to do more practical stuff and go out and see things that are playing', which seems to align with the characteristics of being proactive and taking initiatives (see item 36). Similarly, it may be desirable for art students to 'make contact and work with people' (Guy, FG3, Student) as they develop their social networks and communication skills (see items 22 and 20). More generally, available data suggest that the attribute of hard work is a key characteristic of the ideal art & humanities student.

Summary

In this chapter, we have explored how the ideal student is constructed and described through the lens of university type and broad discipline. Data from the ideal student survey found limited differences between participants from pre-92 and post-92 universities. Qualitatively, the ideal pre-92 university student appears to be an all-rounded high achiever and the ideal post-92 university student as someone who tries their best and makes progress (see also Chapter 8 for how institutional context can influence the ways in which students identify as an ideal student).

Regarding disciplinary differences, the ideal student survey also found modest differences between STEM and SHAPE participants. Qualitatively, the ideal natural science student would be balanced, curious, creative and reflective, and the ideal applied science student should be academically proficient. The ideal social science student would be critical, independent and committed, and the ideal arts & humanities student is epitomised by a strong work ethic.

In sum, we have unveiled some of the nuances about how desirable characteristics of the ideal student can vary by university type and discipline. Next, we consider the ideal university student through the lens of social identity, especially focusing on inequalities of gender, ethnicity, social class and age.

7 The social identities of the ideal student

Whilst the ideal student can be constructed in different ways by staff and students across universities and disciplines (see Chapters 5 and 6), our focus in this chapter is on the social identities of the ideal student. We discuss the extent to which the ideal student is considered by staff and students to be an identity that is available to everyone, or more likely to be individuals from particular social backgrounds. For instance, in UK schools, there is evidence to suggest that white middle-class boys are often seen as the epitome of 'naturally brilliant' students (Francis and Skelton 2005). By the same token, is there a social archetype for the ideal student at university?

Chapter 7 draws primarily on our qualitative data, although as with the previous two chapters we begin with a short descriptive overview of the ideal student survey outcome. However, we are fully aware of the survey's limitations and therefore our emphasis is very much on the focus group discussions. More specifically, our aim is to explore how university staff and students view, describe and envision the ideal student through social identities and inequalities of gender, ethnicity, social class and age. To do so, we explore how the ideal student is constructed according to our participants' own demographic background as well as what staff and students think about the influence of these social backgrounds in our identifications of the ideal student. In short, we ask, is the ideal student gendered, racialised, classed or aged? Is the ideal student an identity that is available to everyone?

Constructions of the ideal student by participants' social background

We begin with a statistical overview of how the ideal student is constructed according to our participants' own social backgrounds. The ideal student survey collected basic demographic information and we can show how responses varied by gender and ethnicity, especially between staff and students. Variations by social class and age are more difficult due to the sample size, which is smaller for staff respondents (n = 303, compared to 730 students), as well as the complexities of social class measurements. In the end, our aspirations for multiple intersectional analyses are scaled down as the participant numbers are too small (and therefore limited in meaning) when we begin to dissect their responses by multiple demographic variables such as role (e.g. staff or student) *and* gender *and* ethnicity and so on. As such, our analysis into social class and age differences will only be on student participants and we used parental education as a proxy for understanding the potential influence of social class. We are aware that social class is complex and can include a multitude of variables such as parental occupation, household income and various indicators of wealth such as savings and properties (Savage 2015; see also Walkerdine 2020). In any case, we recognise that the ideal student survey only asked for basic demographic details, to minimise completion time of the questionnaire and thus, we consider our participants' views towards these social identities in the second part of the chapter when we draw on focus group data. Appendix 3 includes a further breakdown of the responses to the individual ideal student survey items.

Differences by gender

When we split our survey by gender (64% female, 35% male, 1% other, see Appendix 1) for both students and staff, we found females to typically rate the ideal student characteristics higher than their male counterparts. Due to low numbers, 'other' is excluded and our initial analysis also found insignificant results for this small subgroup.

As detailed in Table 7.1, female students rated four dimensions of the ideal student higher than males. These statistically significant comparisons include *Diligence & Engagement, Organisation & Discipline, Supportive of Others* and *Employability skills*, with the largest effect size – and therefore the biggest difference – on the dimension *Organisation & Discipline* ($d = .40$, considered a small effect). As the survey itself does not explain why female students rated these dimensions more important for an ideal student than male students, we do not wish to overinterpret and will therefore revisit the influence of gender with qualitative data later in the chapter. For now, all we can say is that female students generally find these four dimensions to be more important in an ideal student.

For staff, no dimensions produced a significant outcome at the Bonferroni-adjusted alpha value ($p < .006$), with the closest dimension to a meaningful result being *Intelligence & Strategic approach*. Here, male staff ($n = 122$, M = 2.370, SD = .764) rated these items higher than female staff ($n = 172$, M = 2.182, SD: .710), with $U = 9044.5$, $p = .043$ and $d = .25$, although this dimension is rated as the least important dimension.

Differences by ethnicity

In the survey, data collection for ethnicity followed the UK's 2011 census option, with 19 ethnic group classifications (which is also used by the Higher Education Statistics Agency, HESA). Our student respondents are diverse (White, $n = 420$, 57.9%; 'non-White', $n = 294$, 40.5%; and others, $n = 12$, 1.7%), but most staff see themselves as White ($n = 273$, 90.8%). The low number of minority ethnic staff ($n = 26$, 8.6%, and others, $n = 2$, 0.6%) may also explain why there are no significant results in our analysis for staff differences by ethnicity.

Table 7.1 Students: differences on dimensions of the ideal student by gender

Dimension	Females (SD)	Males (SD)	Mann–Whitney U	Sig (2-tailed)	Effect size (Cohen's d)
Diligence & Engagement	4.356 (.501)	4.202 (.511)	42877.5	<.001*	.28
Organisation & Discipline	4.264 (.590)	3.980 (.711)	40232.5	<.001*	.40
Supportive of Others	4.078 (.756)	3.807 (.829)	42910.0	<.001*	.33
Employability skills	3.692 (.781)	3.470 (.833)	45375.0	.001*	.25

Note: Only included dimensions which are significant* at Bonferroni-adjusted alpha value (.006).

Our student data (see Table 7.2) produced significant results for seven of the eight dimensions, the exception being *Organisation & Discipline*. Although the effect sizes were all small, students from non-White backgrounds rated these characteristics as more important than their White counterparts did, with the biggest difference being on the dimension *Positive & Confident outlook* ($d = .32$). Previous research has reported that Black, Asian and Minority Ethnic (BAME) university students tend to lack confidence and self-belief (Bunce et al. 2019; Wong et al. 2020) and so perhaps the importance of *Positive & Confident outlook* also reflects the desires and aspirations of 'non-White' students to further develop and strengthen in these areas in order to be ideal.

Differences by social class

As already mentioned, the proxy for students' social class background was parental education, where we initially offered three options (no degree-educated, one degree-educated and two or more degree-educated parents). In our analysis, we regrouped our students into those with at least one degree-educated parent ($n = 415$, 56.8%) and those with no degree-educated parents ($n = 263$, 36.0%; with unknown, $n = 52$, 7.2% – which were omitted from the analysis).

Here, no dimensions produced a statistically significant outcome at the Bonferroni-adjusted alpha value ($p < .006$). Table 7.3 included two dimensions of the ideal student that are closest to significance. For the dimension *Academic skills*, we can only speculate that students with degree-educated parents may be better informed about the importance of mastering a range of academic skills in order to be successful in higher education (see Wong 2018).

Differences by age

For age, our focus was also on students. A range of age categories were collected but for analysis, we reorganised students into those aged 20 or under ($n = 453$, 62.1%) and those aged 21 or over ($n = 258$, 35.3%; with other, $n = 19$, 2.6%). The group aged 21 or over aligned with the category of mature students commonly used by UK universities. Here, no dimensions produced a statistically significant outcome at the Bonferroni-adjusted alpha value. Table 7.4 highlights *Positive & Confident outlook* as the only dimension close to significance. Here, younger students rated confidence and positivity to be more important than their older counterparts, although we caution the effect size is very small ($d = .14$).

To appreciate the importance of the first year of undergraduate study (especially in the context of student transition into university), we also grouped our students by their level of study. For comparability, we arranged our students into two groups, *first year* ($n = 338$, 46.3%) and *not first year* ($n = 378$, 51.8%; with data unavailable, $n = 14$, 1.9%), which includes second year ($n = 132$), third or fourth year ($n = 166$), postgraduate degree ($n = 75$) and others ($n = 5$). In Table 7.5, we can see that five dimensions of the ideal student had a significant outcome, with *Organisation & Discipline* showing the biggest difference, with

Table 7.2 Students: differences on dimensions of the ideal student by ethnicity

Dimension	White (SD)	Non-white (SD)	Mann–Whitney U	Sig (2-tailed)	Effect size (Cohen's d)
Diligence & Engagement	4.255 (.515)	4.353 (.519)	52035.0	.006*	.21
Reflection & Innovation	4.016 (.609)	4.187 (.608)	49483.0	<.001*	.30
Positive & Confident outlook	4.006 (.883)	4.187 (.608)	49725.0	<.001*	.32
Supportive of Others	3.909 (.783)	4.088 (.797)	51429.0	<.001*	.26
Academic Skills	3.847 (.668)	4.011 (.694)	50934.0	.001*	.26
Employability Skills	3.528 (.806)	3.737 (.808)	51368.0	<.001*	.26
Intelligence & Strategic approach	2.940 (.874)	3.224 (.931)	50060.0	<.001	.30

Note: Only included dimensions which are significant* at Bonferroni-adjusted alpha value (.006).

Table 7.3 Students: differences on dimensions of the ideal student by parental education

Dimension	Degree parent (SD)	No degree parent (SD)	Mann–Whitney U	Sig (2-tailed)	Effect size (Cohen's d)
Reflection & Innovation	4.118 (.598)	4.025 (.623)	48421.5	.045	.15
Academic skills	3.950 (.678)	3.828 (.663)	47642.5	.014	.18

Note: No significant difference reported at Bonferroni-adjusted alpha value (.006), but included results $p < .05$.

Table 7.4 Students: differences on dimensions of the ideal student by age group

Dimension	Age 20 or less (SD)	Age 21 or over (SD)	Mann–Whitney U	Sig (2-tailed)	Effect size (Cohen's d)
Positive & Confident outlook	4.155 (.869)	4.016 (.927)	52748.0	.042	.15

Note: No significant difference reported at Bonferroni-adjusted alpha value (.006), but included results p < .05.

Table 7.5 Students: differences on dimensions of the ideal student by level of study

Dimension	First year (SD)	Not first year (SD)	Mann–Whitney U	Sig (2-tailed)	Effect size (Cohen's d)
Diligence & Engagement	4.370 (.471)	4.232 (.548)	52484.0	.001*	.25
Organisation & Discipline	4.307 (.592)	4.035 (.685)	46860.5	<.001*	.44
Supportive of Others	4.087 (.727)	3.899 (.840)	55105.5	.005*	.21
Employability Skills	3.730 (.751)	3.508 (.850)	53871.5	.001*	.25
Intelligence & Strategic approach	3.187 (.904)	2.944 (.891)	52024.5	.001*	.24

Note: Only included dimensions which are significant* at Bonferroni-adjusted alpha value (.006).

an effect size ($d = .44$) that is close to a medium effect. We are not surprised that *first year* students rate *Organisation & Discipline* as particularly important given new students are often overwhelmed with new information at the beginning of their university journey. Over time, however, once students familiarise themselves with the university structures and systems, the relative importance of *Organisation & Discipline* could decline, as in the case of our *not first year* students.

Perceptions of the ideal student by social identities

So far, we have explored how students' own demographic backgrounds could shape different constructions of the ideal student. Whilst insightful, these statistics do not provide us with reasons as to why particular patterns emerge. For the remainder of this chapter, we focus on the views of staff and students on how different social identities might shape perceptions of the ideal student. In particular, we discuss the extent to which characteristics of the ideal student are more, or less, likely to be seen in particular individuals, especially in the context of gender, ethnicity, social class and age. Here, we are interested to see if the identity of an ideal student is considered and perceived to be easier, or harder, for people to embody from different social backgrounds and identities.

However, before we unpack these four social identities, we want to explore a broader question that might help us to set the scene, that is, *can anyone become an ideal student?* The short answer, as far as our staff and students are concerned, is yes, but with caveats. We are not surprised that some participants, especially students, have articulated *egalitarian discourses* of the ideal student as *for anyone*. In other words, being an ideal student, or embodying the identity of an ideal student, is considered to be possible, available and open for *anyone* who works for it. Yet, as we explore later, there are also competing views and recognitions that some traits and characteristics may favour particular groups. In fact, egalitarian views are sometimes expressed *alongside* discourses that highlight social inequalities (e.g. as available for anyone *but* also gendered), even by the same participant. This does not mean the individual is being untruthful but merely illustrates how fluid our views can be at different points or phases of a discussion, as well as highlighting, again, that the concept of the ideal student can be complex and multifaceted (see Chapter 3). What we are most interested here is the range of meanings and ideas, rather than to critique individuals who may have contradicted themselves.

Anyone can be an ideal student

The egalitarian discourse of the ideal student as available for anyone was mentioned in the majority of our focus groups, even if it was mostly superficial or brief, or discussed only in conjunction with social identities such as gender and ethnicity (which we discuss next). A few students were particularly passionate about how the ideal student should not be defined by any social categories or identities because 'they come in all shape and sizes' (Jofra, FG19, Staff). Kobe (FG21, Student) said he does not 'think any other factor really affect[s] your likelihood to become an ideal student'. For students such as Ben (FG7), becoming an ideal student 'comes down to the person individually', with the emphasis on individual aspirations and effort, more so than wider social inequalities. Perhaps the most optimistic view comes from Gabriel (FG22, Student), who believes that higher education is an opportunity for students to start anew, which includes working towards an ideal student identity:

> I think one of the nicest things about university is that it's a blank canvas for a lot of people. So regardless of where you come from, where your background, you sort of see university as a level playing field at the start, and you can do what you wanna do regardless of what you've done before. And you can choose, like, to work as hard as you want or not as hard as you want. You can choose to take part in as many activities as you want, again or the opposite. You can choose to be as social as you want or not … You can choose to be an ideal student or not.

Whilst we could argue that such freedom of choice is unlikely to be equal for students from different backgrounds, we appreciate the view and vision of higher education as a platform for students to redevelop and reconstruct their sense of selves, including as an ideal university student. The idea that 'anybody can be an ideal student, it's just if you want to be it or not' (Suvi, FG13, Student) is certainly an attractive proposition and ideology, but there is also recognition and realisation that higher education 'is not a level playing field' (Chloe, FG22, Student) and that our social identities 'do matter … in reality' (Marc, FG5, Student), especially experiences of inequalities due to gender, ethnicity, social class and age (see Chapters 1 and 2). Below, we continue by looking at gender and how staff and students perceive gender to shape our views of and identification with the ideal student.

Perceptions of gender

Despite egalitarian views, when staff and students were asked more directly about how gender might influence our constructions and identifications of the ideal student, a broader range of perspectives emerged. Egalitarian discourses are still articulated, with impassioned defences of gender equality – at least as an ideology – and the view that biological differences do not and should not impede anyone's ability to be an ideal student. For instance, Sally (FG2, student) argued that 'you can get a very unfocused woman and a very unfocused guy. You can get a very organised woman and a very organised guy. So, it just depends on the person', whilst Anto (FG16, Staff) asserted that 'I don't think that there's anything inherent' between the genders or sexes in becoming an ideal student.

Yet, there is recognition that expectations of students can vary by gender due to family socialisations and societal or cultural constructions of gendered roles and responsibilities. For example, Nivaan (FG23, Student) recounted that 'my parents have more expectations from me than from my brother … even around with my nieces or my cousins it's the same, the girls are supposed to do better'. Her views are shared by Dior (FG23, Student), who acknowledged the popular 'stereotypes where girls are supposed to be more studious or getting better grades than guys'. In the same conversation, Dillan (FG23, Student) added that girls are typically seen as 'more obedient … and more disciplined' than boys. Given girls are more likely to be expected to hold these traits (and most of which are considered as ideal student characteristics, see Chapter 4), it should not be too surprising that some of our participants, especially students, had girls in mind when speaking about the ideal student.

Sienna (FG1, Student), for instance, admitted that 'I automatically think of a girl. I don't know why, but I just do when you think of the ideal student'. Other students explained that girls are more likely to be ideal students because girls tend to achieve higher than boys, even at university. On the part of staff, there are suggestions that 'female students are genuinely better than the male ones … [because] they tend to have more maturity' (Francis, FG17, Staff) and are therefore more desirable to teach as university students. Of course, the view here is not that male students are immature, but from the experiences of staff in our study, female students are usually more mature, especially those on degree courses dominated by males. According to Kathy (FG17, Staff), women who persevere in male-dominated disciplines, such as the physical sciences, are 'usually in the ideal part because somehow they had to be so resilient to get to the point'. The challenges experienced by women in STEM degrees are well documented, especially when also from a racial minority background (e.g. Hughes et al. 2017; Morton and Parsons 2018; Ong et al. 2018). While the relationship between gender and subject discipline (see Chapter 6) was not a key discussion topic, there is some recognition of traditional gender stereotypes which position boys as more adept in technical skills or scientific knowledge and girls as better attuned in the arts, humanities and social sciences. However, it is unclear the extent to which these gendered stereotypes actually shape the ways in which the ideal student is perceived or constructed.

What we do know is that possible traits of the ideal student are mostly discussed in relation to female students, such as being studious, disciplined, high-achieving and mature. By comparison, the only characteristic that was mentioned as more likely to be found in male students is confidence, because girls tend to have 'a little more self-doubt than guys' (Doris, FG20, Student). Funnily enough, Eva (FG18, Staff) said that 'cocky, arrogant students … are more likely to be male', which reminds us that confidence – typically a positive and desirable trait – can also be viewed negatively and undesirable if in excess. With this in mind, one of our students, Stefan (FG12, Student), pondered whether our perceptions of the ideal student should be different for female and male students, especially if expectations of female and male students are generally and even genuinely different.

As such, should there be, say, an ideal female student? Or an ideal male student? With greater recognition and appreciation of non-binary gender identities, we are reminded of the dangers and limitations of associating particular ideal student characteristics with a specific gender or sex, especially as expressions of these identities are more fluid than ever before. Stefan (FG12, Student) ultimately concluded that 'when you go into a classroom, you should look for an ideal student and not for a gender *per se*'. In other words, our focus should be on characteristics we find desirable in an ideal student, rather than the apparent gender of the person who embodies these traits. Whilst we end this subsection with a reference back to egalitarian views and aspirations, we acknowledge that it is inevitable that certain desirable characteristics of the ideal student would be seen as more typical or expected of a particular gender.

Perceptions of ethnicity and cultural background

When the discussion was on ethnicity, the content of these conversations also extended to cultural backgrounds. As with gender, there were reminders of egalitarian discourses and viewpoints, although most staff and students appear to hold stronger views about the possible role of ethnicity (and to a broader extent, culture) on the likelihood of students to embody ideal characteristics. One of the few, but powerful, egalitarian comments was made by Tricia (FG11, Staff), who believed that:

> Ethnic background does not play any part in, for me personally, in understanding what ideal means. This idea about your ethnic background or cultural background could be used as a blaming point or slander time to say well students from a certain culture are not expected to achieve. But I don't see that as being a key point in defining what an ideal student is.

Here, Tricia was keen to avoid a cultural or racial deficit model of learning, with the argument that being an ideal student should not be dependent, reliant or reflective of our ethnic or cultural background. There were other similar views, but these were often coupled with an acknowledgement that ethnicity and culture are likely to play a key role in the constructions of our educational values, priorities, practices and ideals. As Net (FG21, Student) said, 'I don't believe that race is an inherent factor ... but like all things held equal, two students of different races or ethnicities may have a different idea of what the ideal student is'.

Our student cohort may be diverse but there are more similarities than differences in their views about how different ideal student characteristics might map differently onto students from particular ethnic or cultural backgrounds. Azzie (FG1, Student) drew on national statistics and argued that, as regular high-achievers in school examinations (e.g. for GCSE and A-level qualifications in England and Wales), British Chinese and Indian students might be seen as the ideal student 'because of their cultures and that they're expected to do well and be motivated'. Similarly, Xin (FG13, Student) spoke of the popular

Western stereotype of 'how the Asian kid is always good at maths' and believed that 'minorities will [often] try harder' due to heightened expectations and pressures from family, peers and even teachers. Existing studies appear to support this view (Archer and Francis 2007; Bhopal 2018; Wong 2015).

We also heard from Shelia (FG29, Student) that in the small island of Mauritius, the educational success of students is often publicly ranked and broadcast on national television, which can 'impact on your work ethic, what you see as ideal and your expectations [because] it's very competitive'. We note that similar forms of *celebration* are common in many Asian societies, although more typically in localised news and accolades. As Reham (FG13, Student) can attest herself, 'I think ethnicity does play a part in terms of how driven I am' as she accredited her Eastern background that has instilled in her the importance of work ethic and high achievement, since 'attainment is a massive deal in our community', including the protection and promotion of family *face* or honour (see Archer and Francis 2007; Wong 2016).

Whilst our previous research found attainment to be insignificant in an ideal student, as far as social science lecturers are concerned (Wong and Chiu 2020), the symbolic and extrinsic value of academic outcome appears to command 'a greater weight' (Elon, FG23, Student) for students (and most likely their families) from Eastern cultures. According to James (FG29, Student), 'I think the ideal student for a typical Asian would be good grades. But maybe if you talk about someone who is American or British, their focus is more on doing what you enjoy doing, or personal fulfilment, then their ideal student would be slightly different'. Although the attributes for grades and enjoyment are both captured in our ideal student survey (items 25 and 26, see Chapter 4), further research is merited to explore how different ideal student characteristics are rated and perceived across different nations and cultures (see Chapter 9, 'Future research'). As Meggie (FG30, Student) predicts, 'I feel like for some Eastern cultures the ideal student wouldn't have the social aspects, they'd just be someone who works really hard and gets the top mark'.

As far as perceptions go, Sophie (FG2, Student) speculated that 'in the West, participation is seen as a really important thing to be engaged in, whereas in Asian countries, it's more about taking in the information, stuff like that'. Similarly, Callum (FG15, Staff) said he found 'Asian students are a bit more insular and a little less likely to engage' than Western students, which might reflect cultural differences in learning. In Western countries such as the UK and US, HangMoon (FG26, Student) believed that creativity 'forms a huge part of an ideal student', whereas education in the East is often rooted in rote learning, with limited scope to challenge established knowledge or ideologies (items 37, 46 and 48, see Chapter 4).

In sum, the narratives here appear to be that students from the East, or with an Eastern ethnic heritage, are more likely to be constructed as hardworking, disciplined and outcome-oriented, whilst students with a Western ethnic background are more likely to be seen as creative, sociable and interest-driven individuals. Of course, these are broad and simplistic generalisations, and certainly not shared by all staff and students. Saying that, it seems to be a popular view, even though these perceptions do not really suggest that students from any particular ethnic or cultural background are more, or less, likely to embody the identity of an ideal student. There is a recognition that desirable characteristics of the ideal student 'really depends on what kind of group and what kind of cultural values, different backgrounds of people you ask' (Cindy, FG13, Student). Indeed, we acknowledge that our research is conducted in the UK, with predominantly UK-domiciled staff and students (for both the survey and focus groups), even though ethnically our student population was relatively diverse (see Appendix 1).

Perceptions of social class

A triangulation of existing research and educational theories (see Chapter 2) would probably lead us to assert that those from more privileged socioeconomic backgrounds are the most likely to identify or be identified as the ideal student. Privileged students typically experience fewer issues or challenges, especially when compared to the struggles of non-traditional or underprivileged university students (e.g. issues of finance, identities and 'fitting in', and familiarity with the higher education system more generally). Whilst the concept of class continues to be debated, our focus here is on perceptions of social class in shaping our identification of the ideal student. In other words, do staff and students think those from more privileged backgrounds are more likely to embody the characteristics of an ideal student?

Like gender and ethnicity, there were a few who felt that students' educational aptitude, their will to learn and work ethic are independent of their social class, as students from privileged and underprivileged backgrounds can both embody these traits. For instance, Sally (FG2, Student) believes that the development of ideal student characteristics is not correlated with social class because our life experiences are complex and therefore relatively individualised. She emphasised the responsibility of the individual and said that to be an ideal student, 'it depends on who you are as a person. If you want to learn, you will learn. If you don't want to learn, cool, sit there. You don't want to learn'.

Most staff and students, however, seem to acknowledge that social class, including our family and social upbringing, is an important factor that shapes the opportunities (or lack thereof) for students to develop their educational dispositions and ideal student characteristics. According to Eric (FG11, Staff), 'if you're brought up in a privileged family where your parents model this and expect you to work hard and achieve, you probably have that seed growing from a very young age'. Although there are aspirations that 'anybody from any class could achieve' (Antoinette, FG28, Student), including the ideal student identity, many recognise the advantage that middle-class students are likely to have over their working-class counterparts in the development and acquisition of ideal student characteristics.

Students from more privileged backgrounds often have highly educated parents or family members who can 'help you ... and advise you better, even for career stuff' (Nivaan, FG23, Student). Marc (FG5, Student) said he perceives 'the middle-class kid is the ideal student because they've got a lot of under-standing, they engage with work ... they'll do extra reading ... they do work on their own', while Grace (FG5, Student) explained that the 'middle class tend to get extra tuition' and make better use of their support system or network (see Reay et al. 2011). Fala (FG24, Student) gave an example of doing course assign-ments and how she, from a more privileged background, felt more prepared than some of her peers:

> So I come out being able to do presentations just fine and I don't get stressed over it. And I know some people who have no experience doing presentations or even writing lab reports, scientific papers like that kind of stuff just really depends on what kind of education you get and that's determined by social class.

Such similar views are shared by many other students and staff, who acknowl-edge that social class and family background play a significant role in our edu-cational experiences, especially the knowledge and resources that are at our disposal. As such, the consensus appears to be that it is probably easier for privileged and middle-class students to develop characteristics of the ideal stu-dent, even though for some, 'it really depends on the person as well' (Rufus, FG25, Student).

On the other hand, students from underprivileged backgrounds are believed to 'have a lot of disadvantages already ... [such as] finance, job and time man-agement' and therefore 'it's harder for them' to be academically successful or socially integrated into university life (Dior, FG23, Student). Experienced first-hand, Jofra (FG19, Staff) said he has met working-class students 'who've had a chip on their shoulder' [*holding a grudge*] and are 'very aware' and conscious of 'their [socioeconomic] background as something that might be holding them back', which results in an unlevel playing field. Jofra said that 'some students will overcome that, but some will always have this, just sheer rage, about what it's taken for them to get there. So, I think that can sometimes stand in the way' of their potential. Reflecting on her own experience as a working-class student at a prestigious university, Shelia (FG29, Student) said:

> All my flatmates, they're so worldly. They've travelled everywhere. They're from international schools or private schools, and I'm the only one that's been from a really crappy school. So, they're on a different wavelength. They all have that work ethic and since they've been pushed to do different things, different events, they're very proactive with their work. And the other day, they were so surprised to find out that my school didn't have any clubs or anything, or even sports teams. And they've all had that privilege, in a sense. And when I look at it, I feel really bad for where I come from because you can see they've been pushed and they've been given the support they need. Whereas with us, it was literally fend for yourself.

The excerpt above is telling and clearly demonstrates how inequality of opportunities can impede the development of educational dispositions that are generally valued, rewarded and even considered as ideal student characteristics (e.g. extracurricular activities and work experiences, see items 45 and 49 in Chapter 4). In the same conversation, Jamal (FG29, Student) believed that the experiences of students like Shelia can also be interpreted in a positive way, 'the fact that you made it here [at a prestigious university] without much pushing, it means that your motivation comes from yourself, and not because people are pushing you. So, you can actually be happy about it'. In other words, if students from underprivileged backgrounds can overcome the barriers to access university, then they are likely to have developed ideal traits such as motivation, as well as tenacity, grit and resilience (see items 1, 2 and even 43 in Chapter 4).

Similarly, Holly (FG1, student) asserted that 'I haven't necessarily come from the best class to start me off in life, but that could give more motivation' because of the desire to prove herself (see Wong 2018). Whilst it was difficult to determine the social class backgrounds of our participants (due to the nature of focus groups), there were some endorsing views about the *stronger* character of working-class students – as a result of the various disadvantages they faced. For example, Dior (FG23, Student) envisioned that 'people from a lower class, they're more motivated to work really hard at uni and make it in life ... they won't take it for granted as much'. As well as wanting to do better than their non-degree-educated parents, working-class students will probably want to achieve highly because 'they want to make sure that they can give everything to their family and buy a better future' (Jean, FG7, Student). From these perspectives, it is fair to say that there are also perceptions and constructions of working-class students as possibly extra driven and motivated to achieve academic success, with certain qualities that are in sync with the characteristics of the ideal student. Of course, these views are only realistically applicable to those who *survive* the various challenges and inequalities.

Despite differing views, there seems to be a general recognition that social class, and socioeconomic background, does matter in the context of being seen as an ideal student – but how these matter is not unanimous. A couple of our participants also spoke of the multiple identities of the ideal student, with suggestions that the ideal student is most likely 'White middle-class' (Kanye, FG5, Student) or 'Chinese female' (Teresa, FG15, Staff). We acknowledge the importance of intersectional identities and inequalities, especially by gender, social class and 'race'/ethnicity (Collins and Bilge 2016; Crenshaw 1991; Leathwood and Read 2009; Nichols and Stahl 2019), but as with the statistics in the first part of the chapter, our data were not rich enough to unpick how staff and students made sense of multiple and intersecting identities. Another topic for future research.

Perceptions of age

Our final subsection focuses on age, by which we mean perceptions of student age and their likelihood of being seen as an ideal student. We were open as to how our participants interpreted age, although as mentioned earlier UK universities use the category 'mature student' for record purposes (i.e. age 21 or over on admittance). When asked to talk about the role of age in their perceptions of the ideal student, two other keywords were frequently mentioned: *maturity* and *experience*, which delve a little deeper into the difference between biological and mental age, where the latter often refers to intellectual ability and emotional intelligence.

Although we are again reminded of egalitarian viewpoints, with comments such as 'you can't judge a book by its cover [as] everybody handles things differently' (David, FG10, Staff), there appears to be a clear distinction in how participants discussed age when compared to the equality discourses that were more confidently articulated around gender, ethnicity and social class. Conversations about age almost always glided into discussions of student maturity and experience, which, for most, do seem to matter in their perceptions of the ideal student. Even for those, such as Ha-Yoon (FG31, Student), who initially said that 'age doesn't necessarily affect' her views of the ideal student, she acknowledged that she became a better student as she progressed into the final year of her degree study. Ha-Yoon concluded, 'it's more like maturity, kind of. Because you mature you get more experience as well'. Fala (FG24, Student) summarised that 'age is not the cause of experience but it correlates'.

In our statistical analysis for age, we included students' level of study as a proxy to understand potential differences between first-year students and non-first-year students. While we did not intentionally ask, there were a few conversations that deliberated how perceptions of the ideal student may differ according to their level of study. For instance, Shirley (FG20, Student) said that 'I feel like third-year students would be much better or closer to that ideal than first years in a way because they have more experience, they learn to reflect and learn from their mistakes'. Similarly, Ilan (FG26, student) noted a clear difference in learning attitudes between postgraduate and undergraduate students and gave an example of a lecture which was attended by both. He said, 'you can definitely see the master's students are sitting in the front taking notes and undergraduates are sitting in the back and looking at the ceiling. So, I feel like maturity levels are important, for sure'. Although our focus is on the undergraduate ideal student, we think the postgraduate context will be fascinating to look into (especially across disciplines, institutions and degree types such as MA/MSc, MBA, PGDip/PGCert and PhD). Further research is merited.

Within the undergraduate context, the importance of maturity is widely acknowledged, and maturity is generally seen as a reflection of age, where older students are considered and constructed as wiser, more experienced and know what they want. Some even reflected on their own experiences, such as Sian (FG19, Staff), who said:

> When I was younger, I didn't really see the purpose of certain avenues that my teachers might have preferred. But as I get older, I sort of understand the benefit of certain things. And I also find myself more motivated to learn than what I was before. I think that's sort of associated with the maturity that comes with age.

Most students seem to agree that 'age brings experience' (Dennis, FG3, Student) and therefore envision older students as more likely to have developed characteristics of the ideal student. Jay (FG28, Student) felt older students are more mature and closer to being an ideal student because they should have 'enough maturity to reflect' and work on themselves 'to be more like ideal', such as a better work–life balance, time-management and organisation skills (see items 24 and 18 in Chapter 4). Older and mature students are also considered to be more motivated, disciplined and respectful because their enrolment in undergraduate study constitutes a conscious decision to study again, unlike the typical pathways of younger students who continue from compulsory education. Here, younger students may be 'slightly immature and not necessarily thinking too much about their duties or roles as a student' (Roman, FG21, Student). And note, Roman is a younger student.

Amongst staff, some admitted from their own experiences that mature students are more likely to embody the qualities of an ideal student, because they have had more time for 'personal development' (Kathy, FG17, Staff) and are therefore generally 'more engaged' (Callum, F15, Staff) and would 'meet more of these ideals' (Maria, FG18, Staff). However, Teresa (FG15, Staff) reminds us 'that doesn't mean that a young student can't have that' even though 'you're more likely to find it in older students'.

Although older and more mature students are generally perceived as the more likely of students to personify ideal characteristics, there are some arguments which position younger students as the prime candidates. Lottie (FG9, Staff) speculated that with fewer responsibilities and life burdens, younger students who live on campus can be energetic and enthusiastic, fully engaged with university life and affairs. Such students would be a form of ideal student. Another member of staff, Anto (FG16, Staff), believed that the ideal characteristic of creativity (item 37) is probably more common amongst younger students because 'the longer you're in [a discipline/field] you're starting to head down a [particular] direction' or way of thinking. Here, younger students are deemed to be better at thinking outside the box because their knowledge and ideas are supposedly still being formed.

In a similar vein, Guy (FG3, Student) argued that mature or older students may be more reluctant and resistant to change, because 'once you hit a certain age, the beliefs that you've already learned are so instilled within you that it could be quite difficult coming to a new course'. Whilst Guy referred to the motto, 'you never stop learning', his views also aligned with the idiom, *you can't teach an old dog new tricks*. Fellow student Dennis (FG3, Student) believed that mature students are socially disadvantaged due to their older age, having more difficultly than younger students to fit in with university life, especially participating in extracurricular activities, often due to family or work commitments. Dennis felt they are 'very much going to be lone wolves'. As a mature student with children, Natasha (FG6, Student) concurred and spoke of competing priorities, typically between university study and family responsibility, which, for mothers like her, the latter must take precedence ('at the end of the day, if your child is unwell, you won't be able to attend class'). The experiences of mature students, especially those with caring responsibilities, may have limited opportunities to freely develop desirable student qualities, suggesting that certain ideal student characteristics may indeed be harder for some mature students to attain.

While our participants did not explicitly discuss whether our ideals and expectations of students should be different for students of different ages, indications from earlier discussions (e.g. under gender, ethnicity and social class) suggest that perceptions of the ideal student should not be different or dependent on demographic background, including age. In sum, older students are generally thought to be more experienced and mature, and perhaps closer to the identity of an ideal student, even though younger students are also considered by some as more creative and open to learn.

Summary

The first part of this chapter focused on the ideal student survey and explored how social identities, namely gender, ethnicity, social class and age, shape the ways we construct the ideal student. Students who are female, from an ethnic minority, with degree-educated parents, in their first year and aged 20 or younger tend to give higher ratings than their counterparts (i.e. male, White, without degree-educated parents, non-first year and aged 21 or over), which gave us an insight into the relative importance of each ideal student dimension within these groups.

The second part of the chapter explored perceptions of the ideal student and whether students from particular gender, ethnic, social class and age backgrounds are more, or less, likely to be seen as an ideal student. A range of perspectives were articulated, including egalitarian standpoints, although most viewpoints appear to lean towards the identity of the ideal student as female, possibly Asian, from a privileged background or perhaps a mature student. Admittedly, these are not intersectional analyses as, for example, few mature undergraduate students are likely to come from privileged backgrounds. This limitation should form the inspiration for future research (see Chapter 9).

8 | Is the ideal student me?

In the previous chapter, we discussed the ways in which identities and inequalities of gender, ethnicity, social class and age can influence perceptions of the ideal student. In Chapter 8, our focus is on being identified as an ideal student, either by the self or by others, as we examine the difficulties, dilemmas and pressures for students to claim or associate with this identity (or not). In other words, *is the ideal student me?* We begin with a comparison of the ideal student with a similar but different, yet seemingly more intelligible identity of the *good student* as we aim to further our understanding of student identities in higher education. Here, we compare how students identify with the good student and the ideal student, with the former seemingly more popular and the latter somewhat undesirable. From recognition by self to the influences of others, we also consider the role of external factors that appear to shape how students identify with the ideal student. In short, this chapter aims to shed light on student identities and identifications as students negotiate the concept and identity of the ideal student.

Describing students as good and ideal

In Chapter 1, we explained why the word *ideal* is the most appropriate keyword to conceptualise our attempts to explore and unveil different desirable student characteristics. In practice, we appreciate that descriptions of what is ideally expected of students can be fluid, with the use of different vocabularies and terminologies to describe students. Whilst it would be useful to differentiate the nuances of every related term and keyword, that would be impractical and so our focus is on the prominent identities and descriptions of being a good student and being an ideal student.

In the dictionary, *good* is defined as 'having the required qualities; of a high standard' (Lexico.com). In other words, being good infers something positive, acceptable and even praiseworthy. Compared to ideal, the use of the word good is arguably broader and used more frequently in everyday discourse and informal conversations. In educational research, the term *good student* is also referenced more commonly than the term *ideal student*, especially in non-UK-based literature (Karakitsiou et al. 2012; Llamas 2006; Vinther and Slethaug 2014) and schools-based studies (Thompson 2010; Worthman and Troiano 2019). In fact, the study by Thunborg et al. (2012) we cited in Chapters 1 and 6 actually used the term good student, rather than ideal student, even though it elicited desirable and ideal expectations of students. It is therefore important for us to first consider the differences and nuances between what it means to be good and ideal. In this chapter, our focus is only on the views of students because we want to understand how students perceive, negotiate and identify with the ideal student identity.

For students, the difference between the good and the ideal student appears to be the latter being a better or more committed version of the former. As Guy (FG3, Student) remarked, a good student 'would be someone who does what is expected of them' but an ideal student 'would be someone who does what is expected and a bit more'. In other words, the ideal student seems to encompass the good student by 'incorporating the extra part of being a student' (Doris, FG20, Student), 'going the extra mile' (Shelia, FG29, Student) and 'taking on extra things' (Jane, FG12, Student). Here, being good entails mastering the basics and minimum expectations, such as attendance, preparation and class-room engagement. According to Stefan (FG12, Student), a good student is 'one that is dedicated, is engaged [and] turns up for the lessons' as he infers that a commitment to learning may be sufficient to indicate a good student. Similarly, other students have mentioned positive learning behaviour and work ethic as the essence of a good student.

Another key difference between a good and an ideal student appears to be the end result, where the former is 'more your attitude rather than the outcome' (Lorna, FG1, Student), whilst the latter is also evidenced through the achieve-ment of 'top grades ... all the time' (Ricardo, FG4, Student), in addition to good learning attitudes. In other words, students seem to describe the good student as someone who works hard regardless of the eventual grade, but an ideal stu-dent ought to be a persistent high achiever as well as a hard worker (see Wong 2016 on the discourse of 'being the best'). As highlighted in previous chapters (especially Chapter 5) and elsewhere, the importance of attainment is debat-able in an ideal student, especially when students and staff both appreciate that grades and outcomes do not always reflect the attitude and effort of the stu-dent. This mismatch could reflect the nature of the assessment, the difference between learning for knowledge and learning to achieve (a grade), as well as individual circumstances and challenges (see Mickelson 1990 and the 'attitude–attainment paradox'). Students in our study seem to appreciate that academic attitude or effort is just as important as – maybe even more important than – grades. That said, most students did appear to construct the ideal student to be a *higher* achiever than a good student. However, there are overlapping charac-teristics that can further blur the distinctiveness of these identities.

As Sienna (FG1, Student) reflects, 'when you think about it, I'm not sure there really is a massive difference. If someone's an ideal student, you'd proba-bly describe them as a good student, so the terms sort of end up being inter-changeable'. Her comment suggests that the differences between good and ideal students are far from obvious and unanimous. Most perceived ideal as 'a better version of good' (Jamal, FG29, Student) but the ambiguities around attainment also shed light on the value of effort over the outcome in an ideal student. Specifically, high achievers are unlikely to be ideal if their attitude, engagement or participation are considered to be inappropriate or poor. For some, the label of high achiever can even be synonymous with the identity of a good student, because the descriptor good (and very good) is frequently used in assessment metrics that permit high grades. We also appreciate that the labels and identities of good and ideal can have different meanings across cultures and social contexts, which can influence how students self-identify as being good or ideal (see also Chapter 7). For instance, the discourse of feeling 'never good enough' seems to be more prominent for students from particular gender and social class backgrounds (Lucey and Reay 2002; Power et al. 1998). Below, we discuss some of the concerns that students raised in being seen or labelled (including by themselves) as an ideal student, which infers that such an identity can also be unattractive (see also Chapter 2).

Ideal as undesirable

Few students, when asked, confidently identified themselves as an ideal student. Many were reluctant. Some saw being an ideal student as a fantasy because 'ideal is like perfection … and nobody's perfect' (Mia, FG4, Student), whilst others were self-critical of 'not doing enough' (Nasreen, FG20, Student) to merit this identity. Students seem cautious about the ideal student identity, especially in the context of their own associations.

Perhaps it is because most felt that the identity of ideal student should not be self-proclaimed, as 'no one wants to claim that [they are] perfect' (Finlay, FG1, Student) or sound 'big-headed [and] over-confident' (Owen, FG1, Student). In other words, self-identification as an ideal student can be undesirable as it infers egoism and arrogance. Here, students said that 'it's for others to judge if me is [an ideal] student or not, according to their parameters' (Olympia, FG33, Student), indicating that the ideal student identity is more creditable and appropriate if endorsed and attributed by others, such as by staff or even fellow students, rather than as 'something you can say about yourself' (Reham, FG13, Student). As elaborated later in the chapter, student identification with the ideal student appears to require legitimation, approval and recognition by others (see also Chapter 2).

Interestingly, our students seem hesitant or unsure about the prospect of being labelled as an ideal student, even when nominated or praised by others, especially their peers. The best example comes from our FG1 with students. In one exchange, Azzie identified Holly as an ideal student because she 'always did the pre-reading, made extra notes and … always put [her] hand up'. Holly, in response, distanced herself as an ideal student and explained that 'the ideal student has to be x, y, z, and if you're not all of these, then you're not the ideal student … [so] I wouldn't say I'm the ideal student'. She reasoned that 'I could always improve … do more reading … access more resources in my own time'. Here, Holly attempts to justify why she is *not* an ideal student, magnifying her apparent shortfalls and downplaying her aptitudes. Perhaps she was modest (see also item 30, Chapter 4) or felt embarrassed and uncomfortable being singled out by her peers, even if the context was seemingly positive. While her disidentification may also be partly due to the never-ending effort that she believed is required to become ideal, it seems clear that being called an ideal student has caused enough unease to prompt Holly to actively explain her inadequacy to embody this identity.

Another example is Henry (FG6, Student), who also rejected the compliments of his peers. Henry explains that the apparent perceptions that others have of him as an ideal student do not correspond with how he thinks about himself. He said that 'other people may not notice ... but deep inside me, I know that something is quite wrong ... I managed to fix it, but it wasn't to my satisfaction'. Here, Henry referred to his personal circumstances and highlighted his internal dissatisfaction and shortfalls according to his own standards and ideals, which meant he was unable to see himself as an ideal student. The example of Henry reminds us of the delicate balance between being recognised by self as well as by others as the ideal student (Gee 2000). Students who are recognised by others to be an ideal student can also reject and refuse such recognition themselves, which means such an identity might not be sustainable. Whilst Henry was clear that 'how I look at myself matters most to me' in his defence against being labelled as an ideal student, his peer Elaine (FG6, Student) pointed out that:

> It's the way people look at you that matters, not really how you look at yourself ... that is why you must be very careful in whatever you are doing. You might look at yourself to be very good [or bad], but to others what you are doing is bad [or good].

Although students appreciate the importance of self-recognition in identifying as the ideal student, given our perceptions of ideal can be 'very individual' (Jean, FG7, Student), there is also a wider recognition that the formation of student identities, including being an ideal student, is also influenced by the views, opinions and expectations of others. These external factors are explored later.

In summary, most students can partially identify as an ideal student, but only a handful claimed full identification, even if jokingly. Consistent with Weber's theory of *ideal types* (see Chapter 2), characteristics of the ideal student are not meant to be all embodied by any individual, but rather be found across a spectrum of students. More interestingly, the identity of ideal student can even burden students with expectations that may be too demanding or unrealistic to sustain, which brings us to question the extent to which being ideal is actually an intelligible, achievable and desirable identity for students. The anticipated pressures of being an ideal student have led some to assert that the ideal student identity is not even worth while. For example, Guy (FG3, Student) said that 'I don't want to stretch myself so thinly to be the ideal student' if that meant adjusting or giving up his other interests. In other words, being ideal can be an undesirable identity for some students, especially those who are concerned of the negative impact such an identity can have on their state of wellbeing or existing practices, as well as the stigma that may be attached to it.

With this in mind, the lack of students who identified with the ideal student identity is not unexpected, although we are slightly surprised and somewhat alarmed at how some students have perceived being ideal as undesirable (which, as discussed in Chapter 3, contradicts the purpose of the concept if being ideal is ironically seen as *not* ideal). Below, we move on to the identity of the good student, which appears to be more intelligible and feasible.

Good as popular and achievable

Being good appears more popular or even normal when compared to being ideal, which is typically seen as rare or an outlier. Whilst the ideal student can appear exclusive, the identity of the good student seems to be more inclusive 'because it is more of a broader term and ... less demanding' (Nasreen, FG20, Student). Being good is seen to be a positive identity that aligns with normative expectations. In general, our students appear more receptive to the good student identity as most were content to identify themselves as 'doing good ... not the best and not the worst' (Doris, FG20, Student). The identity of good seems to be more desirable, achievable and less contentious compared to the ideal student. For some, especially those in post-92 universities, being a good student is about balance (see item 24, Chapter 4):

> An ideal student has being a student as their first priority, whereas a good student may try to balance a working life, a social life, as well as their academic life and may not always put their course first. (Dennis, FG3, Student)

Here, the good student is constructed in a balanced way where students can develop their social as well as academic life. The identity of good appears to enable students to 'have a social life, go out with friends, do whatever they want' (Sally, FG2, Student). The concept of the good student also infers that one is doing something right, at an acceptable and respectable level, but not to the extremes of ideal that appear to entail extraordinary academic commitment. For other students, especially those from pre-92 universities, being a good student is also associated with academic performance and study attitude (see Chapter 6, 'Differences by university type'). Perhaps as a consequence of being in a competitive learning environment, some students felt getting a high grade is normal and even expected.

All in all, students appear more comfortable with the good student identity because good implies growth, progress and effort over the outcome, which is not always an option for the ideal student who is supposedly already 'at the top' (Marc, FG5, Student) and has 'to stay at the top' (Holly, FG1, Student). Instead, our students appreciate that for a good student, there is still 'room for improvement and ... room for error' (Dennis, FG3, Student). Thus, being a good student is seen to be 'a lot more realistic ... [because] you can fail and things like that' (Mai, FG4, Student).

As Joanna (FG6, Student) observed on the perceived differences between ideal and good students, 'ideal is a very theoretical term and good student is more practical ... because good student is more possible to achieve rather than the ideal'. In other words, the good student is recognised to be more reflective of reality, as well as an identity that is more intelligible and possible because it signifies respectable but not exceptional (and somewhat unrealistic) accomplishments. Thus, being good is considered to be normal, so much so that it is 'achievable for everyone if they like work hard enough ... just like be on top of things and get the most out of the degree' (Doris, FG20, Student). By comparison, Doris feared that 'ideal is more of this abstract notion of someone ... that's realistically not completely obtainable'.

In short, most students would be happy with a good student identity because it entails a respectable (but not ideal) embodiment of student characteristics that can be improved. For most, the identity of the good student is attractive, achievable and not overwhelming, although making progress, for instance, is also a central feature of the ideal student (see Chapter 3).

Identifying as the ideal student: Different spheres of influence

As hinted earlier, students' identification with the ideal student can also be influenced by external factors and personnel, such as staff or peers. In this part of the chapter, our emphasis is on the different spheres of influence that can shape students' identifications with the ideal student. While we emphasise that these influences are by no means exhaustive or prescriptive, such insights will provide us with a more holistic lens to understand how students construct what it means to be a university student, including an ideal student. Although some of these influences are also covered in earlier chapters, our intention here is to bring together these different influences to appreciate how students negotiate and identify with the ideal student. For transparency, most data in this section were written as part of a separate paper (Chiu et al. forthcoming).

Students' prior cultural and educational experiences

For some students, particularly those with experience of different cultures or educational systems, their conceptions of the ideal student may also reflect wider societal norms (which is elaborated later). Aaron (FG21, Student), for instance, described his learning experiences in Singapore and Thailand where the culture of the former seems to 'focus more on grades' while the latter appears to place more emphasis on 'hard work'. As such, we appreciate that different educational systems could yield different priorities and emphases. According to Doris (FG20, Student):

> I feel like with Chinese or Singaporean people there's a lot more focus on academics and grades which I think is just a product of a school system

which values that a lot more, where as I feel like some European school systems ... people who have come from those value general university experience a bit more.

Here, students' perceptions of the ideal student are at least partially shaped by
their prior educational and societal expectations. Relatedly, some minority ethnic students, such as Maha (FG4, Student), also talked about the pressure from
their parents to be academically successful and work 'towards achieving certain goals' (see also Wong 2015). She believed that being an ideal student 'does
depend on how you are brought up, and the culture'. That said, students' construction of the ideal student is not fixed or static and can certainly be developed as they experience and encounter different education systems:

In Asian education you're used to just being spoon fed like you know how to
memorise information. That's what you've been used to for 12 years in your
life. But I think Western education is based on exploration, you're given more
opportunities to widen your horizon on any topic you like. (Alisha, FG24,
Student)

Alisha's reflections and comparison of Asian/Eastern and European/Western
education reveal the ongoing development and negotiation of what it means to
be a university student for those with transnational educational experiences
(Watkins 2000). As an Asian international student who only experienced UK
education when she started university, HangMoon (FG26, Student) said she
realised that getting good grades is not the only valuable or desirable outcome;
instead, being creative is also highly regarded, which she believes should 'form
a huge part of an ideal student'. Her experiences are not uncommon for international students, especially those from the East, who are likely to have been
socialised with a different philosophy of education, teaching and learning
(Chang et al. 2011), which might inform a different range of desirable student
characteristics. Indeed, international students often need to learn and negotiate
the cultures of their host country, some of which may even come as a shock or
surprise when compared to their own norms and values (Brown and Holloway
2008; Durkin 2008; Zhou et al. 2008).

Overall, there is a sense that what it means to be an ideal student can be
contingent on students' pre-university life experience, at least initially. However, most students are open to engage with different ideas of the ideal student,
especially from the influences of their degree, lecturers and wider institutional
or societal expectations.

Demands of the subject and curriculum

Students' perceptions of the ideal student can be shaped by the structure of
their degree discipline and curriculum (see also Chapter 6, 'Differences by discipline'). For instance, some students from the natural sciences consider the
ideal student to be highly independent and adept to self-study beyond what is

taught in lectures. These students suggest that their curriculum is structured in a way that allows them to 'have full flexibility to manage [their] time ... and not [to be] restricted to nine to five like any other courses' (Lindsay, FG25, Student). Here, students appreciate the freedom of study time, which seems to help and support their development of time management skills and to 'find the [work–life] balance' (Gola, FG25, Student) – a key characteristic in their discipline-specific ideal student.

Other students reported a different learning experience that also highlights the role of the subject curriculum. As one engineering student commented on his roommates who study physics:

> I live with three physicists, and they were talking ... last year they had like deadline after deadline ... I think it's like second week of spring or something like that where they were just worked to the bone to make sure they got all these things out. And the fact that they're expected to do that and it nearly drove them up the wall because there was so much of it. (Alex, FG27, Student)

Here, the physical, emotional and intellectual demands of their degree course seem to have limited the opportunities for students to explore or develop their other interests. The design of the curriculum can influence and impact on how students perceive and identify with the ideal student, especially in the context of their discipline. For example, natural science students are generally perceived to be more focused on their comprehension of key principles, whilst applied science students are typically expected to display more interest in the application of knowledge to solve problems. Kyle (FG26, Student), for instance, said that the ideal engineering student would be expected to apply their learning 'to solve real-life problems'.

For other students, the ideal student is viewed and constructed with considerations of the professional identity related to the discipline. Guy (FG3, Student) studied sports journalism and for him:

> The ideal student is for us to go and try to make contact and work with people and find out what it's actually like in the real world ... so that would be our bread and butter, where a sports student, theirs would be to train hard ... and put in good performances.

Here, we can appreciate that identifications with the ideal student may also include consideration of what professionals associated with their subject discipline are typically expected to embody. As a reminder, more detailed discussions on disciplinary differences can be found in Chapter 6.

Lecturer expectations

In recognition of the influence of others, students' identification and construction of the ideal student are also associated with what they think lecturers expect of them. According to Xin (FG13, Student), 'what is ideal shifts according to who we're being taught. You're like morphing into different images of an ideal student'. Whilst students believe there are characteristics of the ideal student that are likely to be universally shared, such as being passionate, motivated and engaged in their study, that does not mean there would not be particular expectations of students from specific staff. As Shelia experienced (FG29, Student):

> Two of our lecturers, one of them likes when you ask questions and speak and discuss the things, whereas the other one is always like, no talking. So, you could be ideal for one [lecturer] and be a crap student for the other one.

At the individual level, certain student characteristics may be more desirable amongst particular tutors, which means it can be difficult for students to identify as an ideal student in the same way for different lecturers, especially if lecturers have different or even contradictory expectations. Here, we can appreciate the importance of being recognised by others (i.e. lecturer) in students' identification with the ideal student (see also Chapter 5, 'What do students think staff expect of them?').

Institutional context

As elaborated in Chapter 6 ('Differences by university type'), the culture of universities can also shape students' perceptions of what it means to be an ideal student. For most pre-92 university students, an ideal student is someone who goes beyond studying but also engages with extracurricular activities. Strong academic performance can be the basic expectation or requirement in a competitive learning environment. In contrast, post-92 university students made fewer references to institutional expectations when discussing their ideal student. Here, students also mentioned the importance of balance, but between personal and academic life rather than between academic and social activities. Whilst an ideal student from a pre-92 university student may demand going the extra mile, for post-92 students, 'an ideal student would be happy enough just concentrating on the coursework and the actual course itself' (Guy, FG3, Student). In short, students' constructions of the ideal student can potentially be influenced by the context or culture of their institutions.

Societal and employer expectations

Lastly, the ideal student has also been discussed in relation to the terms the *ideal worker* or the *ideal employee*, in recognition of external influences and the importance to adhere or conform to established practices and values. According to Grace (FG5, Student):

> The idea of ideal student is connected to the idea of ideal worker. In the job market, you are requested to be ideal for the role, and it doesn't matter if you're different from me. You must be what they [employers] want you to be ... I feel that like, be the ideal student is like the training to become the ideal worker, in a sense.

Here, the ideal student is interpreted as preparation to be an ideal candidate for employment, which means, as Meggie (FG30, Student) summarises, 'the ideal student is also someone who's attractive to employers'. In other words, what students consider as an ideal student can also be premised on what they think society and employers expect of them. According to Shirley (FG20, Student), academic credentials are one of the quickest and easiest way to filter down job applicants, and is therefore a key marker of an ideal candidate:

> What we view as ideal [is] ... a result of society's expectations in a way. Because um, how society is structured is that it recognises grades, like for graduates, one thing that they really look at after you graduate, whether it's for study or for employment, is grades first.

Whilst the value of degree outcome for employers is debatable, especially alongside the importance of work experience or knowledge of technical/specific skills, Shirley's account has highlighted how students' perceptions of external expectations can also shape their views of the ideal student.

Self-identification as an ideal student: An ambivalent position?

Our short answer to the question, *is the ideal student me?* would be a 'no' for most students, which is understandable given many students initially associated being ideal with perfection when asked about their own identification as an ideal student. More importantly, our students spoke of the different challenges to associate and identify with the ideal student, which, in alignment with social identity theories (see Chapter 2), seems to require recognition and acknowledgment by the self and by others as intelligible. As discussed above, students' construction of the ideal student can also be shaped by what they think are valued by others, such as their peers, lecturers, institutions and employers. From the earlier examples of Holly and Henry, even when students are recognised by others as an ideal student (in this case, by peers), it is conceivable that most students do not identify themselves as an ideal student.

So, there are internal and external spheres of influence that can shape how students identify with the ideal student, which is more complicated if there is misalignment between the expectations of different influences/agents (e.g. a mismatch between personal perspective and the expectations of an external agent, such as the university). Here, students could be in an ambivalent position as they negotiate the challenge of striking a balance between their desire to adhere to their intrinsic motivation and intention, whilst acknowledging the external values and expectations. According to Guy (FG3, Student):

> I'm not an ideal student ... an ideal student would be totally 100% committed and would be nailed and focused on just the course ... Whereas, I've come

to university for primarily the course, but also the social life, the going out and having a few drinks and turning up to a couple lectures hungover and maybe not engaging as much as I should have in those. But that's the experience that I wanted … it might harm my grade in the end but I'm happy enough with a good solid grade, not top-top.

Here, Guy did not see himself as an ideal student because such an identity, he felt, would contradict his desire to embrace, experience and enjoy the student social life, even if such engagement might impact his grades. Similarly, others were also determined to focus on their own aspirations and expectations, rather than to be influenced by the expectations of others: 'it's more about my own expectations, what I want to get out from my degree, what I feel okay with … it's more doing myself justice' (Gola, FG25, Student). Whilst the significance of academic outcome was played down by some students, there are still external pressures that can engender tensions and ambivalences as students navigate what it means to be a university student, especially an ideal student.

We noticed that some students appear to prioritise the values and expectations of external agents (or recognitions by others). In highly competitive learning environments (especially in some pre-92 universities), students such as Shirley (see earlier) suggested that a kind of pragmatic learning identity may be manifested to reflect the ways in which the wider society is typically structured to value academic grades. She elaborated that such a pragmatic and strategic approach might not be the best way to develop deep and sustainable learning, and probably 'not something you should be aiming for', but conceded 'that's how you get a first [class degree]'. In other words, if top grades are generally recognised by society and employers as the marker of success and competence, then it is plausible for students to be strategic in their pursuit of top grades as the way to evidence their abilities.

Here, the emphasis on how individuals or students should respond and react to what society appears to value and reward would certainly resonate with the importance of being recognised by others in the development of a sustainable identity (Gee 2000; Wenger 1998), which thrives on external validation of our sense of self, such as being a high-achiever. In this scenario, the priority for students would be academic outcome, perhaps even at the expense of the holistic, balanced and all-rounded individual that students also seem to value, expect and desire in an ideal student (see Chapter 5, 'How do students describe the ideal student?'). In this case, it is possible that the desire to maintain an identity as someone who is academically capable can inadvertently inhibit students' development as an ideal student who is intrinsically engaged and committed to the learning process.

The importance of external recognition, even if it is students' own perceptions of what they think others expect of them, is clearly significant in understanding how students develop and maintain their identities in higher education. We wonder how students might be able to work towards their own perceptions of the ideal student, but without excessive external influence and expectations. How can staff and universities support students to think about what an ideal student means to them? If students are keen on a pragmatic identity, how can we better support students to embrace the holistic aims of higher education, such as the importance of transferable and higher-order skills development? We revisit these questions in Chapter 9 when we consider the implications of this study for pedagogy and practice.

While most students distanced themselves from their own constructions of an ideal student, the majority were happy to proclaim the identity of a good student. Based on this, perhaps our arguments should just advocate for the concept of the good student. However, we must remind ourselves that the purpose of the concept of the ideal student is to enable conversations and discussions about what is desirable of university students, as visions and imaginations that can be used to make sense of and make comparisons or reflections with reality (see Chapter 2). As well as self-recognition as an ideal student, we highlighted that fellow students, staff, the university and wider society can also shape what it means to be, and what is ideally expected of, students in higher education, be it implicit or explicit. We believe open discussions and negotiations of the different characteristics of the ideal student will improve transparency and reduce hidden expectations of students. Students are also to be empowered to decide on what, if any, ideal features are personally desirable to work towards and embody. We stress that it is not our intention or aim to suggest that the ideal student is *better* than the good student, or vice versa. In truth, the two forms of student identity are equally valuable and likely to serve different purposes in students' educational trajectories and aspirations. What we want to reiterate is the potential of the concept of the ideal student, especially the emphasis placed on being explicit and transparent about our desirable expectations (see Chapter 3).

Summary

Chapter 8 has investigated the difference between being a good student and an ideal student, with the focus on how students perceived and associated with these identities. Generally, being good is popular as it is seen to be more achievable than being ideal.

To appreciate the complexities around how students may identify as the ideal student, we also explored the external factors that can shape their constructions of and identifications with the ideal student. These spheres of influence include students' prior culture and educational experiences, the demands of the subject and curriculum, lecturer expectations, the institutional context and societal and employer expectations.

We debated the relationship between recognition by self and by others and highlighted the dilemmas and difficulties associated with being ideal. Our takeaway message is that the concept of the ideal student provides a concrete frame of reference where different expectations of students can be mapped out for discussion, negotiation and identification.

Conclusion and implications for practice

The ideal student research draws to a close in this chapter. We hope to have intrigued you at some point in the book and the ideas presented should be of particular interest to those working or studying in higher education. To recap, we aimed to unpack the desirable and ideal expectations that we have of students in higher education. By being more explicit and transparent about what we expect and desire from students, we can reduce inequalities that are often exacerbated by implicit rules or unspoken assumptions, which disadvantage certain students (see Chapters 1 and 2). With mutual understanding, the concept of the ideal student can help us to better manage our different expectations, especially between students, staff and the university. We believe the ideal student is a fresh and stimulating concept, with potential for further development and research. However, it is now time to reflect and evaluate on the implications of the work so far. For more reading, further details on the research methodology and data analysis can be found in the Appendices.

In this chapter, we consider the meanings and implications of our research for theory and practice. We begin with a brief but critical reflection on the ideal student study, revisiting the key concerns and possibilities of the concept. Next, we discuss the potential of the ideal student concept to support the development of graduate attributes. Our focus is then on the applications of the concept as we make practical suggestions for teaching and learning, curriculum design and pedagogical development. We include examples of how the concept of the ideal student can be applied in practice, with details and reflections on the use of the ideal student survey. We conclude with our views on further research and final thoughts.

A brief reflection on the research

The underlying aim of this book has been to present our conceptualisation of the ideal student. We used a variety of sources to inform our thinking as we discussed our ideas, aspirations and apprehensions about the concept. In this reflection, we revisit the issues that we think are important in the broader context of the ideal student study.

We are conscious that the concepts of ideal and ideal student can trigger preconceptions and presumptions. As introduced in Chapter 1, ideal is a common word and we should expect preconceived ideas about its meaning. As such, we cannot take for granted that our definitions and interpretations are readily recognised or understood. The term ideal student can be dismissed as non-existent, irrelevant or even pointless. It is therefore important for us to highlight the significance of transparency and explicitness in the construction of our respective ideal students, especially for social justice and equality (see Chapter 2).

Setting aside the concerns as discussed in Chapter 3 about the concept of ideal *per se* (e.g. around definition, metric and achievability), we still feel that the ideal student survey we used has merits but needs to be updated to cater for the context of future studies. As described in Chapter 4, we identified eight dimensions of the ideal student from the survey, which comprised 50 desirable student characteristics (see Appendix 2). These items were informed by existing literature as well as 795 keywords that were brainstormed from 33 focus groups (see Appendix 1). Like any survey of this nature, our analysis is inevitably limited by the number of items we had ($n = 50$), which means the ideal student survey would not capture or recognise student qualities that will be new or unique in a specific context. Indeed, our survey is not meant to be prescriptive or comprehensive. It is therefore important the range of ideal student characteristics is revised and adapted to reflect the research context, which can differ by country, culture, language, discipline or particular social groups. As one student Diana also recognised, 'I think the ideal student changes with time as the market changes ... there's a change of the way of the ideal student is built or educated'. In Appendix 1, we also include our reflections of the ideal student survey based on open-ended comments from our participants.

The question of *who is the ideal student?* does not have a simple answer. Depending on who is asked and by whom, the responses will be different. Our views of ideal can change with time, space/location and circumstance (e.g. our roles and responsibilities). What we hope to have achieved is to provide a sufficiently detailed narrative of the different ways in making sense of how ideal expectations of students are interpreted and conceptualised. In Chapters 5, 6 and 7, we looked at these different constructions and interpretations by staff and students, institution types, broad disciplines, as well as by social identity, including gender, ethnicity, class and age (including students' level of study). Although our evidence was gathered in the UK higher education context, we believe the findings and outcomes will be of interest and relevance to other countries and contexts and we invite further research into the breadth of ideal student characteristics (see 'Future research').

In Chapter 8, we focused on how students may or may not identify with the ideal student. A follow-up question that is particularly relevant for staff is *whether we should actively support students to develop ideal student characteristics, and if so, how?* There is not a straightforward answer. Perhaps, as with most social science inquiries, the most common answer is that *it depends*. This is a tempting response for us as well but to avoid sitting on the fence, so to speak, our overall view is that we should indeed strive to support students to develop ideal student attributes. Here is why.

First, rehearse a statement we have made countless times, implicit and hidden values and expectations can breed inequalities. When we are able to make explicit what student characteristics are desirable, students will be aware of the valuable attributes in their learning contexts and have more opportunities to work towards these, beyond the minimum requirements that are typically required for progression (e.g. minimum grade or attendance to pass). We do recognise and understand that not all students would want, or are able, to pursue these so-called ideal characteristics (especially if students themselves do not share or agree with the stated ideals, for example). Nevertheless, by being explicit about what is expected of students, including the support available to develop these attributes, students are at least able to make a more informed choice as to whether or not they want, or are able, to develop all or some ideal student characteristics, considering personal drive but also individual circumstances and challenges. As Madrona (FG20, Student) commented, the ideal student 'might be very different for everyone. It's just more about … being able to find your sort of best spot within all of that'. Moreover, students should not only elaborate on their thoughts about these desirable attributes but also carefully consider their own action plans, should they wish to develop these qualities. In doing so, students should develop achievable goals that can support their personal development and limit the influences of external pressures (see Chapter 8).

Second, many of the desirable student characteristics we presented are consistent with graduate attributes (see below) and thereby it is important that staff can support students to foster the development of these transferable skills and competencies. Here, we might also question *how can staff support students to develop these ideal characteristics* and *how explicit should staff be when speaking to students about these desirable expectations?* We acknowledge there may be concerns that an explicit approach might engender a sense of rigidity and limitation as to these desirable attributes (see Chapter 3), although we have highlighted that ideal expectations of students can vary by context and respondents' backgrounds (see Chapters 5, 6 and 7). We discuss the practical implications later in the chapter, sharing our reflections and ideas for practitioners.

Rethinking graduate attributes

As a concept, we believe the ideal student has the potential to support the development and conceptualisation of graduate attributes, which are essentially institutional ideals of university students. In Chapter 2, we reviewed how universities in Australia, New Zealand and the UK have deployed the banner of graduate attributes to advertise the qualities that are expected of their graduates. In Chapter 8, our students also interpreted the ideal student as preparation to be an ideal employee. Our argument is that graduate attributes are fundamentally the desirable characteristics that universities want for their students, which can mirror the properties of the ideal student (or more precisely, the *ideal graduate*).

However, unlike the multiple perspectives that we advocate in the constructions of the ideal student, the extent to which graduate attributes consider or represent the views of staff or students is unclear, at least in UK universities. There are indications that graduate attributes are largely envisioned by senior leaders, alongside their marketing or special subcommittees, which may or may not include frontline staff or students. More significantly, our earlier work also suggests that studies on graduate attributes appear to be mostly atheoretical, that is, without a theoretical foundation or basis. Here, we think that the concept of the ideal student has the potential to enrich future discussions on institutional ideals, especially since a key purpose of the ideal student concept is to appreciate and acknowledge the desirable expectations of students from different stakeholders, which can also include universities and their development of graduate attributes.

Our proposition is that the concept of ideal student has the potential to provide a theoretical foundation and platform for key stakeholders to discuss and negotiate their different expectations of students, before universities advertise their institutional ideal student through graduate attributes. In practice, we do not envisage a drastic change to existing practice. Our intention is to offer a different mindset, through the concept of the ideal student where desirable expectations of students are formed through multiple, meaningful and mutual conversations. The emphasis on ideal serves as an important conceptual goal and vision of the possibilities and aspirations for university students, which align with the aims of graduate attributes.

By understanding and appreciating the range of student characteristics that are considered to be ideal at a particular university, the development of graduate attributes is likely to better reflect the views of their staff and students. For example, the eight dimensions of the ideal student we identified could form the basis of discussions on the attributes that graduates should develop. Through deliberation and mutual understanding, such reimagination of graduate attributes is likely to be more accessible and relatable to students. Here, the most thorough approach is probably an internal audit of the ideal student characteristics that senior leaders, staff and students themselves want and expect from graduates. Although senior leaders may still have the final say on what is marketed as the graduate attributes of their university, we believe that curiosities around the concept of the ideal student will enable deeper and more meaningful conversations about what is ideally and realistically expected of university students and graduates.

Ideas for practice

An important part of our work is to ensure that our research has practical relevance and we have been fortunate to have been be able to try, share and collaborate with colleagues on how the concept of the ideal student might be applied in the context of teaching and learning. Ultimately, we want staff and students to have open and regular conversations about what it means to be a university student, especially what is ideally expected of students in their particular contexts, to minimise any mismatches in expectations. In this section we discuss and reflect on the pedagogical implications of our study, including examples of what we did to translate our research into practice. For higher education practitioners, we encourage them to think about the ideas, practices and reflections below, and how these might be adapted to their situated learning and teaching contexts.

Induction and welcome week

For new students, the induction period, especially the early encounters (e.g. welcome or fresher's week), has the potential to set the tone for their university experiences in the first term, if not more. As students are being introduced and generally receptive to learn about their new environment and the range of support services offered, there is an opportunity to ensure that preconceived ideas (if any) about what it means to be a university student are discussed, which can support students with their transition from school to university (Ambrose et al. 2010; Wong and Chiu 2019c).

To promote mutual understanding and recognition of what is expected of students, between students themselves but also by staff, we designed a 'managing expectations' induction activity using the student characteristics/items in the ideal student survey. The activity aims to initiate a discussion between students and staff on what is desirable of students in their degrees. The exercise begins by directing students to complete a simplified version of the ideal student survey (a list of 50 student characteristics alongside a Likert scale), which can be done online as well as on paper. The purpose of the survey is to provide students with a good range of characteristics and qualities that might be expected of university students. In other words, we want to build up their awareness of the breadth of possible student characteristics that might be desirable. As with our actual survey, students can also rate each characteristic from 'not important' to 'very important', which would help to formulate or consolidate their existing thoughts on what attributes are important in a student, as well as any other characteristics that may be outside of the survey. In other words, the survey acts as a stimulus that presents students with some ideas and language in relation to university learning, but the goal is to ignite discussion and open conversation.

The reason for having students complete the survey in the first instance is to promote inclusivity where students are able to share their views based on their existing perceptions of what it means to be a university student before any staff inputs. This sequence addresses the question we raised earlier about how explicit staff should be when introducing and discussing desirable expectations to students. Specifically, instead of *relaying* or *imposing* these expectations on students directly, we opt for an inductive and reflective approach where we encourage students to think, reflect and negotiate their ideas based on their prior knowledge and perceptions.

After students complete the survey, which should take 5–10 minutes, the next stage of the activity is a group discussion. In small groups, students are asked to share and discuss their thoughts on the most important or desirable features of a student in their discipline. To facilitate a whole-class discussion, students are also asked to submit their thoughts to an online poll that collects and displays the keywords in a live word cloud (e.g. *Mentimeter*). Where time allows, there was also an extra task where students are asked to share their thoughts on tutor expectations, with the question, *what do you think the tutors think the most important features are?* To make comparisons of viewpoints more interesting and meaningful, teaching staff in the department could also participate (even if in advance) by submitting their respective keywords to a different word cloud on what they think are desirable of students, and these different outcomes are then shared and discussed, especially if there are notable differences.

For the whole-class discussion towards the end of the activity, students are encouraged to elaborate on what they (as individuals or as a group) had agreed was important and why. Here, students – but also staff – can appreciate and understand different viewpoints but it is important that the facilitator (typically the course tutor) can share and explain what they themselves expect of students and why. What makes this activity effective is that the discussion and conversation are contextualised in a specific discipline. We recognise that the same terms or words might vary in meaning from one discipline to another and hence it is important to advise students to elaborate their thoughts and rationales in their learning context.

For wider adoption of the activity, we created a short guide, with hyperlinks to the ideal student survey items (see also Appendix 2), alongside suggestions for online and interactive engagement. The activity was planned for 30 minutes but is flexible enough in that some discussions could be longer or shorter. We are pleased that the activity was used or adapted by colleagues in the 2019 induction period, reaching over 300 students. In 2020, over 1,000 students took part in an online version of the activity, after it was trialled by a colleague in Australia. The step-by-step instructions we provided for tutors are replicated below, which can be adapted as appropriate:

Step 1 (5–10 minutes)

- *State the purpose of the exercise (i.e. promote mutual understanding of what is expected of students)*
- *Students to complete the ideal student survey and download (where appropriate) their answers in the session*

Step 2 (15 minutes)

- *Student discussion during the session: What are the most important features of a university student?*
- *Students post their individual top 3 important features on an online presentation app, such as Mentimeter (these can be from the survey items but also other views)*

Step 3 (5–10 minutes)

- *Whole-class discussion: Tutor to prompt student rationale and show students top 3 important features from tutor perspectives and link to the degree (e.g. how students will learn in the programme)*
- *Discuss any mismatches and emphasise the key attributes*

The activity does not have to be online or survey based as it can also be adapted as an offline group and class discussion. For instance, teaching staff can preselect a number of ideal student items from the survey (e.g. for example, their own top 10, or the whole 50 characteristics), but also adapt and/or include new attributes as appropriate. These student characteristics can be printed out (and even laminated) as individual slips of paper, where students can be arranged to work in groups and discuss with each other the relative or order of importance from their perspectives (e.g. as a *diamond 9* activity or simply ranked from most to least important). Alternatively, students can also share their thoughts on ideal student characteristics by writing on small pieces of adhesive paper, before physically posting or illustrating on large posters or walls for further discussions. Each group can then present their thoughts and rationales, and where appropriate, staff can reinforce, elaborate, mediate or question these viewpoints. Furthermore, these discussions can facilitate conversations about how the module or even programme learning outcomes and curriculum can support students to develop these key attributes. Depending on class size and the time allocated for discussions, the activity can last from 10 minutes to an hour, with 30 minutes our suggested length.

Beyond induction

Whilst the 'managing expectations' activity above is particularly effective in the induction phase for new students, we are aware that students undergo different challenges and experiences throughout their degree, especially in the first year. With that in mind, we are conscious that students' thoughts and ideas about what it means to be a university student, or what attributes are important, may have already shifted after the induction period. As such, to support their progression, we also worked with a colleague to rerun the activity in the second term/semester, to explore what, if any, differences there may be in terms of how students describe the most important features of a student. We think there is value to provide students with regular opportunities to reflect on their thoughts about university learning and what is expected of them as they progress throughout their course.

In this follow-up activity, which we trialled with first years in the Dyson School of Design Engineering (Imperial College London), we asked students to discuss the following at the start of their second term/semester:

- *So far, is undergraduate study what you expected?*
- *Using one word, how would you describe your experiences so far?*

- *What do you now think are the most important features of a student in design engineering?*

Figure 9.1 Word cloud of Dyson engineering students' learning experience

alright be open-minded exciting eye-opening full-on

good hectic interesting natural selection okay

organisation

overwhelming painfully fun rollercoaster understanding ambiguity

To briefly share the outcome of this exercise, we found that most students struggled to find a work–life balance, as they learnt and realised the importance of time management. Figure 9.1 includes the words that students used to describe their current learning experiences.

One of the benefits of a follow-up activity such as this is the ability to make comparisons with their earlier responses, which allows students to see, react and reflect on their changing views and ideas of what it means to be a university student. The word cloud, especially with the new words or phrases, can also provide tutors with a better understanding of the evolving mindsets and experiences of their students, which is important in the process of being transparent and reflective about what is desirable or expected of students. Having experienced their first term at university, we added new discussion activities that can promote a stronger sense of belonging and community of practice. For instance, students were asked to share in small groups their study strategies and the support they found useful so far. We found students to highly appreciate this opportunity and space to hear and learn from the experiences of others.

In short, we believe regular conversations (once a term/semester or year) between staff and students on their learning experiences would help to ensure that expectations of students are continuously managed and communicated. Where needed, staff can also reiterate the support available to assist students to develop the various desirable characteristics or graduate attributes. Information on student support are often introduced in the induction or early phases of the first year, whereas students may not fully recognise or appreciate their value or usefulness until they have had some time and experience with the different aspects of university life and study, including the submission of assignment. We believe frequent reminders and signposting to the support services will be very useful as students navigate their university life.

Fostering ideal student characteristics: Curriculum and assessment

If staff want to support students to develop specific skills or attributes, including those considered to be ideal and desirable, then one of the most effective routes is through their curriculum and assessment. Our suggestions are very much aligned with the various recommendations made by advocates of inclusive teaching, learning, pedagogy and curriculum (Hitch et al. 2015; Hockings 2010; Lawrie et al. 2017; UCL 2020).

Very often, if the support or provision of study skills is not considered as part of the curriculum, students may not engage because of perceptions of irrelevance or avoid seeking support because of fear as well as pride (Wong and Chiu 2019c). To pre-empt these potential issues, we encourage staff to incorporate the development of different skillsets into the design of their cur-riculums to formalise such learning (Chiu and Rodriguez-Falcon 2018). Ideally, the teaching team and the whole department would work closely with other providers of student support across the university to embed their skills work-shops and teaching into the curriculum. For instance, to enhance student writ-ten communication skills, teaching staff might collaborate with their academic language or writing skills team to deliver timetabled provision to be a part of the curriculum (Wingate et al. 2011). If we want students to develop interview skills in preparation for job applications, teaching staff can work with their career services to design tailored support (Bridgstock et al. 2019). This way, staff would proactively and explicitly encourage students to nurture desirable student characteristics.

Where appropriate, staff should look into their assessment practice to ensure the design does not just focus on content mastery but also the develop-ment of transferable skills or attributes. After all, it is generally desirable that students and graduates can apply what they have learnt in different contexts, beyond just knowledge of the subject. Given that assessment can drive student learning behaviours, especially in competitive learning environments, we urge staff to consider reducing the use of assessments that primarily require stu-dents to memorise content (MacLellan 2001). Instead, assessments should be designed in ways that students can also demonstrate, for example, their critical thinking and other forms of *Academic skills* (see Chapter 4).

To strengthen the value of assessments, beyond pass, fail and a score, we suggest a wider use of authentic assessments as a way to encourage students to apply their acquired knowledge and skills to real-life problems or situations (Swaffield 2011), which can lead to the broader development of ideal student characteristics. Examples may include the use of simulations, role play, research report writing, presentations and journal entries. These assessments tend to require students to perform, apply, evaluate and actively produce some-thing which taps into higher-order thinking and problem-solving skills (Ashford-Rowe et al. 2014; Gulikers et al. 2004). We believe in reality these are likely to be covered or mentioned as broad learning outcomes in most degree programmes, or even specific modules, but the challenge is the interlinked practice of assessment, of how to assess, measure or judge students to have developed or mastered these skills. For instance, we can ask questions such as *what should students be able to do as a result of the module/programme?* and *what indicates students have met these standards (e.g. skills, knowledge)?* Authen-tic assessment tends to be qualitative in nature and so it is useful to develop a marking rubric for consistency between markers. Clear assessment criteria and marking schemes can help markers to evaluate beyond impressionistic judgements and make it transparent to students what is expected from their submissions (Dawson 2017; Villarroel et al. 2018).

We acknowledge that some of the practices or ideas above may already be common practice across institutions. For instance, assignment marking rubrics and grade guidelines are typically available and stated in course or module handbooks, indicating the requirements and expectations of assignments that would merit a first-class/top grade, as well as the minimum that is required to pass. What perhaps could be enhanced is the programme-level skills or attributes development audit. Specifically, staff can prioritise the development of ideal student characteristics that are considered to be most important for graduates in their field. Here, staff may consult with their alumni to identify what knowledge, skills and attitudes their recent graduates found most useful and relevant in their current line of work and feed back to the programme-level learning outcomes (Nghia et al. 2020).

Staff play a central role in supporting students' cultivation of ideal student characteristics, through the ways in which university norms and cultures are communicated and indoctrinated (Roberts 2018). All university staff, from academic to professional to support roles, can shape the values and ethos of an institution, which can encompass desirable student characteristics. For example, if we want to encourage students to be more *Reflective and Innovative*, one of the higher rated dimensions in the ideal student survey (see Chapter 5), then all university staff ought to develop practice that supports students to embody the idea of learning from experience and reflection in all aspects of their university experience. For instance, staff can encourage students to reflect on their learning by providing prompt questions that can scaffold their thinking processes.

We also recognise that the ways in which staff communicate and respond to students, especially their questions and assignments, can influence their learning approaches and behaviours. For instance, when providing feedback to students, staff can make use of process-oriented language and commentaries in their interactions with students such as *not yet, this is a good attempt, how could you improve the work?* and *what would you do differently next time?*. The focus on the process and the feedback can also feed forward to subsequent or future tasks (Hill and West 2020; Hughes et al. 2015; Wimshurst and Manning 2013). These practices can contribute to the improvement of students' self-efficacy, motivation and engagement in learning, and therefore also strengthen students' identification with the ideal student as someone who is, in this case, reflective and improving (Wong and Chiu 2020).

Another approach to support the development of self-reflection is to incorporate it into a summative assessment. The purpose is to move away from the emphasis on the reward that is often placed on the final product or submission, typically a final grade, which inadvertently relays the message that only the outcome is valued. By highlighting and rewarding critical reflection and evaluation in learning, students are given the opportunity to internalise the value of the process for personal growth and learning from mistakes. However, we are not suggesting that we should reward or mark every self-reflection process because in practice, the final outcome is often what matters most. Yet, at the initial stage of students' learning journey, it is worth while to consider a formal reward and recognition of their learning process as a kind of incentive to support students to appreciate and develop a greater range of ideal student attributes. Such practice is particularly well placed for the first year of study, given the weighting is often lower than in subsequent years.

In sum, there may be hidden or micro messages that are unintentionally communicated (or miscommunicated) through the ways in which students interact with their curriculum and assessments, and potentially create a mismatch between the expectations of staff and students (Egan 2011). Staff should therefore ensure that intended learning outcomes, teaching content, pedagogy and assessment and feedback practice, where relevant, are aligned to each other and can foster the development of particular skills or attributes that are valued in their respective disciplinary and institutional context, including those considered to be ideal and desirable. Most importantly, the expectations of students need to be made explicit and transparent, where possible, to minimise the potential mismatches.

Future research

We hope to have planted the seeds for the concept of the ideal student to grow and flourish. Briefly, we want to share our thoughts on how this project could be taken forward. Given our project was very much a test of concept study, there is scope to scale up and improve the breadth and depth of the data collected, particularly in the ideal student survey. As mentioned in Chapter 7, our aspirations for intersectional analysis were limited by the sample size, which could easily be addressed in the next iteration of the research. In addition to higher numbers, the range of participants could also be widened to include more students in postgraduate and doctoral study, as well as students from more diverse social backgrounds. For instance, the ideal student survey could be updated to enable more detailed analysis of how new social identities, such as the status of carer/parent, commuter or disabled student, might also shape students' perceptions of the ideal student.

We highlighted, especially in Chapter 6, how the ideal student can vary across contexts. We mapped these variations by discipline and institution type. A logical next step, particularly for the ideal student survey, is to consider going global and explore similarities and differences by countries (including, of course, intersectional variations by social identities). We think an international perspective on the ideal student can provide interesting new knowledge concerning the transnational and multicultural practices across the global higher education contexts and ensure that differences in cultural norms and practices are considered and reflected, which are key for interdisciplinary and intercultural awareness.

We have actually translated the ideal student survey into Chinese (simplified and traditional versions), in preparation for what would have been a series of workshops for educational developers in China (hosted by the National Academy of Education Administration in Beijing). While the workshops were postponed because of the coronavirus pandemic (Covid-19), the intention was for our international colleagues to learn about the research, try the survey and adopt the 'managing expectations' activity with their students. This can hopefully still happen in the near future when we return to some semblance of normality.

Concluding thoughts

We hope to have done the concept of the ideal student justice, having looked at it from different angles with new data and analysis. Throughout the book, we have set out our visions, perspectives, interpretations and arguments. Writing each chapter has helped us to consolidate our thinking process and provided us with an opportunity to share our ideas and aspirations. As Stefan, one of the students, commented, 'I think the idea of an ideal student is always evolving … this is what we know of an ideal student so far and this can grow'.

In early 2020, just after the conclusion of our research, the UK's and much of the world's higher education experienced the unprecedented challenge of rapid and mass migration to online teaching and learning. Covid-19 has changed the way we work and learn. The longer-term impact on higher education, especially on teaching and learning, remains unclear. But we wondered whether our experiences of lockdown (in the UK at least) and the shift to homeworking might have altered perceptions of ideal student characteristics. More especially, we wonder if good digital skills (part of *Academic skills*, item 16 in the ideal student survey) might be particularly desirable in light of the pandemic.

We hope the concept will develop and mature in a way that continues to promote transparency and explicitness, and encourages open and meaningful conversation amongst different stakeholders in higher education to overcome assumptions and their associated inequalities.

Appendix 1: Research methodology

Further details of our research methodology are provided here, namely the qualitative and quantitative data collection and analysis process, especially the development of the ideal university student survey. As a reminder, our aim was to explore the breadth and nuances of the ideal student, including the concept *per se*. The study was designed to project the perspectives and interpretations of university staff and students as we mapped the different characteristics of the ideal student in higher education.

Using focus groups to explore ideas of ideals

Our data collection began with focus groups because we wanted to promote discussions and interactions between participants to highlight, debate and reflect on similar and different expectations and ideals of university students (Krueger and Casey 2014). For the qualitative data in this book we conducted a total of 33 focus groups with 132 university staff and students. Our focus was on their interpretations of the concept of the ideal student, including the potential problems and possibilities as we refine our understanding of the ideal student. As explained later, the focus groups also provided the foundations for the development of the ideal university student survey. Data were collected between 2017 and 2019. We conduced 23 focus groups with 105 students and 10 focus groups with 27 staff, from the four broad disciplines of the applied sciences, arts & humanities, natural sciences and social sciences.

As seen in Table A1.1, we conducted at least five focus groups for each of the four broad disciplines. Due to availability, the focus group size for staff is smaller than that of students, but we note that our staff participants were mostly expressive, which meant smaller groups actually enabled discussion at greater depth. Participants came from five universities across three English regions (London, South East, and Yorkshire and the Humber), including pre-92 and post-92 institutions.

Potential participants were identified through convenient and snowball sampling, by email invitations, and attempts were made to recruit participants for each focus group by their broad discipline, to promote data on disciplinary viewpoints. As a small token of appreciation, a £10 voucher was offered to students for their participation. Almost all focus groups included staff or students from the same degree programme or department.

Most students were undergraduates ($n = 92$), with some masters and doctoral candidates ($n = 13$), who took part in three of the 23 student focus groups. Our staff came from a range of teaching and research backgrounds, with from one to over 25 years of teaching experience in higher education. In total, we

Table A1.1 Focus group participants

Focus group	Participant	Discipline	University type	Group size
1	Students	Social Sciences	Pre-92	6
2	Students	Arts & Humanities	Post-92	3
3	Students	Arts & Humanities	Post-92	3
4	Students	Natural Sciences	Post-92	5
5	Students	Social Sciences	Post-92	6
6	Students	Social Sciences	Pre-92	5
7	Students	Applied Sciences	Post-92	5
8	Staff	Social Sciences	Post-92	3
9	Staff	Social Sciences	Post-92	4
10	Staff	Arts & Humanities	Pre-92	2
11	Staff	Applied Sciences	Post-92	2
12	Students	Arts & Humanities	Post-92	4
13	Students	Social Sciences	Pre-92	7
14	Staff	Arts & Humanities	Post-92	2
15	Staff	Natural Sciences	Pre-92	2
16	Staff	Natural Sciences	Pre-92	2
17	Staff	Applied Sciences	Pre-92	3
18	Staff	Natural Sciences	Pre-92	3
19	Staff	Applied Sciences	Pre-92	4
20	Students	Natural Sciences	Pre-92	4
21	Students	Applied Sciences	Pre-92	5
22	Students	Applied Sciences	Pre-92	5
23	Students	Natural Sciences	Pre-92	5
24	Students	Natural Sciences	Pre-92	5
25	Students	Natural Sciences	Pre-92	3
26	Students	Applied Sciences	Pre-92	5
27	Students	Applied Sciences	Pre-92	5
28	Students	Applied Sciences	Pre-92	4
29	Students	Applied Sciences	Pre-92	3
30	Students	Natural Sciences	Pre-92	5
31	Students	Natural Sciences	Pre-92	4
32	Students	Applied Sciences	Pre-92	3
33	Students	Natural Sciences	Pre-92	5

recruited slightly more females (n = 77, or 58%, including 14 staff and 63 students) than males (n = 55, or 42%, including 13 staff and 42 students). We would have preferred a better gender balance, but we note that 26 of the 33 focus groups (or 79%) had at least one male participant (and all but three focus groups, or 91%, had at least one female). Most participants self-identified as White, White British or White European (n = 56), although a wide range of other ethnicities were also reported (n = 76), including multiple/mixed backgrounds, Asian, Black and Chinese ethnicities. We did not probe into nationalities, but our educated guess is that around a quarter of our participants would probably be non-UK citizens.

Each focus group lasted an hour on average and was audio-recorded, with the data transcribed verbatim and personal details anonymised. Participants were prompted to discuss their thoughts and views around the notion of the ideal student, including their expectations of students 'in an ideal world' as well as a comparison with their understandings of the good student. Although a few staff admitted their initial scepticism about the notion of ideal *per se*, all participants shared and articulated their own desirable expectations of students. Some found it easier to talk about their minimum (rather than their maximum or ideal) expectations of university students. We acknowledge that such reluctance to describe or, in some cases, to accept this terminology may reflect particular epistemological, philosophical or research perspectives, including concerns around labelling and stereotyping.

We believe such reluctance also illustrates the fluidity and difficulty of the notion of the ideal student, which is discussed in Chapter 3. For clarification purposes, we revisited the key points towards the end of each focus group and asked participants to summarise their views and desirable expectations of students. Fortunately, most participants mentioned at the end that their participation had provided them with 'food for thought', as well as a greater appreciation of the fluidity and potential of the concept of the ideal student. As one member of staff said, 'I mentioned to you before we started that I would actually never use that term … But I think it makes sense now to have this term … I've never really thought about it that deep' (FG15, Staff). We consider these remarks to be a positive indication of the value and potential of the project.

Our data analysis is informed by a social constructionist perspective which recognises social phenomena as socially constructed and discursively produced (Burr 2015). Focus group data were managed and organised using the software *NVivo*. Initial codes were created through the identification of relevant themes that emerged in the initial stages of data analysis as we moved 'back and forth' between the data and analyses in an iterative process through which the dimensions of concepts and themes were refined or expanded through comparison of the data (Corbin and Strauss 2014).

A provisional coding framework was established after we independently coded the same data (for three transcripts) by relevant themes, which we then discussed and compared, with any differences on the application of codes being debated until a consensus was reached. The coding process involved gathering a range of views and expectations of the ideal student. These codes were subject to an iterative process of gradual coding refinement, with the themes being revised with emerging research data and further coding. Intersectional analyses were also applied to our codes, using the *NVivo* function *matrix-coding query*, where references (i.e. coded data) were separated by focus group-level demographics, such as by student and staff, pre-92 and post-92 universities, and broad disciplines (see Chapters 5 and 6).

Discussion of the concept of the ideal student has not only provoked curiosity and cynicism, but also offered insights into its potential value for theory and practice. In Chapter 3, we argue that despite the conceptual challenges and potential misinterpretations, the concept of the ideal student is theoretically important, and even necessary, to champion transparency in expectations of students in higher education.

Developing the ideal university student survey

The ideal university student survey was developed using existing literature and empirical data gathered from focus groups as described above. In our earlier work with social science lecturers, we identified six personal and academic skillsets that were desirable of university students, namely those of preparation, engagement, commitment, as well as being critical, reflective and progressive (Wong and Chiu 2020). The ability to achieve high grades was rarely mentioned as important. Building on this work, we want to explore a wider range of possible characteristics related to the ideal student by using our focus group participants to brainstorm and discuss their ideas and suggestions about the possible characteristics of the ideal student.

The purpose of our survey is to understand how the ideal student is constructed by university staff and students, across the broad disciplines of the natural sciences, applied sciences, social sciences and arts & humanities, as well as their institution types (namely pre-92 and post-92 institutions) and demographic profiles, such as gender and ethnicity. Essentially, we wanted to map out the range of ideal student characteristics and attributes, which were reported in Chapters 5, 6 and 7.

The development of the ideal university survey began with the qualitative data and Table A1.2 organises the focus groups by discipline and type of participant. To brainstorm initial ideas of ideal student characteristics, our participants in each focus group were also allocated an individual activity, which was to write down their five most and five least important characteristics of the ideal university student (see Killen 1994). Each participant was then asked to share and discuss their own list as individuals were probed to explain, elaborate and clarify their meanings and definitions of different student characteristics.

In total, 795 student characteristics were brainstormed, with 636 keywords or phrases attributed to the five most important characteristics of an ideal student and a further 159 for the least important features (see Figure A.1.1 for the 50 most popular words that were articulated). As the numbers indicate, most

Table A1.2 Number of focus groups conducted by disciplines and participant type

	Natural sciences	Applied sciences	Social sciences	Arts & humanities
Student group	8 (*n* = 36 students)	8 (*n* = 35 students)	4 (*n* = 26 students)	3 (*n* = 8 students)
Staff group	3 (*n* = 7 staff)	3 (*n* = 9 staff)	2 (*n* = 7 staff)	2 (*n* = 4 staff)

Figure A1.1 Word cloud of the top 50 words brainstormed from the activity to identify the characteristics of an ideal student

participants did not complete in full both elements of the activity, as many struggled to articulate their five least important characteristics of an ideal student. Nonetheless, with 795 student characteristics, more of which were considered important characteristics, we had plenty of empirical data to begin developing the ideal student survey.

Based on our participants' description and discussion of these ideal student characteristics, we gradually refined, collated and grouped together similar ideas and meanings in an iterative process that involved the conversion of lower-level concepts to higher-level concepts through the 'ladder of abstraction' (Corbin and Strauss 2014). In other words, each student characteristic was recoded where relevant under a broader theme that aimed to encapsulate the similar intended meanings of the keywords and phrases that were brainstormed for the ideal student. Our survey development also took note of the well-developed literature around graduate attributes, especially from Australia, but also increasingly in the UK (Barrie et al. 2009; Bath et al. 2004; Bridgstock 2009; de la Harpe and David 2012; France et al. 2016; Ipperciel and ElAtia 2014; Jackson 2015; Normand and Anderson 2017; Oliver 2013; Su 2014). These attributes are institutional objectives, as well as marketing strategies, which enlist the expected skills that graduates of these institutions will develop over the course of their degree. As argued in Chapter 2, graduate attributes constitute the institution's own ideal student, as the vision of the outcomes ideally expected of their students. As expected, there are various overlaps between the literature and the ideal student characteristics brainstormed by staff and students.

Through a reflective and iterative process of amalgamation and refinement, the breath of student characteristics was consolidated and confined to 51 items to reflect the common features that may constitute the ideal student. Whilst some items may comprise multiple descriptors, these keywords are grouped together due to their synonymous intended meanings, especially as described and explained by participants. Admittedly, not every student characteristic mentioned in focus group activities or the literature are included, due to considerations of practicality and manageability, but we are confident that the ideal student survey we devised will provide us with data to explore the different constructions of the ideal university student.

We also cross-referenced and remapped the 51 items back to the original 795 student characteristics, where 49 items were matched (see Appendix 2 for the final list). In other words, just two items (16 and 21) were informed solely by the literature, which were related to study skills and graduate attributes. Of the 795 keywords, we managed to map 730 (or 92%) onto our survey items, with the remaining keywords deemed to be niche, random or difficult to incorporate with the provisional list of 51 items (which was later reduced to 50, as explained under 'Survey analysis' below). Some of these are included in the subsection 'Honourable mentions' in Chapter 4.

Most keywords mapped onto one item only, as anticipated, but a small number of keywords, often expressed as phrases, could potentially be matched with two items rather than one. For these keywords, we did not force their association with one or the other but decided to include them in both items. In raw numbers, this meant there is a double count of 20 keywords across our 51 items, so that when we summed the number of keywords that informed the survey, our total was 750. All survey items, therefore, have a well-established empirical or theoretical base. The draft survey was reviewed by several colleagues with expertise and experience in survey design, as well as piloted with 20 students for ease of completion and comprehension. Minor changes to language and wording were made before the survey was finalised for wider distribution.

Demographic data were collected as part of the survey to enable interactional and regression analyses, such as participant type (e.g. student, staff), institutional affiliation (pre-92 and post-92 university) and the broad discipline of the respondent (natural sciences, applied sciences, social sciences and arts & humanities). For the 51 ideal student characteristic items, respondents rate on a 5-point Likert scale: 'not important (1)', 'slightly important (2)', 'moderately important (3)', 'important (4)' and 'very important (5)', in relation to their views of an ideal student. All questions are optional.

Survey data collection

Data collection began in June 2018 and concluded in January 2019. The online survey takes around 10 minutes to complete and the survey website was designed to be friendly across desktop and mobile devices. A paper version of the survey for staff and students was also created, although only a handful of copies were distributed and completed as most respondents were approached and communicated electronically. Paper completions were subsequently entered manually into the online version. Our target respondents were university students and staff at UK universities, including foundation, undergraduate and postgraduate students, as well as teaching, research, support and professional staff. Only a handful of respondents fell outside of our target (e.g. not based in the UK), which were excluded from the analysis.

Our recruitment methods were email based, including the use of personal contacts, higher education staff interest group mailing lists and, our main approach, a purposeful but randomised emailing of UK university staff. Using publicly available department websites, we collected (with support from Meggie Copsey-Blake) and sent over 2,500 personal emails to staff (who are mostly tutors but also some support and professional staff) from over 30 universities, which included pre-92 and post-92 institutions in all UK regions. The email asked for their participation in the survey, as well as to forward the invite to their students. We gathered the names and emails of around 20 staff from each of the four broad disciplines, where available, with around 80 emails for each university. A range of departments was identified within each university in this email process and we noted that not all universities we randomly selected had departments across the four broad disciplines. In the end, as an indication, our survey was completed by participants from the following departments, schools or faculties: Agriculture, Art, Biomedical Sciences, Economics, Engineering, Education, Environmental Sciences, Health Sciences, Mathematics, Modern Language, Physics, Psychology and Social Sciences.

We used mail merge and our staff recipients were invited to take part and to share the survey details with their respective students, such as on a notice-board posting on their internal virtual learning environments. The invitation to staff included a brief description of the project, its aims and a link to the survey, where further information can be accessed. Our emails and survey website also included an example lesson plan on the use of the survey to facilitate class discussions on expectations of university students (see Chapter 9). Entry to a prize draw was also promoted to encourage survey submission (10 × £20 voucher). The ideal student survey was completed by 1,043 participants, with at least 10 participants from over 20 different UK universities and a further 50 other UK universities with less than 10 participants, most of whom were staff respondents. Table A1.3 provides further details:

Table A1.3 Breakdown of participants in the ideal student survey ($n = 1{,}043$)

Role	Student (70%)	Staff (29%)	Other (1%)
University	Pre-92 (60%)	Post-92 (40%)	
Gender	Female (64%)	Male (35%)	Other (1%)
Ethnicity	White (68%)	'Non-White' (32%)	
Discipline	Natural sciences (27.4%)	Social sciences (34.5%)	Other (1.9%)
	Applied sciences (19.6%)	Arts & humanities (16.6%)	

Table A1.4 Overview of the ideal university student dimensions

[Rank] Dimensions	Brief description	Mean (SD)
[1] Diligence & Engagement	Strong work ethic and positive learning attitude	4.271 (.511)
[2] Organisation & Discipline	Being prepared, punctual and procedural	4.078 (.664)
[3] Reflection & Innovation	Thoughtful and proactive about decisions and ideas	4.058 (.595)
[4] Positive & Confident outlook	Being positive, happy and confident	3.921 (.949)
[5] Supportive of Others	Being collegial and helpful to others	3.894 (.789)
[6] Academic skills	Study skills typically rewarded by lecturers	3.873 (.673)
[7] Employability skills	Employable skills typically valued by employers	3.453 (.853)
[8] Intelligence & Strategic approach	Someone who is clever, focused and capable	2.825 (.937)

Due to low numbers from several minority ethnic groups, the category 'Non-White' was created to collate all other ethnicities that were not White for the purpose of statistical analysis. For the same reason, we grouped the disciplines of natural and applied sciences together ('STEM'), and the arts & humanities with the social sciences ('SHAPE') (see Chapter 6).

Survey analysis

Analyses began by conducting reliability and validity tests using exploratory factor analysis (EFA) and Cronbach's alpha to determine the respective unidimensionality of scales and internal consistency. The EFA (using principal axis factoring with oblimin rotation) revealed the following eight factors: *Diligence & Engagement, Organisation & Discipline, Reflection & Innovation, Positive & Confident outlook, Supportive of Others, Academic skills, Employability skills*, and *Intelligence & Strategic approach*. Cronbach's alphas ranged from .765 (*Organisation & Discipline*) to .890 (*Employability skills*). One item ('Working smarter, rather than working harder') did not load consistently on any of the eight factors and was dropped from all statistical analysis (thus, the survey was based on 50 items). See Table A1.5 for the factor loadings and Cronbach's alphas for each of the eight factors.

Next, all of the factors that emerged from the first set of analyses were used to form composite variables (by taking scores on the 5-point Likert scale items and averaging across items). These variables were then utilised to explore patterns in the responses, including by role (staff/student), university type, discipline, as well as gender and ethnicity (see Chapter 7, where student participants were also analysed by proxies of social class and age). More specifically, descriptive (e.g. means and rankings) and multivariate analyses (e.g. non-parametric versions of t-tests and analyses of variance, as the data were not normally distributed) were used to gain an overview of the data for each composite variable. Following this, regression analyses were used to explore which variables (background variables of role, discipline, type of university, gender and ethnicity, as well other composite variables) were most closely related to each outcome.

Finally, to delve into the key comparison, such as between staff and students (see Chapter 5), a series of Mann–Whitney U-tests were performed to examine differences within these groups. In these analyses, a significance level of .006 was used, using the Bonferroni correction for multiple tests ($p = 0.05$ divided by eight, for each test that corresponds to each of the eight dimensions). Although there are arguments for the use of independent p-values for individual tests and comparisons (Armstrong 2014), we decided on a more conservative approach with a lower p-value, especially since our sample was large (which tends to decrease the p-value of any tests). More importantly, our interpretations were more focused on the magnitude of these differences, which is illustrated through the effect size. For this, we adopted Cohen's d, as our focus

Table A1.5 Dimensions and items of the ideal student survey with factor loadings and Cronbach's alphas

Composite Variables	Item components	Factor loadings	Cronbach's alpha*
Diligence & Engagement	1 Enthusiastic, passionate, engaged and/or motivated in learning	0.424	0.855
	2 Dedicated, focused and/or determined in learning	0.681	
	3 Disciplined, diligent and/or respectful in learning	0.696	
	4 Responsible and/or professional in learning	0.651	
	5 Good attitude, willingness and/or behaviour in learning	0.633	
	6 Good preparation and/or readiness in learning	0.668	
	7 Hard-working and/or studious in learning	0.589	
	9 Do more than required and/or go the extra mile in learning	0.437	
	10 Always trying their best in learning	0.429	
Organisation & Discipline	11 Good attendance and/or punctuality	0.370	0.765
	18 Good organisational or time-management skills	0.356	
	41 Seek support when needed	0.519	
	42 On-time submission of assignments	0.601	
	46 Follow university or teaching instructions, rules or procedures	0.537	
Reflection & Innovation	8 Curious, inquisitive and/or open-minded about learning	0.432	0.785
	28 Being independent or self-directed	0.218	
	31 Being reflective or self-aware	0.393	
	36 Being proactive and/or taking initiatives	0.186	
	37 Being creative, innovative and/or divergent in thinking	0.373	
	44 Acceptance of own weakness or room for improvement	0.396	
	48 Challenge instructions or existing knowledge/practices	0.527	
Positive & Confident outlook	26 Being positive or happy	0.492	0.793
	27 Being confident	0.548	

319567289153428459

Table A1.5 Continued

Composite Variables	Item components	Factor loadings	Cronbach's alpha*
Supportive of Others	29 Being friendly or approachable	0.544	0.861
	32 Being supportive of others	0.692	
	29 Being friendly or approachable	0.544	
	32 Being supportive of others	0.692	
	34 Being a good team player and/or working well with others	0.429	
	35 Being a trustworthy individual	0.724	
	38 Contribute to discussions and/or learning of others	0.302	
	39 An honest, moral or ethical person	0.675	
Academic skills	12 Good critical thinking, analytical and/or problem-solving skills	0.498	0.822
	13 Good numeric, mathematical and/or statistical skills	0.327	
	14 Good reading and/or writing skills	0.681	
	15 Good presentation, speaking and/or communication skills	0.622	
	16 Good digital and/or technology skills	0.523	
	17 Good research and/or inquiry skills	0.627	
Employability skills	19 Good job searching or job application writing skills	0.500	0.890
	20 Good interpersonal and/or communication skills	0.490	
	21 Good leadership skills	0.601	
	22 Good social skills and/or with wide social networks	0.669	
	23 Good cross-cultural awareness and/or appreciation of global diversity	0.469	
	24 Good balance between academic and social activities	0.534	
	45 Participation in extracurricular activities (societies or clubs)	0.412	
	49 Participate in work experience, placement or volunteering during university	0.338	

(continued)

Table A1.5 Continued

Composite Variables	Item components	Factor loadings	Cronbach's alpha*
Intelligence & Strategic approach	25 Being a high achiever and/or has top grades	0.614	0.861
	30 Being modest, low-profile or quiet	0.558	
	33 Being intelligent, smart or clever	0.614	
	40 Prior knowledge or experience in the discipline	0.510	
	43 Someone with a strong belief in themselves and/or single-minded	0.518	
	47 Has plans or thoughts on post-degree pathways	0.541	
	50 Presentable or professional appearance (well-dressed, 'smart')	0.473	

*For each composite for variable.

is on differences between means (Sawilowsky 2009), although we acknowledge other calculations for effect size can also be used (e.g. Pearson's r or eta-squared), but we stress that the key messages remain.

Regression analyses were also used to explore relationships among the dimensions, as well as to gather insight into background variables that may also be related. Eight models were created, one for each dimension, and these are summarised in Table A1.6 (see also Wong et al. in review).

In terms of salient relationships amongst dimensions, the regression analysis found that the dimension of *Diligence & Engagement* was strongly associated with *Organisation & Discipline* and *Reflection & Innovation* (first model in Table A1.6). We believe that these three dimensions can contribute and enrich the 'personal skillsets' that were qualitatively identified as key elements in an ideal student (Wong and Chiu 2020). Our regression analysis (fourth model) found the dimension *Supportive of Others* to be closely associated with the dimension *Positive & Confident Outlook*. Considering the student characteristics within each dimension, it is not difficult to envisage that these two dimensions could be considered as part of students' sense of self, self-efficacy and self-identity.

Further regression analysis also found a strong association between *Intelligence & Strategic approach* and *Employability skills*, which is reasonable given the ultimate emphasis of both dimensions is on tangible and quantifiable outcomes. Perhaps these two dimensions shed light on the more pragmatic aspects of the ideal student that consider the purpose and outcomes of higher education. In addition, although background variables (e.g. gender, ethnicity, university type, discipline) are not as closely associated with any given dimension as other dimensions, the analyses broadly align with the findings of Mann–Whitney U-tests between students and staff (see Chapter 5, including Table 5.1), reinforcing that participant role (i.e. students vs. staff) would appear to play a key part in influencing individuals' perceptions of the ideal student. Statistical data are reported in Chapters 5, 6 and 7.

Post-survey reflection on open-ended comments

In the ideal student survey, we included two open-ended comment boxes at the end for respondents to provide us with feedback on (1) any other ideal student attributes, especially those specific to their discipline, that are important, and (2) any other thoughts or suggestions about the survey in general. Of the 1,043 participants, 219 inserted text in the first box and 66 in the second box. For participants who completed the survey, some comments rightly raised concerns about the concept of ideal *per se* (see Chapter 3) as well as the meanings of particular items or keywords that we used (see Chapter 4). These are, of course, discussed at length in the book but we appreciate this luxury was not available to participants when they did the survey, often in under 10 minutes.

Most comments in box 1 reinforce the items and keywords in our survey, but we want to reflect on a few interesting suggestions that could be considered and incorporated in future iterations of the survey. One respondent noted the

Table A1.6 Regression models for each of the eight dimensions

Model*		Coefficient (B)	SE	Beta (std)	Adjusted R^2
Diligence & Engagement	Intercept (constant)	1.642	.096	N/A	
	Discipline (Sciences)	-.046	.026	-.045	
	Academic skills	.171	.023	.228	
	Reflection & Innovation	.206	.025	.241	
	Organisation & Discipline	.279	.022	.361	.468
Organisation & Discipline	Intercept (constant)	.943	.136	N/A	
	Gender (male)	-.112	.034	-.081	
	Institution type (post-1992)	.116	.033	.086	
	Intelligence & Strategic approach	.114	.024	.161	
	Diligence & Engagement	.451	.035	.349	
	Supportive of Others	.105	.028	.125	
	Employability skills	.144	.029	.186	.482
Reflection & Innovation	Intercept (constant)	1.527	.088	N/A	
	Institution type (post-1992)	-.088	.029	.072	
	Role (staff)	.169	.034	.128	
	Discipline (sciences)	-.046	.029	-.039	

Table A1.6 Continued

Model*	Coefficient (B)	SE	Beta (std)	Adjusted R²
Intelligence & Strategic approach	.133	.021	.208	
Supportive of Others	.255	.024	.336	
Employability skills	.087	.026	.125	
Academic skills	.219	.025	.247	.533
Positive & Confident outlook				
Intercept (constant)	.874	.124	N/A	
Role (staff)	-.147	.056	-.070	
Discipline (sciences)	.172	.048	.090	
Intelligence & Strategic approach	.132	.034	.130	
Supportive of Others	.494	.039	.409	
Employability skills	.208	.041	.187	.470
Supportive of Others				
Intercept (constant)	.386	.113	N/A	
Gender (male)	-.088	.034	-.053	
Role (staff)	.071	.040	.041	
Employability skills	.353	.026	.384	
Reflection & Innovation	.340	.034	.259	
Positive & Confident Outlook	.235	.021	.284	.605

(continued)

Table A1.6 Continued

Model*		Coefficient (B)	SE	Beta (std)	Adjusted R^2
Academic skills	Intercept (constant)	.423	.142	N/A	
	Role (staff)	.156	.040	.105	
	Discipline (sciences)	.137	.034	.102	
	Intelligence & Strategic approach	.131	.025	.181	
	Diligence & Engagement	.326	.037	.247	
	Employability skills	.213	.027	.269	
	Reflection & Innovation	.203	.036	.181	.495
Employability skills	Intercept (constant)	−.260	.123	N/A	
	Gender (male)	.085	.035	−.048	
	Role (staff)	.236	.041	−.126	
	Discipline (sciences)	−.100	.035	−.059	
	Intelligence & Strategic approach	.233	.025	.255	
	Supportive of Others	.399	.028	.369	
	Academic skills	.283	.031	.224	
	Reflection & Innovation	.131	.039	.092	.654

Table A1.6 Continued

Model*		Coefficient (B)	SE	Beta (std)	Adjusted R^2
Intelligence & Strategic approach	Intercept (constant)	-.990	.147	N/A	
	Gender (being male)	.154	.042	.079	
	Ethnicity (non-white)	.124	.045	.061	
	Institution type (post-1992)	.139	.043	.073	
	Role (Staff)	.460	.049	-.224	
	Supportive of Others	.107	.037	.090	
	Employability skills	.349	.037	.319	
	Academic skills	.237	.039	.171	
	Reflection & Innovation	.300	.047	.192	.568

* *Note:* Only those variables that are statistically significant for a model are included in that model.

importance of the ideal student to have 'a sense of belonging and identifies with institution'. Although this idea appeared only once, we think an item based on this suggestion could potentially enrich the dimension *Positive & Confident outlook* (see Chapter 4). It is plausible that students will be more positive and confident about their learning if they feel a stronger sense of belonging at university (Freeman et al. 2007; Strayhorn 2012; Thomas 2012).

Another interesting comment was 'tolerance of ambiguity'. While embracing uncertainty is not part of the current survey, we feel this characteristic ought to be included in the future, especially post-Covid-19. In fact, the word ambiguity was mentioned by students in our follow-up induction activity to support student transition and progression (see Figure 9.1). In this particular exercise, engineering students recognise 'understanding ambiguity' to be part of their current learning experience, which may reflect the fluidity and uncertainties of real-world problems. We speculate an item on uncertainty would fit within the dimension *Employability skills*.

A few staff respondents mentioned that some of the dispositions in the survey can be nurtured and taught with the support of staff and the university, rather than as something that students should already possess. As one member of staff wrote, 'I would say that many of the qualities I identified as important are what I would hope to see in graduates – not necessarily in students while they are progressing along their pathways of development'. Another member of staff commented that 'the ideal idea puts the emphasis on the student journey prior to application. These journeys are diverse and we should not expect students to be fully prepared when they arrive'. These comments are linked to two different stages of thinking about the ideal student – as a *product* and as a *process* – the latter of which would foreground the perspectives of these staff. In our focus groups, both stages are woven through as staff and students discussed their understandings of the ideal student (see Chapters 5 and 8).

A few respondents raised concerns in their comments about the difficulty to respond to the survey because their views may change according to context. As one respondent wrote, 'this is hard to answer due to the variation in course settings. I have answered this purely based on the lecture and studying aspects of a course, not placements or working elements'. Another also commented, 'it is quite difficult to consider the ideal student at various stages. I think my ideal student at stage 6 [final year] would be different from a student just starting'.

These comments seem to reflect the views of staff who work with students across different levels. Although we framed our study in the context of undergraduate students, we appreciate that there may well be differences if respondents were asked to describe their ideal first-year undergraduate as well as how they might describe their ideal final-year undergraduate. A future study is merited. That said, we did manage to explore differences by students' own level of study on their views about the ideal student (see Chapter 7).

As mentioned throughout, the ideal student survey we developed constitutes a first version in our attempt to better understand how different stakeholders construct their ideal student. New items may be needed, and existing items may be rephrased or removed to reflect the context of the next study.

Appendix 2: The ideal university student survey items

01 Enthusiastic, passionate, engaged and/or motivated in learning

02 Dedicated, focused and/or determined in learning

03 Disciplined, diligent and/or respectful in learning

04 Responsible and/or professional in learning

05 Good attitude, willingness and/or behaviour in learning

06 Good preparation and/or readiness in learning

07 Hard-working and/or studious in learning

08 Curious, inquisitive and/or open-minded about learning

09 Do more than required and/or go the extra mile in learning

10 Always trying their best in learning

11 Good attendance and/or punctuality

12 Good critical thinking, analytical and/or problem-solving skills

13 Good numeric, mathematical and/or statistical skills

14 Good reading and/or writing skills

15 Good presentation, speaking and/or communication skills

16 Good digital and/or technology skills

17 Good research and/or inquiry skills

18 Good organisational or time-management skills

26 Being positive or happy

27 Being confident

28 Being independent or self-directed

29 Being friendly or approachable

30 Being modest, low-profile or quiet

31 Being reflective or self-aware

32 Being supportive of others

33 Being intelligent, smart or clever

34 Being a good team player and/or working well with others

35 Being a trustworthy individual

36 Being proactive and/or taking initiatives

37 Being creative, innovative and/or divergent in thinking

38 Contribute to discussions and/or learning of others

39 An honest, moral or ethical person

40 Prior knowledge or experience in the discipline

41 Seek support when needed

42 On-time submission of assignments

43 Someone with a strong belief in themselves and/or single-minded

19 Good job searching or job application writing skills

20 Good interpersonal and/or communication skills

21 Good leadership skills

22 Good social skills and/or with wide social networks

23 Good cross-cultural awareness and/or appreciation of global diversity

24 Good balance between academic and social activities

25 Being a high achiever and/or has top grades

44 Acceptance of own weakness or room for improvement

45 Participation in extracurricular activities (societies or clubs)

46 Follow university or teaching instructions, rules or procedures

47 Has plans or thoughts on post-degree pathways

48 Challenge instructions or existing knowledge/practices

49 Participate in work experience, placement or volunteering during university

50 Presentable or professional appearance (well-dressed, 'smart')

Appendix 3: Breakdown of the ideal university student survey analysis

Table A3.1 Percentage of responses to individual items in the ideal student survey, by highest overall mean

Survey Item	Not important	Slightly important	Moderately important	Important	Very important	Item mean	SD
1 Enthusiastic, passionate, engaged and/or motivated in learning	0.3	0.8	4.0	32.4	62.5	4.56	0.64
2 Dedicated, focused and/or determined in learning	0.3	0.4	5.5	37.4	56.5	4.49	0.65
8 Curious, inquisitive and/or open-minded about learning	0.4	1.4	8.1	29.9	60.2	4.48	0.74
10 Always trying their best in learning	0.4	1.9	8.3	30.0	59.3	4.46	0.76
5 Good attitude, willingness and/or behaviour in learning	0.3	1.3	8.0	37.8	52.6	4.41	0.72
12 Good critical thinking, analytical and/or problem-solving skills	0.2	1.9	9.1	34.7	54.0	4.40	0.75
42 On-time submission of assignments	1.1	4.4	10.8	29.5	54.3	4.31	0.91
7 Hard-working and/or studious in learning	0.4	2.7	14.2	40.4	42.4	4.22	0.81
18 Good organisational or time-management skills	0.7	2.5	13.9	41.0	42.0	4.21	0.82
28 Being independent or self-directed	0.5	2.5	12.5	44.8	39.7	4.21	0.79
41 Seek support when needed	0.3	3.4	12.8	42.3	41.3	4.21	0.81
3 Disciplined, diligent and/or respectful in learning	0.3	3.3	13.4	44.0	39.0	4.18	0.81

(continued)

Table A3.1 Continued

Survey item	Not important	Slightly important	Moderately important	Important	Very important	Item mean	SD
44 Acceptance of own weakness or room for improvement	1.2	3.0	16.1	39.3	40.5	4.15	0.88
6 Good preparation and/or readiness in learning	0.4	3.2	18.6	42.3	35.5	4.09	0.83
26 Being positive or happy	2.6	6.1	13.9	34.2	43.2	4.09	1.02
4 Responsible and/or professional in learning	0.7	3.4	17.1	45.5	33.4	4.08	0.83
14 Good reading and/or writing skills	0.5	3.6	19.3	43.1	33.5	4.06	0.84
31 Being reflective or self-aware	1.1	5.1	16.1	42.4	35.4	4.06	0.90
17 Good research and/or inquiry skills	0.7	5.3	17.6	43.7	32.7	4.03	0.88
37 Being creative, innovative and/or divergent in thinking	1.2	6.3	17.8	38.1	36.6	4.03	0.95
39 An honest, moral or ethical person	3.1	6.2	17.7	33.8	39.3	4.00	1.05
36 Being proactive and/or taking initiatives	0.9	5.8	20.0	40.6	32.7	3.98	0.92
32 Being supportive of others	2.4	6.1	19.9	38.2	33.4	3.94	1.00
34 Being a good team player and/or working well with others	2.1	5.6	20.9	41.2	30.2	3.92	0.96
35 Being a trustworthy individual	3.8	8.1	17.0	34.1	37.0	3.92	1.10
24 Good balance between academic and social activities	3.8	6.1	19.9	35.1	35.0	3.91	1.07
11 Good attendance and/or punctuality	2.7	6.1	19.5	41.8	29.9	3.90	0.99

Table A3.1 Continued

Survey item	Not important	Slightly important	Moderately important	Important	Very important	Item mean	SD
20 Good interpersonal and/or communication skills	1.1	6.2	23.6	40.0	29.1	3.90	0.93
38 Contribute to discussions and/or learning of others	2.2	5.5	23.9	41.7	26.7	3.85	0.95
15 Good presentation, speaking and/or communication skills	1.2	6.9	25.5	41.6	24.8	3.82	0.93
46 Follow university or teaching instructions, rules or procedures	3.8	8.3	24.8	34.8	28.3	3.76	1.07
23 Good cross-cultural awareness and/or appreciation of global diversity	4.0	8.3	24.0	36.3	27.3	3.75	1.07
27 Being confident	4.1	7.7	24.0	37.2	26.9	3.75	1.06
29 Being friendly or approachable	4.8	8.5	23.7	35.2	27.8	3.73	1.10
9 Do more than required and/or go the extra mile in learning	2.0	9.9	26.7	39.6	21.8	3.69	0.99
16 Good digital and/or technology skills	2.0	13.2	32.8	35.2	16.9	3.52	0.99
48 Challenge instructions or existing knowledge/ practices	4.4	14.1	28.7	33.2	19.6	3.50	1.09
13 Good numeric, mathematical and/or statistical skills	5.9	13.5	32.1	29.1	19.3	3.42	1.12
49 Participate in work experience, placement or volunteering during university	9.9	14.6	23.3	29.8	22.4	3.40	1.26
22 Good social skills and/or with wide social networks	6.7	17.4	27.7	30.0	18.1	3.35	1.16

(continued)

Table A3.1 Continued

Survey Item	Not important	Slightly important	Moderately important	Important	Very important	Item mean	SD
19 Good job searching or job application writing skills	8.8	18.2	30.3	27.7	15.1	3.22	1.17
33 Being intelligent, smart or clever	10.5	17.6	29.3	26.5	16.1	3.20	1.21
21 Good leadership skills	9.3	20.2	33.7	24.4	12.4	3.10	1.14
45 Participation in extracurricular activities (societies or clubs)	14.9	20.2	28.8	22.6	13.6	3.00	1.25
43 Someone with a strong belief in themselves and/or single-minded	14.8	20.2	30.3	21.7	13.1	2.98	1.24
47 Has plans or thoughts on post-degree pathways	16.6	20.8	25.9	23.0	13.6	2.96	1.28
25 Being a high achiever and/or has top grades	18.4	16.2	30.4	24.5	10.5	2.92	1.25
40 Prior knowledge or experience in the discipline	21.7	25.4	27.1	16.5	9.2	2.66	1.24
50 Presentable or professional appearance (well-dressed, 'smart')	30.0	20.6	20.5	16.7	12.1	2.60	1.38
30 Being modest, low-profile or quiet	29.7	23.2	24.4	13.9	8.7	2.49	1.28

Table A3.2 Difference in mean on individual survey items between students and staff, by largest mean difference

Survey item	Student N	Staff N	Student mean (SD)	Staff mean (SD)	Difference in mean
50 Presentable or professional appearance (well-dressed, 'smart')	726	302	2.90 (1.38)	1.89 (1.10)	1.01
25 Being a high achiever and/or has top grades	726	303	3.20 (1.20)	2.26 (1.12)	0.94
30 Being modest, low-profile or quiet	726	303	2.73 (1.31)	1.92 (1.00)	0.81
43 Someone with a strong belief in themselves and/or single-minded	724	303	3.22 (1.24)	2.43 (1.04)	0.79
47 Has plans or thoughts on post-degree pathways	726	302	3.19 (1.26)	2.42 (1.17)	0.77
19 Good job searching or job application writing skills	724	303	3.45 (1.11)	2.69 (1.13)	0.76
24 Good balance between academic and social activities	726	303	4.12 (0.97)	3.41 (1.12)	0.71
45 Participation in extracurricular activities (societies or clubs)	726	303	3.20 (1.24)	2.51 (1.14)	0.69
40 Prior knowledge or experience in the discipline	723	303	2.87 (1.27)	2.18 (1.03)	0.69
29 Being friendly or approachable	724	303	3.93 (1.05)	3.25 (1.08)	0.68
27 Being confident	723	303	3.96 (0.99)	3.29 (1.04)	0.67
21 Good leadership skills	725	302	3.29 (1.13)	2.66 (1.05)	0.63
22 Good social skills and/or with wide social networks	724	301	3.54 (1.15)	2.91 (1.07)	0.63
49 Participate in work experience, placement or volunteering during university	726	302	3.58 (1.19)	2.98 (1.32)	0.60
33 Being intelligent, smart or clever	725	303	3.38 (1.19)	2.79 (1.16)	0.59
26 Being positive or happy	725	303	4.25 (0.97)	3.74 (1.05)	0.51

(continued)

Table A3.2 Continued

Survey item	Student N	Staff N	Student mean (SD)	Staff mean (SD)	Difference in mean
13 Good numeric, mathematical and/or statistical skills	726	303	3.56 (1.07)	3.10 (1.17)	0.46
42 On-time submission of assignments	723	302	4.45 (0.84)	4.02 (0.97)	0.43
32 Being supportive of others	724	301	4.07 (0.98)	3.65 (0.97)	0.42
46 Follow university or teaching instructions, rules or procedures	725	303	3.88 (1.04)	3.47 (1.09)	0.41
34 Being a good team player and/or working well with others	725	303	4.04 (0.93)	3.64 (0.96)	0.40
44 Acceptance of own weakness or room for improvement	726	303	4.27 (0.83)	3.88 (0.90)	0.39
18 Good organisational or time-management skills	722	303	4.32 (0.81)	3.97 (0.81)	0.35
7 Hard-working and/or studious in learning	722	302	4.31 (0.79)	3.99 (0.83)	0.32
20 Good interpersonal and/or communication skills	725	303	3.99 (0.91)	3.70 (0.92)	0.29
35 Being a trustworthy individual	725	302	4.01 (1.08)	3.73 (1.10)	0.28
23 Good cross-cultural awareness and/or appreciation of global diversity	726	303	3.82 (1.06)	3.56 (1.08)	0.26
16 Good digital and/or technology skills	724	303	3.58 (1.00)	3.35 (0.93)	0.23
3 Disciplined, diligent and/or respectful in learning	725	301	4.25 (0.80)	4.04 (0.82)	0.21
39 An honest, moral or ethical person	725	303	4.06 (1.04)	3.86 (1.05)	0.20
10 Always trying their best in learning	725	303	4.52 (0.72)	4.32 (0.83)	0.20
15 Good presentation, speaking and/or communication skills	725	303	3.87 (0.93)	3.69 (0.89)	0.18
11 Good attendance and/or punctuality	726	303	3.95 (1.00)	3.78 (0.93)	0.17

Table A3.2 Continued

Survey item	Student N	Staff N	Student mean (SD)	Staff mean (SD)	Difference in mean
48 Challenge instructions or existing knowledge/practices	723	302	3.54 (1.11)	3.37 (1.04)	0.17
36 Being proactive and/or taking initiatives	726	303	4.03 (0.90)	3.87 (0.96)	0.16
9 Do more than required and/or go the extra mile in learning	724	301	3.73 (0.97)	3.60 (1.00)	0.13
17 Good research and/or inquiry skills	723	302	4.06 (0.88)	3.94 (0.89)	0.12
2 Dedicated, focused and/or determined in learning	726	303	4.53 (0.64)	4.42 (0.64)	0.11
37 Being creative, innovative and/or divergent in thinking	724	303	4.06 (0.96)	3.95 (0.91)	0.11
6 Good preparation and/or readiness in learning	724	302	4.13 (0.84)	4.03 (0.81)	0.10
5 Good attitude, willingness and/or behaviour in learning	726	302	4.44 (0.73)	4.35 (0.70)	0.09
4 Responsible and/or professional in learning	722	301	4.10 (0.84)	4.01 (0.81)	0.09
28 Being independent or self-directed	725	303	4.23 (0.79)	4.15 (0.79)	0.08
41 Seek support when needed	724	302	4.23 (0.83)	4.17 (0.76)	0.06
31 Being reflective or self-aware	724	303	4.07 (0.91)	4.04 (0.87)	0.03
12 Good critical thinking, analytical and/or problem-solving skills	726	302	4.40 (0.76)	4.44 (0.71)	−0.04
14 Good reading and/or writing skills	723	302	4.04 (0.87)	4.10 (0.78)	−0.06
1 Enthusiastic, passionate, engaged and/or motivated in learning	726	303	4.54 (0.66)	4.63 (0.58)	−0.09
38 Contribute to discussions and/or learning of others	725	303	3.82 (1.00)	3.93 (0.82)	−0.11
8 Curious, inquisitive and/or open-minded about learning	723	302	4.42 (0.77)	4.63 (0.61)	−0.21

Table A3.3 Difference in mean on individual survey items between pre-1992 and post-1992 participants, by largest mean difference

Survey item	Pre-92 participants N	Post-92 participants N	Pre-92 mean (SD)	Post-92 mean (SD)	Difference in mean
33 Being intelligent, smart or clever	617	417	3.28 (1.19)	3.07 (1.24)	0.21
45 Participation in extracurricular activities (societies or clubs)	618	416	3.07 (1.26)	2.89 (1.24)	0.18
13 Good numeric, mathematical and/or statistical skills	618	417	3.48 (1.12)	3.35 (1.12)	0.13
27 Being confident	616	416	3.80 (1.09)	3.68 (1.03)	0.12
25 Being a high achiever and/or has top grades	618	417	2.96 (1.24)	2.86 (1.27)	0.10
26 Being positive or happy	618	416	4.13 (1.02)	4.04 (1.02)	0.09
44 Acceptance of own weakness or room for improvement	618	417	4.18 (0.88)	4.10 (0.88)	0.08
37 Being creative, innovative and/or divergent in thinking	617	416	4.05 (0.97)	3.98 (0.92)	0.07
12 Good critical thinking, analytical and/or problem-solving skills	618	416	4.43 (0.74)	4.36 (0.76)	0.07
24 Good balance between academic and social activities	618	417	3.93 (1.10)	3.88 (1.01)	0.05
31 Being reflective or self-aware	618	415	4.07 (0.90)	4.03 (0.91)	0.04
1 Enthusiastic, passionate, engaged and/or motivated in learning	618	417	4.57 (0.64)	4.55 (0.65)	0.02
29 Being friendly or approachable	617	416	3.73 (1.12)	3.71 (1.07)	0.02
28 Being independent or self-directed	617	417	4.21 (0.80)	4.19 (0.77)	0.02
34 Being a good team player and/or working well with others	618	416	3.92 (0.98)	3.91 (0.93)	0.01

Table A3.3 Continued

Survey item	Pre-92 participants N	Post-92 participants N	Pre-92 mean (SD)	Post-92 mean (SD)	Difference in mean
8 Curious, inquisitive and/or open-minded about learning	617	414	4.48 (0.76)	4.48 (0.72)	0.00
17 Good research and/or inquiry skills	617	414	4.02 (0.90)	4.02 (0.86)	0.00
32 Being supportive of others	615	417	3.94 (1.00)	3.94 (0.99)	0.00
30 Being modest, low-profile or quiet	618	417	2.48 (1.26)	2.49 (1.31)	−0.01
35 Being a trustworthy individual	617	416	3.92 (1.12)	3.93 (1.07)	−0.01
2 Dedicated, focused and/or determined in learning	618	417	4.49 (0.67)	4.51 (0.60)	−0.02
18 Good organisational or time-management skills	616	415	4.20 (0.86)	4.22 (0.76)	−0.02
36 Being proactive and/or taking initiatives	618	417	3.97 (0.92)	3.99 (0.91)	−0.02
3 Disciplined, diligent and/or respectful in learning	617	415	4.18 (0.83)	4.20 (0.76)	−0.02
39 An honest, moral or ethical person	618	416	3.99 (1.08)	4.02 (1.01)	−0.03
5 Good attitude, willingness and/or behaviour in learning	617	417	4.39 (0.75)	4.44 (0.67)	−0.05
15 Good presentation, speaking and/or communication skills	618	416	3.79 (0.95)	3.85 (0.88)	−0.06
20 Good interpersonal and/or communication skills	617	417	3.87 (0.97)	3.94 (0.87)	−0.07
48 Challenge instructions or existing knowledge/practices	618	413	3.46 (1.10)	3.54 (1.08)	−0.08
22 Good social skills and/or with wide social networks	617	414	3.32 (1.18)	3.41 (1.13)	−0.09

(continued)

Table A3.3 Continued

Survey item	Pre-92 participants N	Post-92 participants N	Pre-92 mean (SD)	Post-92 mean (SD)	Difference in mean
21 Good leadership skills	616	417	3.06 (1.15)	3.16 (1.13)	−0.10
38 Contribute to discussions and/or learning of others	617	417	3.81 (0.98)	3.91 (0.90)	−0.10
23 Good cross-cultural awareness and/or appreciation of global diversity	618	417	3.70 (1.11)	3.81 (1.00)	−0.11
10 Always trying their best in learning	617	417	4.42 (0.80)	4.53 (0.68)	−0.11
7 Hard-working and/or studious in learning	614	416	4.17 (0.83)	4.29 (0.78)	−0.12
43 Someone with a strong belief in themselves and/or single-minded	618	415	2.93 (1.23)	3.06 (1.25)	−0.13
41 Seek support when needed	618	414	4.15 (0.82)	4.30 (0.79)	−0.15
19 Good job searching or job application writing skills	618	415	3.16 (1.18)	3.31 (1.15)	−0.15
6 Good preparation and/or readiness in learning	615	416	4.04 (0.85)	4.19 (0.80)	−0.15
42 On-time submission of assignments	616	415	4.25 (0.93)	4.40 (0.88)	−0.15
16 Good digital and/or technology skills	616	417	3.45 (1.00)	3.61 (0.96)	−0.16
40 Prior knowledge or experience in the discipline	617	415	2.60 (1.21)	2.76 (1.30)	−0.16
4 Responsible and/or professional in learning	617	412	4.01 (0.86)	4.17 (0.78)	−0.16

Table A3.3 Continued

Survey item	Pre-92 participants N	Post-92 participants N	Pre-92 mean (SD)	Post-92 mean (SD)	Difference in mean
14 Good reading and/or writing skills	617	414	3.99 (0.86)	4.15 (0.81)	−0.16
47 Has plans or thoughts on post-degree pathways	617	417	2.89 (1.29)	3.06 (1.27)	−0.17
46 Follow university or teaching instructions, rules or procedures	617	417	3.68 (1.09)	3.86 (1.03)	−0.18
9 Do more than required and/or go the extra mile in learning	616	415	3.61 (1.01)	3.82 (0.94)	−0.21
50 Presentable or professional appearance (well-dressed, 'smart')	618	416	2.51 (1.36)	2.73 (1.41)	−0.22
49 Participate in work experience, placement or volunteering during university	618	416	3.29 (1.30)	3.56 (1.18)	−0.27

Table A3.4 Difference in mean on individual survey items between STEM and SHAPE disciplinary background, by largest mean difference

Survey item	STEM participants N	SHAPE participants N	STEM mean (SD)	SHAPE mean (SD)	Difference in mean
13 Good numeric, mathematical and/or statistical skills	489	529	3.84 (0.97)	3.06 (1.12)	0.78
33 Being intelligent, smart or clever	489	528	3.42 (1.15)	3.03 (1.23)	0.39
45 Participation in extracurricular activities (societies or clubs)	489	528	3.18 (1.22)	2.83 (1.26)	0.35
26 Being positive or happy	489	528	4.25 (0.92)	3.95 (1.09)	0.30
27 Being confident	489	526	3.90 (1.00)	3.61 (1.10)	0.29
25 Being a high achiever and/or has top grades	489	529	3.09 (1.20)	2.81 (1.27)	0.28
30 Being modest, low-profile or quiet	489	529	2.64 (1.27)	2.37 (1.28)	0.27
29 Being friendly or approachable	489	527	3.85 (1.05)	3.61 (1.14)	0.24
16 Good digital and/or technology skills	487	529	3.63 (0.97)	3.41 (0.99)	0.22
24 Good balance between academic and social activities	489	529	4.02 (1.04)	3.81 (1.08)	0.21
34 Being a good team player and/or working well with others	489	528	4.02 (0.94)	3.82 (0.97)	0.20
44 Acceptance of own weakness or room for improvement	489	529	4.22 (0.89)	4.08 (0.88)	0.14
43 Someone with a strong belief in themselves and/or single-minded	489	527	3.05 (1.23)	2.92 (1.25)	0.13
47 Has plans or thoughts on post-degree pathways	489	528	3.03 (1.26)	2.91 (1.31)	0.12
50 Presentable or professional appearance (well-dressed, 'smart')	488	529	2.68 (1.37)	2.56 (1.39)	0.12

Table A3.4 Continued

Survey item	STEM participants N	SHAPE participants N	STEM mean (SD)	SHAPE mean (SD)	Difference in mean
40 Prior knowledge or experience in the discipline	489	526	2.72 (1.25)	2.63 (1.24)	0.09
35 Being a trustworthy individual	489	527	3.97 (1.08)	3.89 (1.11)	0.08
36 Being proactive and/or taking initiatives	489	529	4.02 (0.89)	3.95 (0.94)	0.07
32 Being supportive of others	488	527	3.97 (1.01)	3.91 (0.98)	0.06
12 Good critical thinking, analytical and/or problem-solving skills	489	528	4.43 (0.74)	4.37 (0.76)	0.06
19 Good job searching or job application writing skills	488	528	3.26 (1.15)	3.20 (1.19)	0.06
5 Good attitude, willingness and/or behaviour in learning	488	529	4.44 (0.70)	4.39 (0.74)	0.05
28 Being independent or self-directed	488	529	4.23 (0.78)	4.18 (0.80)	0.05
18 Good organisational or time-management skills	486	528	4.24 (0.86)	4.19 (0.79)	0.05
21 Good leadership skills	489	527	3.13 (1.15)	3.08 (1.15)	0.05
22 Good social skills and/or with wide social networks	488	526	3.38 (1.18)	3.34 (1.14)	0.04
42 On-time submission of assignments	487	527	4.34 (0.89)	4.30 (0.92)	0.04
48 Challenge instructions or existing knowledge/practices	488	526	3.51 (1.10)	3.47 (1.10)	0.04
31 Being reflective or self-aware	489	527	4.07 (0.90)	4.04 (0.91)	0.03
46 Follow university or teaching instructions, rules or procedures	488	529	3.77 (1.05)	3.74 (1.10)	0.03

(continued)

Table A3.4 Continued

Survey item	STEM participants N	SHAPE participants N	STEM mean (SD)	SHAPE mean (SD)	Difference in mean
49 Participate in work experience, placement or volunteering during university	489	528	3.41 (1.23)	3.39 (1.28)	0.02
10 Always trying their best in learning	489	528	4.47 (0.77)	4.45 (0.75)	0.02
39 An honest, moral or ethical person	489	528	4.01 (1.08)	3.99 (1.03)	0.02
3 Disciplined, diligent and/or respectful in learning	488	527	4.19 (0.82)	4.18 (0.79)	0.01
37 Being creative, innovative and/or divergent in thinking	487	529	4.03 (0.97)	4.02 (0.94)	0.01
15 Good presentation, speaking and/or communication skills	488	529	3.81 (0.96)	3.82 (0.90)	−0.01
1 Enthusiastic, passionate, engaged and/or motivated in learning	489	529	4.56 (0.62)	4.57 (0.65)	−0.01
2 Dedicated, focused and/or determined in learning	489	529	4.49 (0.64)	4.51 (0.64)	−0.02
17 Good research and/or inquiry skills	488	526	4.02 (0.90)	4.04 (0.86)	−0.02
41 Seek support when needed	488	527	4.19 (0.83)	4.22 (0.80)	−0.03
8 Curious, inquisitive and/or open-minded about learning	487	527	4.47 (0.74)	4.50 (0.73)	−0.03
7 Hard-working and/or studious in learning	485	528	4.20 (0.80)	4.25 (0.83)	−0.05
4 Responsible and/or professional in learning	488	524	4.03 (0.84)	4.12 (0.84)	0.09
20 Good interpersonal and/or communication skills	488	529	3.85 (0.97)	3.94 (0.88)	−0.09

Table A3.4 Continued

Survey item	STEM participants *N*	SHAPE participants *N*	STEM mean (SD)	SHAPE mean (SD)	Difference in mean
9 Do more than required and/or go the extra mile in learning	486	528	3.65 (1.00)	3.75 (0.96)	−0.10
14 Good reading and/or writing skills	487	527	3.98 (0.87)	4.12 (0.83)	−0.14
6 Good preparation and/or readiness in learning	487	527	4.02 (0.89)	4.18 (0.78)	−0.16
38 Contribute to discussions and/or learning of others	489	528	3.76 (0.98)	3.92 (0.93)	−0.16
11 Good attendance and/or punctuality	489	529	3.80 (0.98)	4.02 (0.98)	−0.22
23 Good cross-cultural awareness and/or appreciation of global diversity	489	529	3.61 (1.13)	3.87 (1.01)	−0.26

Table A3.5 Difference in mean on individual survey items between female and male participants, by largest mean difference

Survey item	Female participants N	Male participants N	Female mean (SD)	Male mean (SD)	Difference in mean
23 Good cross-cultural awareness and/or appreciation of global diversity	654	358	3.87 (1.00)	3.48 (1.15)	0.39
46 Follow university or teaching instructions, rules or procedures	654	357	3.87 (0.98)	3.55 (1.16)	0.32
11 Good attendance and/or punctuality	654	358	4.02 (0.93)	3.70 (1.04)	0.32
21 Good leadership skills	652	358	3.19 (1.12)	2.91 (1.16)	0.28
10 Always trying their best in learning	653	358	4.56 (0.68)	4.29 (0.82)	0.27
32 Being supportive of others	652	356	4.03 (0.95)	3.77 (1.04)	0.26
6 Good preparation and/or readiness in learning	652	356	4.19 (0.77)	3.93 (0.91)	0.26
34 Being a good team player and/or working well with others	653	358	4.01 (0.89)	3.75 (1.02)	0.26
19 Good job searching or job application writing skills	652	358	3.31 (1.13)	3.06 (1.20)	0.25
38 Contribute to discussions and/or learning of others	653	358	3.95 (0.92)	3.70 (0.97)	0.25
41 Seek support when needed	651	358	4.30 (0.78)	4.05 (0.82)	0.25
39 An honest, moral or ethical person	654	358	4.08 (0.98)	3.84 (1.14)	0.24
24 Good balance between academic and social activities	654	358	3.99 (1.00)	3.78 (1.14)	0.21
18 Good organisational or time-management skills	653	355	4.29 (0.77)	4.09 (0.88)	0.20
22 Good social skills and/or with wide social networks	653	355	3.42 (1.17)	3.23 (1.14)	0.19

Table A3.5 Continued

Survey item	Female participants N	Male participants N	Female mean (SD)	Male mean (SD)	Difference in mean
50 Presentable or professional appearance (well-dressed, 'smart')	653	358	2.66 (1.38)	2.48 (1.38)	0.18
49 Participate in work experience, placement or volunteering during university	653	358	3.47 (1.23)	3.30 (1.29)	0.17
36 Being proactive and/or taking initiatives	654	358	4.04 (0.92)	3.87 (0.91)	0.17
14 Good reading and/or writing skills	650	358	4.11 (0.82)	3.95 (0.88)	0.16
26 Being positive or happy	653	358	4.15 (0.98)	3.99 (1.08)	0.16
15 Good presentation, speaking and/or communication skills	653	358	3.87 (0.91)	3.72 (0.94)	0.15
5 Good attitude, willingness and/or behaviour in learning	654	357	4.46 (0.69)	4.32 (0.77)	0.14
7 Hard-working and/or studious in learning	653	354	4.27 (0.79)	4.13 (0.85)	0.14
20 Good interpersonal and/or communication skills	654	357	3.95 (0.89)	3.82 (0.97)	0.13
4 Responsible and/or professional in learning	650	356	4.12 (0.81)	3.99 (0.87)	0.13
42 On-time submission of assignments	651	357	4.37 (0.86)	4.24 (0.96)	0.13
27 Being confident	651	358	3.79 (1.04)	3.67 (1.11)	0.12
28 Being independent or self-directed	654	357	4.26 (0.75)	4.14 (0.83)	0.12
35 Being a trustworthy individual	653	357	3.96 (1.09)	3.84 (1.11)	0.12

(continued)

Table A3.5 Continued

Survey item	Female participants N	Male participants N	Female mean (SD)	Male mean (SD)	Difference in mean
40 Prior knowledge or experience in the discipline	652	357	2.70 (1.25)	2.60 (1.24)	0.10
29 Being friendly or approachable	652	358	3.75 (1.12)	3.66 (1.08)	0.09
3 Disciplined, diligent and/or respectful in learning	651	358	4.21 (0.79)	4.14 (0.82)	0.07
9 Do more than required and/or go the extra mile in learning	652	356	3.72 (0.96)	3.65 (1.02)	0.07
17 Good research and/or inquiry skills	650	358	4.06 (0.86)	4.00 (0.90)	0.06
45 Participation in extracurricular activities (societies or clubs)	654	357	3.02 (1.25)	2.97 (1.25)	0.05
1 Enthusiastic, passionate, engaged and/or motivated in learning	654	358	4.58 (0.63)	4.54 (0.63)	0.04
31 Being reflective or self-aware	652	358	4.07 (0.92)	4.04 (0.85)	0.03
2 Dedicated, focused and/or determined in learning	654	358	4.51 (0.64)	4.48 (0.64)	0.03
8 Curious, inquisitive and/or open-minded about learning	650	357	4.49 (0.72)	4.47 (0.75)	0.02
37 Being creative, innovative and/or divergent in thinking	653	358	4.03 (0.93)	4.02 (0.97)	0.01
43 Someone with a strong belief in themselves and/or single-minded	652	358	2.98 (1.23)	2.99 (1.25)	−0.01
12 Good critical thinking, analytical and/or problem-solving skills	654	357	4.40 (0.76)	4.42 (0.73)	−0.02

Table A3.5 Continued

Survey item	Female participants *N*	Male participants *N*	Female mean (SD)	Male mean (SD)	Difference in mean
25 Being a high achiever and/or has top grades	654	358	2.92 (1.25)	2.94 (1.26)	−0.02
16 Good digital and/or technology skills	652	358	3.51 (0.97)	3.55 (1.01)	−0.04
44 Acceptance of own weakness or room for improvement	654	358	4.14 (0.88)	4.18 (0.86)	−0.04
47 Has plans or thoughts on post-degree pathways	654	357	2.95 (1.28)	2.99 (1.30)	−0.04
30 Being modest, low-profile or quiet	654	358	2.45 (1.31)	2.53 (1.23)	−0.08
48 Challenge instructions or existing knowledge/practices	651	357	3.46 (1.12)	3.57 (1.03)	−0.11
33 Being intelligent, smart or clever	653	358	3.16 (1.20)	3.28 (1.24)	−0.12

Table A3.6 Difference in mean on individual survey items between ethnic groups, by largest mean difference

Survey item	Non-white N	White N	Non-white mean (SD)	White mean (SD)	Difference in mean
50 Presentable or professional appearance (well-dressed, 'smart')	324	704	3.08 (1.39)	2.37 (1.32)	0.71
30 Being modest, low-profile or quiet	324	705	2.93 (1.34)	2.27 (1.20)	0.66
47 Has plans or thoughts on post-degree pathways	324	704	3.38 (1.26)	2.76 (1.25)	0.62
25 Being a high achiever and/or has top grades	324	705	3.27 (1.21)	2.75 (1.24)	0.52
27 Being confident	322	704	4.09 (1.00)	3.59 (1.06)	0.50
21 Good leadership skills	324	703	3.43 (1.12)	2.94 (1.12)	0.49
45 Participation in extracurricular activities (societies or clubs)	324	704	3.33 (1.22)	2.84 (1.24)	0.49
40 Prior knowledge or experience in the discipline	322	704	2.96 (1.31)	2.51 (1.19)	0.45
13 Good numeric, mathematical and/or statistical skills	324	705	3.71 (1.03)	3.30 (1.14)	0.41
19 Good job searching or job application writing skills	323	704	3.49 (1.14)	3.08 (1.17)	0.41
43 Someone with a strong belief in themselves and/or single-minded	322	705	3.25 (1.30)	2.84 (1.18)	0.41
49 Participate in work experience, placement or volunteering during university	324	704	3.65 (1.20)	3.28 (1.27)	0.37
44 Acceptance of own weakness or room for improvement	324	705	4.38 (0.79)	4.04 (0.90)	0.34
29 Being friendly or approachable	323	704	3.94 (1.06)	3.61 (1.11)	0.33
23 Good cross-cultural awareness and/or appreciation of global diversity	324	705	3.96 (0.95)	3.64 (1.11)	0.32

Table A3.6 Continued

Survey item	Non-white N	White N	Non-white mean (SD)	White mean (SD)	Difference in mean
39 An honest, moral or ethical person	324	705	4.21 (0.96)	3.89 (1.07)	0.32
35 Being a trustworthy individual	323	704	4.13 (1.06)	3.82 (1.10)	0.31
46 Follow university or teaching instructions, rules or procedures	323	705	3.95 (1.05)	3.66 (1.07)	0.29
22 Good social skills and/or with wide social networks	321	704	3.54 (1.14)	3.26 (1.16)	0.28
6 Good preparation and/or readiness in learning	324	701	4.27 (0.76)	4.01 (0.85)	0.26
15 Good presentation, speaking and/or communication skills	324	704	3.98 (0.93)	3.73 (0.92)	0.25
48 Challenge instructions or existing knowledge/practices	322	703	3.66 (1.07)	3.42 (1.10)	0.24
33 Being intelligent, smart or clever	324	704	3.36 (1.23)	3.12 (1.20)	0.24
26 Being positive or happy	323	705	4.24 (1.01)	4.01 (1.02)	0.23
34 Being a good team player and/or working well with others	323	705	4.07 (0.96)	3.84 (0.95)	0.23
4 Responsible and/or professional in learning	321	702	4.23 (0.85)	4.00 (0.82)	0.23
32 Being supportive of others	324	701	4.09 (0.99)	3.86 (0.99)	0.23
24 Good balance between academic and social activities	324	705	4.06 (1.04)	3.84 (1.08)	0.22
16 Good digital and/or technology skills	322	705	3.66 (1.04)	3.45 (0.96)	0.21
31 Being reflective or self-aware	322	705	4.19 (0.93)	3.99 (0.89)	0.20
42 On-time submission of assignments	322	703	4.44 (0.87)	4.25 (0.92)	0.19
20 Good interpersonal and/or communication skills	324	704	4.02 (0.92)	3.83 (0.93)	0.19

(continued)

Table A3.6 Continued

Survey item	Non-white N	White N	Non-white mean (SD)	White mean (SD)	Difference in mean
3 Disciplined, diligent and/or respectful in learning	324	702	4.31 (0.81)	4.12 (0.80)	0.19
5 Good attitude, willingness and/or behaviour in learning	324	704	4.53 (0.67)	4.35 (0.74)	0.18
18 Good organisational or time-management skills	322	703	4.33 (0.80)	4.15 (0.83)	0.18
36 Being proactive and/or taking initiatives	324	705	4.09 (0.88)	3.92 (0.93)	0.17
7 Hard-working and/or studious in learning	322	702	4.30 (0.81)	4.17 (0.81)	0.13
11 Good attendance and/or punctuality	324	705	3.97 (1.04)	3.86 (0.96)	0.11
12 Good critical thinking, analytical and/or problem-solving skills	324	704	4.48 (0.70)	4.37 (0.77)	0.11
28 Being independent or self-directed	323	705	4.28 (0.80)	4.17 (0.79)	0.11
17 Good research and/or inquiry skills	321	704	4.10 (0.91)	3.99 (0.87)	0.11
37 Being creative, innovative and/or divergent in thinking	324	703	4.10 (0.97)	3.99 (0.94)	0.11
2 Dedicated, focused and/or determined in learning	324	705	4.56 (0.66)	4.46 (0.64)	0.10
41 Seek support when needed	322	704	4.26 (0.84)	4.18 (0.80)	0.08
9 Do more than required and/or go the extra mile in learning	323	702	3.73 (1.04)	3.67 (0.96)	0.06
10 Always trying their best in learning	324	704	4.50 (0.76)	4.44 (0.76)	0.06
14 Good reading and/or writing skills	321	704	4.09 (0.88)	4.03 (0.83)	0.06
38 Contribute to discussions and/or learning of others	324	704	3.88 (1.02)	3.84 (0.92)	0.04
8 Curious, inquisitive and/or open-minded about learning	323	701	4.46 (0.76)	4.49 (0.73)	−0.03

Table A3.7 Difference in mean on individual survey items between first-year (Y1) students and other-year (Non-Y1) students, by largest mean difference (students only)

Survey item	Y1 student N	Non-Y1 student N	Y1 student mean (SD)	Non-Y1 student mean (SD)	Difference in mean
50 Presentable or professional appearance (well-dressed, 'smart')	338	378	3.12 (1.33)	2.69 (1.39)	0.43
40 Prior knowledge or experience in the discipline	336	377	3.09 (1.20)	2.66 (1.30)	0.43
21 Good leadership skills	338	377	3.49 (1.06)	3.10 (1.16)	0.39
11 Good attendance and/or punctuality	338	378	4.15 (0.89)	3.78 (1.07)	0.37
46 Follow university or teaching instructions, rules or procedures	337	378	4.07 (0.92)	3.70 (1.12)	0.37
43 Someone with a strong belief in themselves and/or single-minded	336	378	3.40 (1.20)	3.06 (1.25)	0.34
19 Good job searching or job application writing skills	337	377	3.61 (1.00)	3.28 (1.19)	0.33
22 Good social skills and/or with wide social networks	338	376	3.68 (1.05)	3.40 (1.22)	0.28
48 Challenge instructions or existing knowledge/practices	336	377	3.68 (1.05)	3.40 (1.15)	0.28
6 Good preparation and/or readiness in learning	338	376	4.27 (0.77)	3.99 (0.89)	0.28
41 Seek support when needed	336	378	4.37 (0.76)	4.10 (0.87)	0.27
47 Has plans or thoughts on post-degree pathways	338	378	3.32 (1.26)	3.06 (1.24)	0.26
35 Being a trustworthy individual	337	378	4.14 (0.97)	3.89 (1.16)	0.25

(continued)

Table A3.7 Continued

Survey item	Y1 student N	Non-Y1 student N	Y1 student mean (SD)	Non-Y1 student mean (SD)	Difference in mean
49 Participate in work experience, placement or volunteering during university	338	378	3.70 (1.10)	3.46 (1.24)	0.24
29 Being friendly or approachable	336	378	4.05 (0.98)	3.82 (1.11)	0.23
34 Being a good team player and/or working well with others	337	378	4.16 (0.83)	3.93 (1.01)	0.23
4 Responsible and/or professional in learning	337	375	4.21 (0.80)	3.99 (0.87)	0.22
38 Contribute to discussions and/or learning of others	338	377	3.92 (0.91)	3.71 (1.07)	0.21
13 Good numeric, mathematical and/or statistical skills	338	378	3.66 (1.03)	3.47 (1.10)	0.19
45 Participation in extracurricular activities (societies or clubs)	338	378	3.30 (1.18)	3.11 (1.30)	0.19
30 Being modest, low-profile or quiet	338	378	2.82 (1.32)	2.64 (1.30)	0.18
42 On-time submission of assignments	337	376	4.54 (0.77)	4.36 (0.90)	0.18
7 Hard-working and/or studious in learning	336	376	4.40 (0.76)	4.23 (0.81)	0.17
26 Being positive or happy	338	377	4.33 (0.92)	4.17 (1.01)	0.16
3 Disciplined, diligent and/or respectful in learning	337	378	4.33 (0.76)	4.17 (0.83)	0.16
37 Being creative, innovative and/or divergent in thinking	338	376	4.14 (0.88)	3.98 (1.03)	0.16
36 Being proactive and/or taking initiatives	338	378	4.11 (0.82)	3.96 (0.97)	0.15
25 Being a high achiever and/or has top grades	338	378	3.27 (1.14)	3.13 (1.24)	0.14

Table A3.7 Continued

Survey item	Y1 student N	Non-Y1 student N	Y1 student mean (SD)	Non-Y1 student mean (SD)	Difference in mean
18 Good organisational or time-management skills	337	375	4.39 (0.71)	4.25 (0.89)	0.14
32 Being supportive of others	338	376	4.14 (0.93)	4.00 (1.02)	0.14
44 Acceptance of own weakness or room for improvement	338	378	4.34 (0.79)	4.20 (0.85)	0.14
9 Do more than required and/or go the extra mile in learning	337	377	3.80 (0.94)	3.66 (1.00)	0.14
10 Always trying their best in learning	337	378	4.59 (0.63)	4.46 (0.79)	0.13
24 Good balance between academic and social activities	338	378	4.18 (0.87)	4.05 (1.06)	0.13
39 An honest, moral or ethical person	338	377	4.11 (0.99)	4.01 (1.09)	0.10
5 Good attitude, willingness and/or behaviour in learning	338	378	4.49 (0.69)	4.39 (0.76)	0.10
15 Good presentation, speaking and/or communication skills	338	377	3.91 (0.90)	3.82 (0.97)	0.09
16 Good digital and/or technology skills	338	376	3.62 (0.98)	3.53 (1.03)	0.09
20 Good interpersonal and/or communication skills	338	377	4.03 (0.83)	3.94 (0.98)	0.09
1 Enthusiastic, passionate, engaged and/or motivated in learning	338	378	4.59 (0.63)	4.50 (0.69)	0.09
23 Good cross-cultural awareness and/or appreciation of global diversity	338	378	3.86 (1.03)	3.77 (1.09)	0.09
2 Dedicated, focused and/or determined in learning	338	378	4.57 (0.60)	4.51 (0.67)	0.06

(continued)

Table A3.7 Continued

Survey item	Y1 student N	Non-Y1 student N	Y1 student mean (SD)	Non-Y1 student mean (SD)	Difference in mean
27 Being confident	337	376	3.98 (0.95)	3.92 (1.03)	0.06
17 Good research and/or inquiry skills	336	377	4.09 (0.85)	4.03 (0.91)	0.06
31 Being reflective or self-aware	336	378	4.09 (0.89)	4.05 (0.93)	0.04
14 Good reading and/or writing skills	337	376	4.05 (0.87)	4.03 (0.87)	0.02
33 Being intelligent, smart or clever	338	377	3.38 (1.15)	3.37 (1.22)	0.01
12 Good critical thinking, analytical and/or problem-solving skills	338	378	4.39 (0.78)	4.39 (0.76)	0.00
8 Curious, inquisitive and/or open-minded about learning	337	377	4.42 (0.71)	4.42 (0.83)	0.00

Table A3.8 Difference in mean on individual survey items between students age 20 or under and students age 21 or over, by largest mean difference (students only)

Survey item	Age 20 or under N	Age 21 or over N	Age 20 or under mean (SD)	Age 21 or over mean (SD)	Difference in mean
45 Participation in extracurricular activities (societies or clubs)	453	259	3.34 (1.20)	2.95 (1.30)	0.39
43 Someone with a strong belief in themselves and/or single-minded	452	258	3.35 (1.19)	3.01 (1.30)	0.34
50 Presentable or professional appearance (well-dressed, 'smart')	453	259	2.98 (1.37)	2.75 (1.38)	0.23
29 Being friendly or approachable	451	259	4.01 (1.01)	3.80 (1.11)	0.21
26 Being positive or happy	452	259	4.32 (0.94)	4.13 (0.99)	0.19
21 Good leadership skills	452	259	3.36 (1.10)	3.17 (1.15)	0.19
22 Good social skills and/or with wide social networks	452	258	3.60 (1.12)	3.44 (1.20)	0.16
24 Good balance between academic and social activities	453	259	4.18 (0.92)	4.02 (1.04)	0.16
34 Being a good team player and/or working well with others	453	258	4.09 (0.90)	3.95 (0.98)	0.14
19 Good job searching or job application writing skills	453	258	3.49 (1.05)	3.36 (1.22)	0.13
40 Prior knowledge or experience in the discipline	452	257	2.91 (1.23)	2.78 (1.35)	0.13
13 Good numeric, mathematical and/or statistical skills	453	259	3.60 (1.06)	3.49 (1.09)	0.11
35 Being a trustworthy individual	453	258	4.04 (1.07)	3.93 (1.11)	0.11
44 Acceptance of own weakness or room for improvement	453	259	4.30 (0.82)	4.19 (0.86)	0.11

(continued)

Table A3.8 Continued

Survey item	Age 20 or under N	Age 21 or over N	Age 20 or under mean (SD)	Age 21 or over mean (SD)	Difference in mean
47 Has plans or thoughts on post-degree pathways	453	259	3.22 (1.25)	3.12 (1.27)	0.10
49 Participate in work experience, placement or volunteering during university	453	259	3.61 (1.14)	3.51 (1.26)	0.10
46 Follow university or teaching instructions, rules or procedures	452	259	3.91 (1.04)	3.82 (1.07)	0.09
11 Good attendance and/or punctuality	453	259	3.98 (0.98)	3.90 (1.04)	0.08
27 Being confident	450	259	3.99 (0.98)	3.91 (1.03)	0.08
42 On-time submission of assignments	453	256	4.47 (0.83)	4.39 (0.88)	0.08
36 Being proactive and/or taking initiatives	453	259	4.06 (0.86)	3.98 (0.98)	0.08
48 Challenge instructions or existing knowledge/practices	452	257	3.56 (1.10)	3.49 (1.14)	0.07
30 Being modest, low-profile or quiet	453	259	2.74 (1.30)	2.68 (1.35)	0.06
32 Being supportive of others	452	258	4.09 (0.98)	4.03 (0.99)	0.06
41 Seek support when needed	452	258	4.25 (0.81)	4.20 (0.86)	0.05
6 Good preparation and/or readiness in learning	452	258	4.14 (0.83)	4.09 (0.88)	0.05
10 Always trying their best in learning	452	259	4.53 (0.72)	4.50 (0.74)	0.03
33 Being intelligent, smart or clever	453	258	3.39 (1.14)	3.36 (1.27)	0.03
37 Being creative, innovative and/or divergent in thinking	453	257	4.07 (0.96)	4.04 (0.97)	0.03

Table A3.8 Continued

Survey item	Age 20 or under N	Age 21 or over N	Age 20 or under mean (SD)	Age 21 or over mean (SD)	Difference in mean
20 Good interpersonal and/or communication skills	453	258	4.00 (0.90)	3.97 (0.94)	0.03
18 Good organisational or time-management skills	451	257	4.33 (0.80)	4.31 (0.82)	0.02
25 Being a high achiever and/or has top grades	453	259	3.21 (1.17)	3.19 (1.25)	0.02
7 Hard-working and/or studious in learning	451	257	4.32 (0.80)	4.31 (0.78)	0.01
16 Good digital and/or technology skills	452	258	3.58 (1.02)	3.57 (0.99)	0.01
1 Enthusiastic, passionate, engaged and/or motivated in learning	453	259	4.54 (0.69)	4.55 (0.62)	−0.01
15 Good presentation, speaking and/or communication skills	453	258	3.85 (0.95)	3.86 (0.92)	−0.01
31 Being reflective or self-aware	452	258	4.07 (0.90)	4.08 (0.94)	−0.01
38 Contribute to discussions and/or learning of others	453	258	3.81 (1.00)	3.83 (1.00)	−0.02
4 Responsible and/or professional in learning	451	257	4.09 (0.83)	4.12 (0.87)	−0.03
17 Good research and/or inquiry skills	451	258	4.04 (0.90)	4.08 (0.87)	−0.04
2 Dedicated, focused and/or determined in learning	453	259	4.52 (0.67)	4.56 (0.58)	−0.04
5 Good attitude, willingness and/or behaviour in learning	453	259	4.42 (0.74)	4.47 (0.71)	−0.05
9 Do more than required and/or go the extra mile in learning	452	258	3.70 (0.98)	3.76 (0.98)	−0.06
23 Good cross-cultural awareness and/or appreciation of global diversity	453	259	3.79 (1.06)	3.86 (1.07)	−0.07

(continued)

Table A3.8 Continued

Survey item	Age 20 or under N	Age 21 or over N	Age 20 or under mean (SD)	Age 21 or over mean (SD)	Difference in mean
3 Disciplined, diligent and/or respectful in learning	452	259	4.22 (0.82)	4.29 (0.76)	−0.07
12 Good critical thinking, analytical and/or problem-solving skills	453	259	4.36 (0.79)	4.44 (0.73)	−0.08
14 Good reading and/or writing skills	451	258	4.01 (0.90)	4.09 (0.81)	−0.08
28 Being independent or self-directed	452	259	4.20 (0.81)	4.29 (0.76)	−0.09
39 An honest, moral or ethical person	452	259	4.02 (1.05)	4.12 (1.01)	−0.10

Table A3.9 Difference in mean on individual survey items between students with and without degree educated parents, by largest mean difference (students only)

Survey item	Degree-educated parent N	No parental degree N	Degree-educated parent mean (SD)	No parental degree mean (SD)	Difference in mean
13 Good numeric, mathematical and/or statistical skills	415	289	3.67 (1.09)	3.42 (1.04)	0.25
37 Being creative, innovative and/or divergent in thinking	413	289	4.13 (0.96)	3.96 (0.94)	0.17
45 Participation in extracurricular activities (societies or clubs)	415	289	3.27 (1.22)	3.10 (1.28)	0.17
12 Good critical thinking, analytical and/or problem-solving skills	415	289	4.46 (0.75)	4.30 (0.77)	0.16
39 An honest, moral or ethical person	415	289	4.13 (1.01)	3.98 (1.04)	0.15
44 Acceptance of own weakness or room for improvement	415	289	4.32 (0.80)	4.18 (0.86)	0.14
16 Good digital and/or technology skills	413	289	3.62 (0.99)	3.49 (1.02)	0.13
31 Being reflective or self-aware	415	288	4.12 (0.91)	3.99 (0.90)	0.13
25 Being a high achiever and/or has top grades	415	289	3.24 (1.18)	3.12 (1.23)	0.12
33 Being intelligent, smart or clever	415	288	3.42 (1.16)	3.30 (1.23)	0.12
32 Being supportive of others	413	289	4.11 (0.98)	4.01 (0.95)	0.10
30 Being modest, low-profile or quiet	415	289	2.76 (1.31)	2.67 (1.32)	0.09
8 Curious, inquisitive and/or open-minded about learning	414	288	4.45 (0.77)	4.37 (0.77)	0.08
24 Good balance between academic and social activities	415	289	4.14 (1.00)	4.07 (0.92)	0.07

(continued)

Table A3.9 Continued

Survey item	Degree-educated parent N	No parental degree N	Degree-educated parent mean (SD)	No parental degree mean (SD)	Difference in mean
17 Good research and/or inquiry skills	414	288	4.08 (0.89)	4.02 (0.86)	0.06
26 Being positive or happy	415	289	4.27 (0.97)	4.21 (0.96)	0.06
27 Being confident	413	288	3.98 (1.00)	3.93 (0.99)	0.05
1 Enthusiastic, passionate, engaged and/or motivated in learning	415	289	4.56 (0.64)	4.52 (0.68)	0.04
28 Being independent or self-directed	414	289	4.25 (0.77)	4.22 (0.79)	0.03
15 Good presentation, speaking and/or communication skills	415	288	3.87 (0.95)	3.85 (0.91)	0.02
29 Being friendly or approachable	415	287	3.93 (1.07)	3.91 (1.02)	0.02
38 Contribute to discussions and/or learning of others	414	289	3.82 (1.01)	3.80 (0.97)	0.02
36 Being proactive and/or taking initiatives	415	289	4.02 (0.91)	4.01 (0.89)	0.01
20 Good interpersonal and/or communication skills	414	289	3.98 (0.93)	3.98 (0.87)	0.00
23 Good cross-cultural awareness and/or appreciation of global diversity	415	289	3.80 (1.08)	3.80 (1.03)	0.00
14 Good reading and/or writing skills	414	289	4.03 (0.88)	4.04 (0.85)	−0.01
18 Good organisational or time-management skills	414	287	4.32 (0.84)	4.33 (0.74)	−0.01
22 Good social skills and/or with wide social networks	415	288	3.52 (1.14)	3.54 (1.15)	−0.02
10 Always trying their best in learning	415	288	4.51 (0.73)	4.55 (0.68)	−0.04

Table A3.9 Continued

Survey item	Degree-educated parent N	No parental degree N	Degree-educated parent mean (SD)	No parental degree mean (SD)	Difference in mean
48 Challenge instructions or existing knowledge/practices	414	287	3.52 (1.11)	3.56 (1.10)	−0.04
4 Responsible and/or professional in learning	413	287	4.08 (0.86)	4.13 (0.81)	−0.05
9 Do more than required and/or go the extra mile in learning	414	288	3.70 (0.97)	3.75 (0.98)	−0.05
47 Has plans or thoughts on post-degree pathways	415	289	3.17 (1.24)	3.22 (1.28)	−0.05
35 Being a trustworthy individual	415	288	3.99 (1.08)	4.05 (1.06)	−0.06
41 Seek support when needed	415	287	4.20 (0.86)	4.26 (0.79)	−0.06
3 Disciplined, diligent and/or respectful in learning	414	289	4.22 (0.82)	4.28 (0.75)	−0.06
34 Being a good team player and/or working well with others	415	288	4.01 (0.94)	4.08 (0.89)	−0.07
2 Dedicated, focused and/or determined in learning	415	289	4.51 (0.67)	4.59 (0.56)	−0.08
50 Presentable or professional appearance (well-dressed, 'smart')	415	289	2.85 (1.37)	2.94 (1.40)	−0.09
19 Good job searching or job application writing skills	415	288	3.40 (1.11)	3.50 (1.12)	−0.10
49 Participate in work experience, placement or volunteering during university	415	289	3.53 (1.20)	3.63 (1.15)	−0.10
42 On-time submission of assignments	414	287	4.41 (0.86)	4.52 (0.78)	−0.11

(continued)

Table A3.9 Continued

Survey item	Degree-educated parent N	No parental degree N	Degree-educated parent mean (SD)	No parental degree mean (SD)	Difference in mean
46 Follow university or teaching instructions, rules or procedures	414	289	3.82 (1.05)	3.94 (1.01)	−0.12
5 Good attitude, willingness and/or behaviour in learning	415	289	4.39 (0.77)	4.51 (0.65)	−0.12
7 Hard-working and/or studious in learning	413	287	4.26 (0.79)	4.38 (0.77)	−0.12
21 Good leadership skills	414	289	3.23 (1.16)	3.36 (1.07)	−0.13
6 Good preparation and/or readiness in learning	415	287	4.07 (0.87)	4.20 (0.81)	−0.13
43 Someone with a strong belief in themselves and/or single-minded	414	289	3.15 (1.25)	3.31 (1.21)	−0.16
40 Prior knowledge or experience in the discipline	415	286	2.78 (1.25)	2.98 (1.29)	−0.20

References

Abdulghani, H.M., Al-Drees, A.A., Khalil, M.S., et al. (2014) What factors determine academic achievement in high achieving undergraduate medical students? A qualitative study, *Medical Teacher* 36 (suppl. 1): S43–S48.

AdvanceHE (2019) *Equality in Higher Education: Students Statistical Report 2019.* York: AdvanceHE.

Ambrose, S.A., Bridges, M.W., DiPietro, M., et al. (2010) *How Learning Works: Seven Research-Based Principles for Smart Teaching.* San Francisco, CA: Jossey-Bass.

Anderson, B. (1983) *Imagined Communities: Reflections on the Origin and Spread of Nationalism.* London: Verso.

Archer, L. and Francis, B. (2007) *Understanding Minority Ethnic Achievement: Race, Gender, Class and 'Success'.* London: Routledge.

Archer, M.S. (1995) *Realist Social Theory: The Morphogenetic Approach.* Cambridge: Cambridge University Press.

Armstrong, R.A. (2014) When to use the Bonferroni correction. *Ophthalmic and Physiological Optics* 34 (5): 502–508.

Arnon, S. and Reichel, N. (2007) Who is the ideal teacher? Am I? Similarity and difference in perception of students of education regarding the qualities of a good teacher and of their own qualities as teachers, *Teachers and Teaching* 13 (5): 441–464.

Ashford-Rowe, K., Herrington, J. and Brown, C. (2014) Establishing the critical elements that determine authentic assessment, *Assessment and Evaluation in Higher Education* 39 (2): 205–222.

Baik, C., Larcombe, W. and Brooker, A. (2019) How universities can enhance student mental wellbeing: the student perspective, *Higher Education Research and Development* 38 (4): 674–687.

Balloo, K., Pauli, R. and Worrell, M. (2017) Undergraduates' personal circumstances, expectations and reasons for attending university, *Studies in Higher Education* 42 (8): 1373–1384.

Bandura, A. (1982) Self-efficacy mechanism in human agency, *American Psychologist* 37 (2): 122–147.

Barnett, R. (2007) *A Will to Learn: Being a Student in an Age of Uncertainty.* Maidenhead: Open University Press.

Barrie, S.C. (2012) A research-based approach to generic graduate attributes policy, *Higher Education Research and Development* 31 (1): 79–92.

Barrie, S.C., Hughes, C. and Smith, C. (2009) *The National Graduate Attributes Project: Integration and Assessment of Graduate Attributes in Curriculum.* Strawberry Hills, NSW: Australian Learning and Teaching Council.

Bath, D., Smith, C., Stein, S., et al. (2004) Beyond mapping and embedding graduate attributes: bringing together quality assurance and action learning to create a validated and living curriculum, *Higher Education Research and Development* 23 (3): 313–328.

Bathmaker, A-M., Ingram, N. and Waller, R. (2013) Higher education, social class and the mobilisation of capitals: recognising and playing the game, *British Journal of Sociology of Education* 34 (5/6): 723–743.

BBC (2019) University of Reading staff warned of 'up to 100%' pay deduction. Available at: https://www.bbc.co.uk/news/uk-england-berkshire-50652305 (accessed 4 December 2019).

Becher, T. and Trowler, P.R. (2001) *Academic Tribes and Territories*, 2nd edition. Buckingham: Open University Press.

Becker, H.S. (1952) Social-class variations in the teacher–pupil relationship, *Journal of Educational Sociology* 25 (8): 451–465.

Bekhradnia, B. (2012) *The Academic Experience of Students in English Universities*. Oxford: HEPI.

Bernstein, B. (2000) *Pedagogy, Symbolic Control, and Identity: Theory, Research, Critique*. Lanham, MD: Rowman & Littlefield.

Bhopal, K. (2018) *White Privilege: The Myth of a Post-Racial Society*. Bristol: Policy Press.

BIS (2016) *Success as a Knowledge Economy: Teaching Excellence, Social Mobility and Student Choice*. London: Department for Business, Innovation & Skills.

Bourdieu, P. (1977) *Outline of a Theory of Practice*. Cambridge: Cambridge University Press.

Bourdieu, P. (1986) The forms of capital, in J. Richardson (ed.) *Handbook of Theory and Research for the Sociology of Education*. Westport, CT: Greenwood Press.

Bourdieu, P. and Passeron, J-C. (1990) *Reproduction in Education, Society and Culture*. London: Sage.

Bowden, J., Hart, G., King, B., et al. (2000) *Generic Capabilities of ATN University Graduates*. Canberra, ACT: Department of Education, Training and Youth Affairs.

Bowles, T.V. and Brindle, K.A. (2017) Identifying facilitating factors and barriers to improving student retention rates in tertiary teaching courses: a systematic review, *Higher Education Research and Development* 36 (5): 903–919.

Bradbury, A. (2013) Education policy and the 'ideal learner': producing recognisable learner-subjects through early years assessment, *British Journal of Sociology of Education* 34 (1): 1–19.

Bradbury, A. (2019) Making little neo-liberals: the production of ideal child/learner subjectivities in primary school through choice, self-improvement and 'growth mindsets', *Power and Education* 11 (3): 309–326.

Bradley, A., Quigley, M. and Bailey, K. (2019) How well are students engaging with the careers services at university?, *Studies in Higher Education*. Available at: https://doi.org/10.1080/03075079.2019.1647416.

Brewer, M.L., van Kessel, G., Sanderson, B., et al. (2019) Resilience in higher education students: a scoping review, *Higher Education Research and Development* 38 (6): 1105–1120.

Bridgstock, R. (2009) The graduate attributes we've overlooked: enhancing graduate employability through career management skills, *Higher Education Research and Development* 28 (1): 31–44.

Bridgstock, R., Grant-Iramu, M. and McAlpine, A. (2019) Integrating career development learning into the curriculum: collaboration with the careers service for employability, *Journal of Teaching and Learning for Graduate Employability* 10 (1): 56–72.

Brooks, R. (2018a) The construction of higher education students in English policy documents, *British Journal of Sociology of Education* 39 (6): 745–761.

Brooks, R. (2018b) Understanding the higher education student in Europe: a comparative analysis, *Compare: A Journal of Comparative and International Education* 48 (4): 500–517.

Brooks, R. (2019a) Asserting the nation: the dominance of national narratives in policy influencers' constructions of higher education students, *Sociological Research Online* 25 (2): 273–288.

Brooks, R. (2019b) Europe as spatial imaginary? Narratives from higher education 'policy influencers' across the continent, *Journal of Education Policy*. Available at: https://doi.org/10.1080/02680939.2019.1672212.

Brooks, R. (2019c) The construction of higher education students within national policy: a cross-European comparison, *Compare: A Journal of Comparative and International Education*. Available at: https://doi.org/10.1080/03057925.2019.1604118.

Brooks, R. (2020) Diversity and the European higher education student: policy influencers' narratives of difference, *Studies in Higher Education* 45 (7): 1507–1518.

Brooks, R. and O'Shea, S. (2021) *Reimagining the Higher Education Student*. London: Routledge.

Brown, D.R. (1960) Non-intellective qualities and the perception of the ideal student by college faculty, *Journal of Educational Sociology* 33 (6): 269–278.

Brown, L. and Holloway, I. (2008) The initial stage of the international sojourn: excitement or culture shock?, *British Journal of Guidance and Counselling* 36 (1): 33–49.

Brown, P. (2016) *The Invisible Problem? Improving Students' Mental Health*. Oxford: Higher Education Policy Institute.

Brown, P., Lauder, H. and Ashton, D. (2011) *The Global Auction: The Broken Promises of Education, Jobs, and Incomes*. Oxford: Oxford University Press.

Brown, R. and Carasso, H. (2013) *Everything for Sale? The Marketisation of UK Higher Education*. Abingdon: Routledge.

Bunce, L., Baird, A. and Jones, S.E. (2017) The student-as-consumer approach in higher education and its effects on academic performance, *Studies in Higher Education* 42 (11): 1958–1978.

Bunce, L., King, N., Saran, S., et al. (2019) Experiences of black and minority ethnic (BME) students in higher education: applying self-determination theory to understand the BME attainment gap, *Studies in Higher Education*. Available at: https://doi.org/10.1080/03075079.2019.1643305.

Burger, A. and Naude, L. (2019) In their own words – students' perceptions and experiences of academic success in higher education, *Educational Studies* 46 (5): 624–639.

Burke, P.J. (2012) *The Right to Higher Education: Beyond Widening Participation*. Abingdon: Routledge.

Burke, P.J., Bennett, D.A., Burgess, C., et al. (2016) *Capability, Belonging and Equity in Higher Education: Developing Inclusive Approaches*. Callaghan, NSW: University of Newcastle.

Burke, P.J., Crozier, G. and Misiaszek, L.I. (2017) *Changing Pedagogical Spaces in Higher Education: Diversity, Inequalities and Misrecognition*. Abingdon: Routledge.

Burr, V. (2015) *Social Constructionism*, 3rd edition. London: Routledge.

Butler, J. (1990) *Gender Trouble*. London: Routledge.

Cameron, H. (2019) Bookishness, blue skies, bright hats and brickies: discourse and positioning in academics' conversations around 'academic intelligence' and the 'good' student, *Studies in Higher Education* 44 (2): 318–332.

Chang, L., Mak, M.C.K., Li, T., et al. (2011) Cultural adaptations to environmental variability: an evolutionary account of East–West differences, *Educational Psychology Review* 23 (1): 99–129.

Chiu, Y-LT. (2019) 'It's a match, but is it a good fit?': admissions tutors' evaluation of personal statements for PhD study, *Oxford Review of Education* 45 (1): 136–150.

Chiu, Y-LT. and Rodriguez-Falcon, O. (2018) Raising attainment with diverse students: an inclusive approach to the teaching of academic literacy, *Journal of Academic Writing* 8 (2): 36–47.

Chiu, Y-LT., Wong, B. and Charalambous, M. (forthcoming) 'It's for others to judge': what influences students' construction of the ideal student?, *Journal of Further and Higher Education*.

Cohen, J. (1988) *Statistical Power Analysis for the Behavioral Sciences*, 2nd edition. Hillsdale, NJ: Lawrence Erlbaum Associates.

Collier, P.J. and Morgan, D.L. (2008) 'Is that paper really due today?': differences in first-generation and traditional college students' understandings of faculty expectations, *Higher Education* 55 (4): 425–446.

Collins, P.H. and Bilge, S. (2016) *Intersectionality*. Cambridge: Polity Press.

Collins, R.L. (1996) For better or worse: the impact of upward social comparison on self-evaluations, *Psychological Bulletin* 119 (1): 51–69.

Corbin, J. and Strauss, A. (2014) *Basics of Qualitative Research: Techniques and Procedures for Developing Grounded Theory*. London: Sage.

Cotton, D.R.E., Joyner, M., George, R., et al. (2016) Understanding the gender and ethnicity attainment gap in UK higher education, *Innovations in Education and Teaching International* 53 (5): 475–486.

Crenshaw, K. (1991) Mapping the margins: intersectionality, identity politics, and violence against women of color, *Stanford Law Review* 43 (6): 1241–1299.

Crozier, G., Reay, D., Clayton, J., et al. (2008) Different strokes for different folks: diverse students in diverse institutions – experiences of higher education, *Research Papers in Education* 23 (2): 167–177.

d'Aguiar, S. and Harrison, N. (2016) Returning from earning: UK graduates returning to postgraduate study, with particular respect to STEM subjects, gender and ethnicity, *Journal of Education and Work* 29 (5): 584–613.

Dawson, P. (2017) Assessment rubrics: towards clearer and more replicable design, research and practice, *Assessment and Evaluation in Higher Education* 42 (3): 347–360.

Day, D.V. (2000) Leadership development: a review in context, *Leadership Quarterly* 11 (4): 581–613.

de la Harpe, B. and David, C. (2012) Major influences on the teaching and assessment of graduate attributes, *Higher Education Research and Development* 31 (4): 493–510.

De Ruyter, D. and Conroy, J. (2002) The formation of identity: the importance of ideals, *Oxford Review of Education* 28 (4): 509–522.

De Vries, R. (2014) *Earnings by Degrees*. London: Sutton Trust.

de Waal, A. (2019) *The Job-Ready Guide: Employability Skills and Strategies for Career Success*. London: Kogan Page.

DeWitt, J., Archer, L. and Osborne, J. (2013) Nerdy, brainy and normal: children's and parents' constructions of those who are highly engaged with science, *Research in Science Education* 43 (4): 1455–1476.

Diver, A. (ed.) (2019) *Employability via Higher Education: Sustainability as Scholarship*. Dordrecht: Springer Nature.

Dong, S. and Lucas, M.S. (2016) An analysis of disability, academic performance, and seeking support in one university setting, *Career Development and Transition for Exceptional Individuals* 39 (1): 47–56.

Durkin, K. (2008) The adaptation of East Asian masters students to western norms of critical thinking and argumentation in the UK, *Intercultural Education* 19 (1): 15–27.

Duval, S. and Wicklund, R.A. (1972) *A Theory of Objective Self Awareness*. London: Academic Press.

Dweck, D.C. (2017) *Mindset – Updated Edition: Changing the Way You Think to Fulfil Your Potential*, 6th edition. London: Robinson.

Egan, R. (2011) Adjusting curricular design to 'CREATE' a culture of self-regulation, *Canadian Journal for the Scholarship of Teaching and Learning* 2 (2). Available at: https://doi.org/10.5206/cjsotl-rcacea.2011.2.6.

Elliot, D.L., Bengtsen, S.S.E., Guccione, K., et al. (2020) *The Hidden Curriculum in Doctoral Education*. London: Palgrave Pivot.

Erikson, M.G. (2007) The meaning of the future: toward a more specific definition of possible selves, *Review of General Psychology* 11 (4): 348–358.

Esson, J. and Ertl, H. (2016) No point worrying? Potential undergraduates, study-related debt, and the financial allure of higher education, *Studies in Higher Education* 41 (7): 1265–1280.

Evans, C., Muji, D. and Tomlinson, M. (2015) *High-Impact Strategies to Enhance Student Achievement*. York: Higher Education Academy.

Fitzmaurice, M. (2013) Constructing professional identity as a new academic: a moral endeavour, *Studies in Higher Education* 38 (4): 613–622.

France, D., Powell, V., Mauchline, A.L., et al. (2016) Ability of students to recognize the relationship between using mobile apps for learning during fieldwork and the development of graduate attributes, *Journal of Geography in Higher Education* 40 (2): 182–192.

Francis, B. and Skelton, C. (2005) *Reassessing Gender and Achievement: Questioning Contemporary Key Debates*. London: Routledge.

Freeman, T.M., Anderman, L.H. and Jensen, J.M. (2007) Sense of belonging in college freshmen at the classroom and campus levels, *Journal of Experimental Education* 75 (3): 203–220.

Fuller, C. (2014) Social capital and the role of trust in aspirations for higher education, *Educational Review* 66 (2): 131–147.

Gee, J.P. (2000) Identity as an analytic lens for research in education, *Review of Research in Education* 25 (1): 99–125.

Gerhardt, U. (1994) The use of Weberian ideal-type methodology in qualitative data interpretation: an outline for ideal-type analysis, *Bulletin of Sociological Methodology* 41(1): 74–126.

Giraleas, D. (2019) Can we assess teaching quality on the basis of student outcomes? A stochastic frontier application. *Studies in Higher Education*. Available at: https://doi.org/10.1080/03075079.2019.1679762.

Green, W., Hammer, S. and Star, C. (2009) Facing up to the challenge: why is it so hard to develop graduate attributes?, *Higher Education Research and Development* 28 (1): 17–29.

Groves, O. and O'Shea, S. (2019) Learning to 'be' a university student: first in family students negotiating membership of the university community, *International Journal of Educational Research* 98: 48–54.

Gulikers, J.T.M., Bastiaens, T.J. and Kirschner, P.A. (2004) A five-dimensional framework for authentic assessment, *Educational Technology Research and Development* 52: 67. Available at: https://doi.org/10.1007/BF02504676.

Habermas, J. and Blazek, J. (1987) The idea of the university: learning processes, *New German Critique* 41: 3–22.

Hall, S. (1990) Cultural identity and diaspora, in J. Rutherford (ed.) *Identity: Community, Culture, Difference*. London: Lawrence & Wishart.

Harkness, S., Blom, M., Oliva, A., et al. (2007) Teachers' ethnotheories of the 'ideal student' in five western cultures, *Comparative Education* 43 (1): 113–135.

Harris, S. (2005) Rethinking academic identities in neo-liberal times, *Teaching in Higher Education* 10 (4): 421–433.

Harrison, N. (2018) Using the lens of 'possible selves' to explore access to higher education: a new conceptual model for practice, policy, and research, *Social Sciences* 7: 10. Available at: https://doi.org/10.3390/socsci7100209.

Hassel, S. and Ridout, N. (2018) An investigation of first-year students' and lecturers' expectations of university education, *Frontiers in Psychology* 8: 2218. Available at: https://doi.org/10.3389/fpsyg.2017.02218.

Healey, M., Flint, A. and Harrington, K. (2014) *Engagement through Partnership: Students as Partners in Learning and Teaching in Higher Education*. York: Higher Education Academy.

HEFCE (2015) *Understanding Provision for Students with Mental Health Problems and Intensive Support Needs*. London: Higher Education Funding Council for England.

Helyer, R. and Lee, D. (2014) The role of work experience in the future employability of higher education graduates, *Higher Education Quarterly* 68 (3): 348–372.

Henderson, H., Stevenson, J. and Bathmaker, A-M. (eds.) (2019) *Possible Selves and Higher Education: New Interdisciplinary Insights*. London: Routledge.

Hill, J. and West, H. (2020) Improving the student learning experience through dialogic feed-forward assessment, *Assessment and Evaluation in Higher Education* 45 (1): 82–97.

Hitch, D., Macfarlane, S. and Nihill, C. (2015) Inclusive pedagogy in Australian universities: a review of current policies and professional development activities, *International Journal of the First Year in Higher Education* 6 (1): 135–145.

Hockings, C. (2010) *Inclusive Learning and Teaching in Higher Education: A Synthesis of Research*. York: Higher Education Academy.

Holdsworth, S., Turner, M. and Scott-Young, C.M. (2018) … Not drowning, waving. Resilience and university: a student perspective, *Studies in Higher Education* 43 (11): 1837–1853.

Holland, D.C., Lachicotte, W., Jr., Skinner, D., et al. (1998) *Identity and Agency in Cultural Worlds*. Cambridge, MA: Harvard University Press.

Holmegaard, H.T., Madsen, L.M. and Ulriksen, L. (2017) Why should European higher education care about the retention of non-traditional students?, *European Educational Research Journal* 16 (1): 3–11.

Houghton, A. and Anderson, J. (2017) *Embedding Mental Wellbeing in the Curriculum: Maximising Success in Higher Education*. York: Higher Education Academy.

Hughes, C.C., Schilt, K., Gorman, B.K., et al. (2017) Framing the faculty gender gap: a view from STEM doctoral students, *Gender, Work and Organization* 24 (4): 398–416.

Hughes, G. and Smail, O. (2015) Which aspects of university life are most and least helpful in the transition to HE? A qualitative snapshot of student perceptions, *Journal of Further and Higher Education* 39 (4): 466–480.

Hughes, G., Smith, H. and Creese, B. (2015) Not seeing the wood for the trees: developing a feedback analysis tool to explore feed forward in modularised programmes, *Assessment and Evaluation in Higher Education* 40 (8): 1079–1094.

Ingram, N. and Allen, K. (2019) 'Talent-spotting' or 'social magic'? Inequality, cultural sorting and constructions of the ideal graduate in elite professions, *Sociological Review* 67 (3): 723–740.

Ipperciel, D. and ElAtia, S. (2014) Assessing graduate attributes: building a criteria-based competency model, *International Journal of Higher Education* 3 (3): 27–38.

Jackson, D. (2015) Employability skill development in work-integrated learning: barriers and best practice, *Studies in Higher Education* 40 (2): 350–367.

Johnston, B. (2010) *The First Year at University: Teaching Students in Transition*. Maidenhead: Open University Press.

Jones, A. (2009a) Generic attributes as espoused theory: the importance of context, *Higher Education* 58 (2): 175–191.

Jones, A. (2009b) Redisciplining generic attributes: the disciplinary context in focus, *Studies in Higher Education* 34 (1): 85–100.

Jones, S. (2018) Expectation vs. experience: might transition gaps predict undergraduate students' outcome gaps?, *Journal of Further and Higher Education* 42 (7): 908–921.

Jorre de St. Jorre, T. and Oliver, B. (2018) Want students to engage? Contextualise graduate learning outcomes and assess for employability, *Higher Education Research and Development* 37 (1): 44–57.

Kahu, E.R. (2013) Framing student engagement in higher education, *Studies in Higher Education* 38 (5): 758–773.

Karakitsiou, D.E., Markou, A., Kyriakou, P., et al. (2012) The good student is more than a listener – the 12+1 roles of the medical student, *Medical Teacher* 34 (1): e1–e8.

Kaufman, J.C. and Sternberg, R.J. (eds.) (2010) *The Cambridge Handbook of Creativity*. Cambridge: Cambridge University Press.

Killen, R. (1994) Differences between students' and lecturers' perceptions of factors influencing students' academic success at university, *Higher Education Research and Development* 13 (2): 199–211.

Komarraju, M., Karau, S.J., Schmeck, R.R., et al. (2011) The Big Five personality traits, learning styles, and academic achievement, *Personality and Individual Differences* 51 (4): 472–477.

Kreber, C. (2010) Academics' teacher identities, authenticity and pedagogy, *Studies in Higher Education* 35 (2): 171–194.

Krueger, R.A. and Casey, M.A. (2014) *Focus Groups: A Practical Guide for Applied Research*, 5th edition. Thousand Oaks, CA: Sage.

Kuh, G.D., Kinzie, J., Buckley, J.A., et al. (2006) *What Matters to Student Success: A Review of the Literature*. Washington, DC: National Postsecondary Education Cooperative.

Kusurkar, R.A., Cate, T.J.T., van Asperen, M., et al. (2011) Motivation as an independent and a dependent variable in medical education: a review of the literature, *Medical Teacher* 33 (5): e242–e262.

Laclau, E. and Mouffe, C. (2014) *Hegemony and Socialist Strategy: Towards a Radical Democratic Politics*, 2nd edition. London: Verso Trade.

Laidlaw, A., McLellan, J. and Ozakinci, G. (2016) Understanding undergraduate student perceptions of mental health, mental well-being and help-seeking behaviour, *Studies in Higher Education* 41 (12): 2156–2168.

Laing, C., Chao, K-M. and Robinson, A. (2005) Managing the expectations of non traditional students: a process of negotiation, *Journal of Further and Higher Education* 29 (2): 169–179.

Latour, B. (2013) *An Inquiry into Modes of Existence*. London: Harvard University Press.

Lawler, S. (2014) *Identity: Sociological Perspectives*. Cambridge: Polity Press.

Lawrie, G., Marquis, E., Fuller, E., et al. (2017) Moving towards inclusive learning and teaching: a synthesis of recent literature, *Teaching and Learning Inquiry* 5 (1): 9–21.

Leathwood, C. (2006) Gender, equity and the discourse of the independent learner in higher education, *Higher Education* 52 (4): 611–633.

Leathwood, C. and O'Connell, P. (2003) 'It's a struggle': the construction of the 'new student' in higher education, *Journal of Education Policy* 18 (6): 597–615.

Leathwood, C. and Read, B. (2009) *Gender and the Changing Face of Higher Education: A Feminized Future?* Maidenhead: Open University Press.

Lee, H-J. and Lee, J. (2012) Who gets the best grades at top universities? An exploratory analysis of institution-wide interviews with the highest achievers at a top Korean University, *Asia Pacific Education Review* 13 (4): 665–676.

Leese, M. (2010) Bridging the gap: supporting student transitions into higher education, *Journal of Further and Higher Education* 34 (2): 239–251.

Lehmann, W. (2007) 'I just didn't feel like I fit in': the role of habitus in university dropout decisions, *Canadian Journal of Higher Education* 37 (2): 89–110.

Lindvig, K. (2018) The implied PhD student of interdisciplinary research projects within monodisciplinary structures, *Higher Education Research and Development* 37 (6): 1171–1185.

Llamas, J.M.C. (2006) Technologies of disciplinary power in action: the norm of the 'good student', *Higher Education* 52 (4): 665–686.

Lowe, H. and Cook, A. (2003) Mind the gap: are students prepared for higher education?, *Journal of Further and Higher Education* 27 (1): 53–76.

Lucey, H. and Reay, D. (2002) Carrying the beacon of excellence: social class differentiation and anxiety at a time of transition, *Journal of Education Policy* 17 (3): 321–336.

MacIntosh, D. (2012) Plato: a theory of forms, *Philosophy Now* 90: 6–7.

MacLellan, E. (2001) Assessment for learning: the differing perceptions of tutors and students, *Assessment and Evaluation in Higher Education* 26 (4): 307–318.

Maltese, A.V. and Tai, R.H. (2011) Pipeline persistence: examining the association of educational experiences with earned degrees in STEM among U.S. students, *Science Education* 95 (5): 877–907.

Marginson, S. (2011) Higher education and public good, *Higher Education Quarterly* 65 (4): 411–433.

Marginson, S. (2016) The worldwide trend to high participation higher education: dynamics of social stratification in inclusive systems, *Higher Education* 72 (4): 413–434.

Markus, H. and Nurius, P. (1986) Possible selves, *American Psychologist* 41 (9): 954–969.

Marshall, C.A., Nolan, S.J. and Newton, D.P. (2016) *Widening Participation, Higher Education and Non-Traditional Students*. London: Palgrave Macmillan.

Maslovaty, N., Cohen, A. and Furman, S. (2008) The structural validity of the perceived traits of the 'ideal student' multi-faceted theory among education students, *Studies in Educational Evaluation* 34 (3): 165–172.

Masnick, A.M., Valenti, S.S., Cox, B.D., et al. (2010) A multidimensional scaling analysis of students' attitudes about science careers, *International Journal of Science Education* 32 (5): 653–667.

Maton, K. (2000) Languages of legitimation: the structuring significance for intellectual fields of strategic knowledge claims, *British Journal of Sociology of Education* 21 (2): 147–167.

McDonald, I. (2014) Supporting international students in UK higher education institutions, *Perspectives: Policy and Practice in Higher Education* 18 (2): 62–65.

Meehan, C. and Howells, K. (2018) 'What really matters to freshers?': evaluation of first year student experience of transition into university, *Journal of Further and Higher Education* 42 (7): 893–907.

Merton, R.K. (1968) *Social Theory and Social Structure*. New York: Free Press.

Meuleman, A-M., Garrett, R., Wrench, A., et al. (2015) 'Some people might say I'm thriving but … ': non-traditional students' experiences of university, *International Journal of Inclusive Education* 19 (5): 503–517.

Mickelson, R.A. (1990) The attitude–achievement paradox among Black adolescents, *Sociology of Education* 63 (1): 44–61.

Mills, C.W. (2005) 'Ideal theory' as ideology, *Hypatia* 20 (3): 165–183.

Mireles-Rios, R. and Garcia, N.M. (2019) What would your ideal graduate mentoring program look like?: Latina/o student success in higher education, *Journal of Latinos and Education* 18 (4): 376–386.

Molesworth, M., Nixon, E. and Scullion, R. (2009) Having, being and higher education: the marketisation of the university and the transformation of the student into consumer, *Teaching in Higher Education* 14 (3): 277–287.

Money, J., Nixon, S., Tracy, F., et al. (2017) Undergraduate student expectations of university in the United Kingdom: what really matters to them?, *Cogent Education* 4 (1): 1–11.

Morrow, W.E. (2009) *Bounds of Democracy: Epistemological Access in Higher Education*. Cape Town: HSRC Press.

Morton, T.R. and Parsons, E.C. (2018) #BlackGirlMagic: the identity conceptualization of Black women in undergraduate STEM education, *Science Education* 102 (6): 1363–1393.

Munro, L. (2011) 'Go boldly, dream large!': the challenges confronting non-traditional students at university, *Australian Journal of Education* 55 (2): 115–131.

Murray, N. (2016) Dealing with diversity in higher education: awareness-raising and a linguistic perspective on teachers' intercultural competence, *International Journal for Academic Development* 21 (3): 166–177.

Nelson, R. (2018) Failing with student success: the hidden role of bad luck and false empowerment, *Higher Education Research and Development* 37 (5): 1050–1061.

Nghia, T.L.H., Pham, T., Tomlinson, M., et al. (2020) *Developing and Utilizing Employability Capitals: Graduates' Strategies across Labour Markets*. London: Routledge.

Nichols, S. and Stahl, G. (2019) Intersectionality in higher education research: a systematic literature review, *Higher Education Research and Development* 38 (6): 1255–1268.

Nicolaisen, L.B. and Achiam, M. (2019) The implied visitor in a planetarium exhibition, *Museum Management and Curatorship* 35 (2): 143–159.

Normand, C. and Anderson, L. (2017) *Graduate Attributes in Higher Education: Attitudes on Attributes from Across the Disciplines*. London: Routledge.

Nyström, A-S., Jackson, C. and Karlsson, M.S. (2019) What counts as success? Constructions of achievement in prestigious higher education programmes, *Research Papers in Education* 34 (4): 465–482.

O'Brien, B.C., Hirsh, D., Krupat, E., et al. (2016) Learners, performers, caregivers, and team players: descriptions of the ideal medical student in longitudinal integrated and block clerkships, *Medical Teacher* 38 (3): 297–305.

OECD (2017) *Education at a Glance 2017: OECD Indicators*. Paris: OECD Publishing.

OECD (2018) Population with tertiary education. Available at: https://www.oecd-ilibrary.org/content/data/0b8f90e9-en (accessed 17 March 2020).

OfS (2019) *Mental Health: Are All Students Being Properly Supported?* London: Office for Students.

Oliver, B. (2013) Graduate attributes as a focus for institution-wide curriculum renewal: innovations and challenges, *Higher Education Research and Development* 32 (3): 450–463.

Oliver, B. and Jorre de St. Jorre, T. (2018) Graduate attributes for 2020 and beyond: recommendations for Australian higher education providers, *Higher Education Research and Development* 37 (4): 821–836.

Ong, M., Smith, J.M. and Ko, L.T. (2018) Counterspaces for women of color in STEM higher education: marginal and central spaces for persistence and success, *Journal of Research in Science Teaching* 55 (2): 206–245.

O'Shea, S. (2014) Transitions and turning points: exploring how first-in-family female students story their transition to university and student identity formation, *International Journal of Qualitative Studies in Education* 27 (2): 135–158.

O'Shea, S. (2015) Filling up silences – first in family students, capital and university talk in the home, *International Journal of Lifelong Education* 34 (2): 139–155.

O'Shea, S. and Delahunty, J. (2018) Getting through the day and still having a smile on my face! How do students define success in the university learning environment?, *Higher Education Research and Development* 37 (5): 1062–1075.

Osmani, M., Weerakkody, V. and Hindi, N. (2017) Graduate attributes in higher education: examining academics' perception in the Middle East, *Journal of Education for Business* 92 (2): 53–64.

Oxford Dictionaries (2010) *Oxford Dictionary of English*. Oxford: Oxford University Press.

Oyserman, D., Bybee, D., Terry, K., et al. (2004) Possible selves as roadmaps, *Journal of Research in Personality* 38 (2): 130–149.

Picton, C., Kahu, E.R. and Nelson, K. (2018) 'Hardworking, determined and happy': first-year students' understanding and experience of success, *Higher Education Research and Development* 37 (6): 1260–1273.

Pizzolato, J.E. (2007) Impossible selves: investigating students' persistence decisions when their career-possible selves border on impossible, *Journal of Career Development* 33 (3): 201–223.

Portelli, J.P. (1993) Exposing the hidden curriculum, *Journal of Curriculum Studies* 25 (4): 343–358.

Power, S., Whitty, G., Edwards, T., et al. (1998) Schoolboys and schoolwork: gender identification and academic achievement, *International Journal of Inclusive Education* 2 (2): 135–153.

Putnam, R. (2000) *Bowling Alone: The Collapse and Revival of American Community*. New York: Simon & Schuster.

Reay, D., Crozier, G. and Clayton, J. (2010) 'Fitting in' or 'standing out': working-class students in UK higher education, *British Educational Research Journal* 36 (1): 107–124.

Reay, D., Crozier, G. and James, D. (2011) *White Middle-Class Identities and Urban Schooling*. Basingstoke: Palgrave Macmillan.

Richardson, J.T.E. (2008) *Degree Attainment, Ethnicity and Gender: A Literature Review*. London: HEA/ECU.

Richardson, M., Abraham, C. and Bond, R. (2012) Psychological correlates of university students' academic performance: a systematic review and meta-analysis, *Psychological Bulletin* 138 (2): 353–387.

Roberts, J. (2018) Professional staff contributions to student retention and success in higher education, *Journal of Higher Education Policy and Management* 40 (2): 140–153.

Robson, J. (2018) Performance, structure and ideal identity: reconceptualising teachers' engagement in online social spaces, *British Journal of Educational Technology* 49 (3): 439–450.

Rockoff, J.E. (2004) The impact of individual teachers on student achievement: evidence from panel data, *American Economic Review* 94 (2): 247–252.

Rossiter, M. (2009) Possible selves and career transition: implications for serving nontraditional students, *Journal of Continuing Higher Education* 57 (2): 61–71.

Rust, C. and Froud, L. (2011) 'Personal literacy': the vital, yet often overlooked, graduate attribute, *Journal of Teaching and Learning for Graduate Employability* 2 (1): 28–40.

Ryan, R.M. and Deci, E.L. (2000) Self-determination theory and the facilitation of intrinsic motivation, social development, and well-being, *American Psychologist* 55 (1): 68–78.

Sadowski, C., Stewart, M. and Pediaditis, M. (2018) Pathway to success: using students' insights and perspectives to improve retention and success for university students from low socioeconomic (LSE) backgrounds, *International Journal of Inclusive Education* 22 (2): 158–175.

Said, E. (1978) *Orientalism*. London: Routledge & Kegan Paul.

Savage, M. (2015) *Social Class in the 21st Century*. London: Pelican.

Sawilowsky, S. (2009) New effect size rules of thumb. *Journal of Modern Applied Statistical Methods* 8 (2): 597–599.

Schömer, F. and González-Monteagudo, J. (2013) Participation in higher education: barriers and opportunities for non-traditional students in higher education in Germany and Spain, *Studies in the Education of Adults* 45 (2): 148–161.

Shiner, M. and Noden, P. (2015) 'Why are you applying there?': 'race', class and the construction of higher education 'choice' in the United Kingdom, *British Journal of Sociology of Education* 36 (8): 1170–1191.

Sotiriadou, P., Logan, D., Daly, A., et al. (2019) The role of authentic assessment to preserve academic integrity and promote skill development and employability, *Studies in Higher Education*. Available at: https://doi.org/10.1080/03075079.2019.1582015.

Speight, S., Lackovic, N. and Cooker, L. (2013) The contested curriculum: academic learning and employability in higher education, *Tertiary Education and Management* 19 (2): 112–126.

Spronken-Smith, R., Bond, C., McLean, A., et al. (2013) *How to Engage with a Graduate Outcomes' Agenda: A Guide for Tertiary Education Institutions*. Ako Aotearoa, NZ: The National Centre for Tertiary Teaching Excellence.

Stemplowska, Z. (2008) What's ideal about ideal theory?, *Social Theory and Practice* 34 (3): 319–340.

Stevenson, J. and Clegg, S. (2011) Possible selves: students orientating themselves towards the future through extracurricular activity, *British Educational Research Journal* 37 (2): 231–246.

Strayhorn, T.L. (2012) *College Students' Sense of Belonging*. London: Routledge.

Street, B. (1994) The New Literacy Studies: implications for education and pedagogy, *Changing English* 1 (1): 113–126.

Su, Y. (2014) Self-directed, genuine graduate attributes: the person-based approach, *Higher Education Research and Development* 33 (6): 1208–1220.

Swaffield, S. (2011) Getting to the heart of authentic Assessment for Learning, *Assessment in Education: Principles, Policy and Practice* 18 (4): 433–449.

Swedberg, R. (2018) How to use Max Weber's ideal type in sociological analysis, *Journal of Classical Sociology* 18 (3): 181–196.

Tan, A-L., Jocz, J.A. and Zhai, J. (2017) Spiderman and science: how students' perceptions of scientists are shaped by popular media, *Public Understanding of Science* 26 (5): 520–530.

Taylor, C. (2004) *Modern Social Imaginaries*. Durham, NC: Duke University Press.

Teigen. K.H., Normann, H-TE., Bjorkheim, J.O., et al. (2000) Who would you most like to like? Adolescents' ideals at the beginning and the end of the century, *Scandinavian Journal of Educational Research* 44 (1): 5–26.

The Guardian (2016) University mental health services face strain as demand rises 50%. Available at: https://www.theguardian.com/education/2016/sep/23/university-mental-health-services-face-strain-as-demand-rises-50 (accessed 14 February 2020).

Thinyane, H. (2013) Academic perceptions of the ideal computer science student, *South African Computer Journal* 50 (1): 28–40.

Thomas, L. (2011) Do pre-entry interventions such as 'Aimhigher' impact on student retention and success? A review of the literature, *Higher Education Quarterly* 65 (3): 230–250.

Thomas, L. (2012) *Building Student Engagement and Belonging in Higher Education at a Time of Change: Final report from the What Works? Student Retention & Success Programme*. York: Higher Education Academy.

Thomas, L., Hockings, C., Ottaway, J., et al. (2015) *Independent Learning: Student Perspectives and Experiences*. York: Higher Education Academy.

Thompson, G. (2010) Acting, accidents and performativity: challenging the hegemonic good student in secondary schools, *British Journal of Sociology of Education* 31 (4): 413–430.

Thunborg, C. and Bron, A. (2019) Being in constant transition or recurrent formation: non-traditional graduates' life transitions before, during and after higher education in Sweden, *Studies in the Education of Adults* 51 (1): 36–54.

Thunborg, C., Bron, A. and Edström, E. (2012) Forming learning identities in higher education in Sweden, *Studies for the Learning Society* 2/3: 23–34.

Tight, M. (2011) How many universities are there in the United Kingdom? How many should there be?, *Higher Education* 62 (5): 649–663.

Times Higher Education (2019) Why can't students recognise transferable skills? Available at: https://www.timeshighereducation.com/features/why-cant-students-recognise-transferable-skills (accessed 18 March 2020).

Tinto, V. (1993) *Leaving College: Rethinking the Causes and Cures of Student Attrition*, 2nd edition. Chicago, IL: University of Chicago Press.

Torrance, E.P. (1965) *Rewarding Creative Behaviour*. Englewood Cliffs, NJ: Prentice-Hall.

Trowler, V. (2010) *Student Engagement Literature Review*. York: Higher Education Academy.

Turner, L. and Tobbell, J. (2018) Learner identity and transition: an ethnographic exploration of undergraduate trajectories, *Journal of Further and Higher Education* 42 (5): 708–720.

Twenge, J.M., Sherman, R.A. and Lyubomirsky, S. (2016) More happiness for young people and less for mature adults: time period differences in subjective well-being in the United States, 1972–2014, *Social Psychological and Personality Science* 7 (2): 131–141.

UCL (2020) *BAME Awarding Gap Project: Staff Toolkit 2020*. London: University College London.

Uiboleht, K., Karm, M. and Postareff, L. (2016) How do university teachers combine different approaches to teaching in a specific course? A qualitative multi-case study, *Teaching in Higher Education* 21 (7): 854–869.

Ulriksen, L. (2009) The implied student, *Studies in Higher Education* 34 (5): 517–532.

Ulriksen, L., Madsen, L.M. and Holmegaard, H.T. (2017) The first-year experience of non-traditional students in Danish science and engineering university programmes, *European Educational Research Journal* 16 (1): 45–61.

Universities UK (2015) *Student Mental Wellbeing in Higher Education: Good Practice Guide*. London: Universities UK.

Villarroel, V., Bloxham, S., Bruna, D., et al. (2018) Authentic assessment: creating a blueprint for course design, *Assessment and Evaluation in Higher Education* 43 (5): 840–854.

Vinther, J. and Slethaug, G. (2014) Changing conceptions of the international classroom and the good student?, *HERMES: Journal of Language and Communication in Business* 27 (53): 25–42.

Vitae (2011) *Researcher Development Framework*. Cambridge: The Careers Research and Advisory Centre.

Wakeling, P. and Savage, M. (2015) Entry to elite positions and the stratification of higher education in Britain, *Sociological Review* 63 (2): 290–320.

Walkerdine, V. (2011) Neoliberalism, working-class subjects and higher education, *Contemporary Social Science* 6 (2): 255–271.

Walkerdine, V. (2020) What's class got to do with it?, *Discourse: Studies in the Cultural Politics of Education*. Available at: https://doi.org/10.1080/01596306.2020.1767939.

Watkins, D. (2000) Learning and teaching: a cross-cultural perspective, *School Leadership and Management* 20 (2): 161–173.

Watkins, J. (2015) Spatial imaginaries research in geography: synergies, tensions, and new directions, *Geography Compass* 9 (9): 508–522.

Weber, M. (1949) *Essays in the Methodology of the Social Sciences*. New York: Free Press.

Weber, M. (1978) *Economy and Society: An Outline of Interpretive Sociology*. Berkeley, CA: University of California Press.

Wenger, E. (1998) *Communities of Practice: Learning, Meaning, and Identity*. Cambridge: Cambridge University Press.

Willcoxson, L., Cotter, J. and Joy, S. (2011) Beyond the first year experience: the impact on attrition of student experiences throughout undergraduate degree studies in six diverse universities, *Studies in Higher Education* 36 (3): 331–352.

Wimshurst, K. and Manning, M. (2013) Feed-forward assessment, exemplars and peer marking: evidence of efficacy, *Assessment and Evaluation in Higher Education* 38 (4): 451–465.

Wingate, U., Andon, N. and Cogo, A. (2011) Embedding academic writing instruction into subject teaching: a case study, *Active Learning in Higher Education* 12 (1): 69–81.

Wong, B. (2012) Identifying with science: a case study of two 13-year-old 'high achieving working class' British Asian girls, *International Journal of Science Education* 34 (1): 43–65.

Wong, B. (2015) A blessing with a curse: model minority ethnic students and the construction of educational success, *Oxford Review of Education* 41 (6): 730–746.

Wong, B. (2016) *Science Education, Career Aspirations and Minority Ethnic Students*. Basingstoke: Palgrave Macmillan.

Wong, B. (2018) By chance or by plan? The academic success of nontraditional students in higher education, *AERA Open* 4 (2). Available at: https://doi.org/10.1177/2332858418782195.

Wong, B. and Chiu, Y-LT. (2019a) Exploring the concept of 'ideal' university student, *Studies in Higher Education*. Available at: https://doi.org/10.1080/03075079.2019.1643302.

Wong, B. and Chiu, Y-LT. (2019b) Let me entertain you: the ambivalent role of university lecturers as educators and performers, *Educational Review* 71 (2): 218–233.

Wong, B. and Chiu, Y-LT. (2019c) 'Swallow your pride and fear': the educational strategies of high-achieving non-traditional university students, *British Journal of Sociology of Education* 40 (7): 868–882.

Wong, B. and Chiu, Y-LT. (2020) University lecturers' construction of the 'ideal' undergraduate student, *Journal of Further and Higher Education* 44 (1): 54–68.

Wong, B., Elmorally, R., Copsey-Blake, M., et al. (2020) Is race still relevant? Student perceptions and experiences of racism in higher education, *Cambridge Journal of Education*. Available at: https://doi.org/10.1080/0305764X.2020.1831441.

Wong, B., Chiu, Y-LT., Copsey-Blake, M., et al. (forthcoming) A mapping of graduate attributes: what can we expect from UK university students?, *Higher Education Research & Development*.

Wong, B., DeWitt, J. and Chiu, Y-LT. (in review) Mapping the eight dimensions of the ideal student in higher education.

Wood, M. and Su, F. (2017) What makes an excellent lecturer? Academics' perspectives on the discourse of 'teaching excellence' in higher education, *Teaching in Higher Education* 22 (4): 451–466.

Worthman, C. and Troiano, B. (2019) A good student subject: a Foucauldian discourse analysis of an adolescent writer negotiating subject positions, *Critical Studies in Education* 60 (2): 263–280.

York, T., Gibson, C. and Rankin, S. (2015) Defining and measuring academic success, *Practical Assessment, Research, and Evaluation* 20 (1): 1–20.

Zhou, Y., Jindal-Snape, D., Topping, K., et al. (2008) Theoretical models of culture shock and adaptation in international students in higher education, *Studies in Higher Education* 33 (1): 63–75.

Index